Exciting Classrooms

The internal teacher is born within you and does not need to be seen. The external teacher shows up to remind you of the inward path.

Stephanie Russell
Everyday Zen

Exciting Classrooms

Practical Information to Ensure Student Success

Frank Thoms

ROWMAN & LITTLEFIELD
Lanham • Boulder • New York • London

Published by Rowman & Littlefield
A wholly owned subsidiary of The Rowman & Littlefield Publishing Group, Inc.
4501 Forbes Boulevard, Suite 200, Lanham, Maryland 20706
www.rowman.com

Unit A, Whitacre Mews, 26-34 Stannary Street, London SE11 4AB

Copyright © 2015 by Frank Thoms

All rights reserved. No part of this book may be reproduced in any form or by any electronic or mechanical means, including information storage and retrieval systems, without written permission from the publisher, except by a reviewer who may quote passages in a review.

British Library Cataloguing in Publication Information Available

Library of Congress Cataloging-in-Publication Data

Names: Thoms, Frank, 1938–
Title: Exciting classrooms : practical information to ensure student success / Frank Thoms.
Description: Lanham : Rowman & Littlefield, [2015] | Includes bibliographical references and index.
Identifiers: LCCN 2015026436| ISBN 9781475823028 (cloth : alk. paper) | ISBN 9781475823035 (pbk. : alk. paper) | ISBN 9781475823042 (electronic)
Subjects: LCSH: Reflective teaching. | Classroom environment.
Classification: LCC LB1025.3 .T532 2015 | DDC 371.102—dc23 LC record available at http://lccn.loc.gov/2015026436

♾ ™ The paper used in this publication meets the minimum requirements of American National Standard for Information Sciences—Permanence of Paper for Printed Library Materials, ANSI/NISO Z39.48-1992.

Printed in the United States of America

Contents

Meet Dan Hilliard	vii
Preface	ix
Introduction	xiii

PART I: WHAT CAN WE DO IMMEDIATELY? — 1

1	Implement 10-2 Thinking	3
2	Instill Skills	13
3	Teach Literacy	19
4	Design Invitations	25
5	Make Meaning	31

PART II: HOW CAN WE EXPAND OUR TEACHING PRACTICE? — 43

6	See the Big Picture	45
7	Search for Wisdom	55
8	Stay Current	63
9	Seek the Higher Road	73

PART III: WHAT MUST WE CHANGE? — 81

10	Abolish Tracking	83
11	Abandon the Crabs in the Cage	93

| 12 | Stop the Interruptions | 103 |
| 13 | End One-Size-Fits-All Teaching | 111 |

PART IV: WHAT CAN WE LEARN FROM BEYOND THE CULTURE OF SCHOOLS? — **119**

14	Become a Gadfly	121
15	Leverage Tipping Points	127
16	Teach As If	135
17	Take the Long View	141
18	Imagine the Ideal	147
19	Invoke the Cosmos	153

PART V: HOW DO WE FIND OUR CALLING? — **159**

20	Grow Our Seeds	161
21	Rethink Our Philosophy	167
22	Achieve Our Dreams	173
23	Become Stakeholders	179
24	Begin at the End	189

CODA: Make a Difference	197
Epilogue: Hidden Expectations	201
Appendix: Teaching Manifesto	205
Acknowledgments	209
Index	211
About the Author	223

Meet Dan Hilliard

Dan Hilliard has been teaching for more than ten years. He is good at it—at least that's what his students tell him. They like his quirky qualities and sense of humor, especially his bad puns. His colleagues respect his ideas in the faculty room and at department meetings. His classroom is arranged much as he found it, desks in neat rows and columns facing his desk and a whiteboard.

He arrives early and leaves late every day—except Fridays. He prepares his lessons to engage minds. While he would not call himself a lecture-style teacher, he orchestrates discussions, rarely hesitating to jump in to offer elaborate explanations. His students enjoy his involvement. They rarely fail to pay attention. Time passes quickly in Mr. Hilliard's class.

He loves teaching, no doubt about it. He looks forward to Mondays. Yet, he yearns for something more, something different. He has tried role-plays and simulations. Once, he and his students published a Soviet newspaper proclaiming the wisdom of Lenin and Stalin. In that same year, he arranged for a Latin American festival in his classroom, complete with a live goat. He was doing his best, but he sensed a longing to move beyond his comfort zone.

One day as he is taking attendance, he notices that Sam, who sits in the middle of the middle row, is absent. Sam never misses class. A streak of sunlight crosses Sam's desk. Slowly, Dan steps forward, hesitates, and then moves toward Sam's seat. He sits down, remaining still and pensive. His students shift in their seats and begin to whisper to each other but soon become quiet.

As he slowly looks around, he sees them looking at him—and at each other. He senses those behind him, as well. Occasionally, he has moved his desks into a horseshoe arrangement, but his students are used to seeing his face. Except for those sitting in the front row, they also see only the backs of the heads of peers. Now they are looking at one another, puzzled about what their teacher is about to do—he has surprised them before. Dan remains quiet and pensive.

He asks a question. Later, when telling the story, he could not remember the question, but it was one to encourage discussion. After a long minute, Juanita responds. Dan remains quiet. After some silence, Peter comments on Juanita's point, which alerts several others. After a few minutes, Rebecca asks Mr. Hilliard for his thoughts. As he is about to launch forth, he hesitates. He asks another question. The discussion resumes and soon breaks up into small-group conversations.

Normally positioned in the front of the room, Dan usually would ask students to stop talking among themselves and pay attention to whoever is talking. This time, he lets the process play itself out. The room becomes noisier than usual, and somewhat chaotic—surely not a time for his principal to walk in.

He looks at the clock and sees that about five minutes are left. Normally, he makes his last one or two points; he often speaks beyond the bell, hoping his students will remember his words. Today, he gives them time to absorb what they have been discussing. He wants to know what's on their minds, as he does not know the content of the small-group conversations, except of those students nearer to him. He raises his hand to get their attention and asks them to take out a piece of paper and write on the following topics:

1. a big idea they discovered today
2. how they plan to pursue their learning at home
3. a question they would like to focus on in class tomorrow

For the next few moments, he could hear a pin drop.

The bell rings, he dismisses them, they stand up, put their responses in the outbox, and leave. Dan remains in Sam's seat for a moment. "I think I'm on to something," he says to himself. "Something exciting!"

Preface

One October day ten years ago, I observed fourteen ninth-grade teachers talking nonstop at their students. These were the same young, energetic teachers who, in a three-day workshop before the opening of school, expressed impatience with our discussions on interactive teaching techniques. They were eager to set up their small learning communities—an innovation I admired—in preparation for their first days and weeks. I agreed to give over my third workshop day for this purpose. However, I cautioned them that the most important ingredient in their success would be the quality of their teaching.

My contract included returning to the school to coach and provide workshops. I was eager to observe them in their respective classrooms, particularly to see how they designed lessons, engaged students, formed relationships, and activated thinking. The coordinators of the program did not tell them when I would be observing.

I was unprepared for what I saw. In each classroom I observed students sitting passively at desks in rows looking at the teacher or whispering to one another. Teachers did virtually all the talking. None of them pursued questions or encouraged student interaction. Not once. By the end of the day, I imagined the students as seated bronzed figures carried from class to class. Several teachers told me later that day that they wished they had known I was coming so they could have prepared better. After all, the idea of delivering a dog-and-pony show when it counts resides deep in the profession.

The next day, I composed a six-page letter to the teachers, which became the foundation for my becoming a writer.

As a lifelong teacher, I've written *Exciting Classrooms: Practical Information to Ensure Student Success* as an invitation for teachers to embrace change. Teachers are frustrated by a double-edged predicament. Reformers plead for them to teach critical thinking skills, creativity, and effective communication to meet the challenges of a global world. At the same time, school officials insist that they meet the tireless demands of annual state and federal testing.

In addition, teachers face expanding curriculums, larger classes, and smaller budgets. It's no wonder they retreat into the cocoons of their classrooms, which remain the same private, isolated worlds of *their* childhood classrooms.

I empathize with our profession's successful resistance to the reform efforts of the past century. We have never been invited to participate as decision-makers or leaders. So, we feign compliance, and as we have, we unfortunately persist to teach as our teachers taught us. The evidence is obvious by the continuing prevalence of whole-class lessons that we deliver talking at students from the front of the room.

At the same time, some of us initiated changes at the classroom level but failed to make much headway. In the 1970s, for example, I participated in the open-education movement. My colleagues and I implemented an exemplary open-education classroom with strong parent support that was based on my teaching at a progressive primary school in Oxfordshire, England. Before the end of the decade, however, our alternative program was reabsorbed into a traditionally structured middle school. So much for change.

I sense that today's teachers feel like frustrated mail carriers with mailbags overstuffed with the demands of No Child Left Behind and Race to the Top. These federal mandates combined with the pressure of raising state standards, demands by local boards, and ever-expanding curriculums require them to teach more in less time. The more they're required to teach, the more they feel pressure to deliver as much as they can—and as quickly as they can.

Many teachers have told me that they prefer administrators to take the initiative to undo what is no longer working. Others indicate that they want to be included at the decision-making table. And, some take it upon themselves to make changes in their classrooms. In schools that support professional learning communities, teachers work closely with administrators to reform teaching. However, most of them still remain in isolated classrooms. When they want help, often they are afraid to ask for fear of being judged. Staying in their rooms, not causing a stir, keeps them safe—and preserves their contracts.

Ironically, teachers are the deciders in their classrooms. They spend every day alone with their students. *Exciting Classrooms* invites them to choose to stop doing what no longer works, start to use better practices, and nurture what they already do well. They do not have to wait for leadership to initiate changes. They do not have to act out of fear. Except for those who are required to execute scripted lessons, they decide how to teach.

Teachers can find the courage to take creative steps to meet the needs of their students. They can design effective lessons with honest content, relevant skills, and enduring understandings. They can commit to exciting classrooms. They can make the difference between an education geared toward the past and one headed for the future.

The emphasis on academic abilities—verbal and mathematical reasoning—represents only two forms of intelligence. Schools must incorporate all forms at equal levels, including the creative and emotional, if they are to serve students well. When the arts are cut to make more room to teach academics—often replaced by "drill and kill" sessions to prepare for assessments—they deprive children of the right and opportunity to discover and develop their gifts. When physical education and recess are eliminated, it sends the message that exercise is not necessary for a healthy life.

Read *Exciting Classrooms: Practical Information to Ensure Student Success* to find ways to let go of what no longer works in your school and classroom. Discover innovations, new strategies, and wisdom to guide you to better practice. Find your gifts. Become free to be the real teacher you are.

Introduction

Dan Hilliard's story at the front of this book illustrates the conundrum facing teachers. Dan is well-respected and works hard, but he senses something is missing. Standing at the front of the room limits his options. By sitting in Sam's seat he discovers new possibilities.

Dan made this decision on his own. Had he been told to make this move, he may well have resisted and held on to his own ways, ones he practiced daily. Instead, he accepted the invitation of the empty desk. He's accepted other invitations, such as one from his colleague, Allegra Bernardi, to return homework without grading to see if students would continue to do it. He and his colleagues are open to new ideas and often try them. However, when the administration insists they use a new approach, they often feign to use it and continue with their own practices. Real change comes best from invitations, not from edicts.

Students are different today. They hardly spend time outdoors without adults where my friends and I used to spend hours using our imaginations. Now they are alone watching TV, plying the Internet, playing video games, text messaging, sexting, tweeting, and conversing on cellphones. They have less time to think and absorb, less time to spend time in their minds. They are becoming conduits of information without reflection—without ownership.

The digital culture holds their attention by demanding immediate responses with hardly any concern for content; not to respond immediately means, "you're not my friend." They feel this anxiety. Multitasking—as good as students may claim they can do it and as much as we may admire it—means to dart in and out of different media without taking ownership of any part. The mind attends to one cognitive task at a time.

Children's brains become wired through their upbringing. Had they grown up learning to do chores, to engage in free play, and to postpone gratification, they would be better suited to learn as previous generations have. Already children spend only four-to-seven minutes a day relating to nature and from seven-to-ten hours in front of screens.[1] They are not us.

They've not had opportunities to learn frustration tolerance, because they get instant gratification from electronic devices and from overindulgent, anxiety-ridden, helicopter parents. Few children have free time with peers, as their lives are closely supervised and heavily scheduled. Increasing numbers live in single-family households without extended family support.

As Marc Prensky stridently identified nearly fifteen years ago, "Our students have changed radically. Today's students are no longer the people our educational system was designed to teach."[2] Given the overwhelming social upheavals that children face—combined with their digitally wired brains—teachers have little choice but to respond to them in new and innovative ways.

Exciting Classrooms: Practical Information to Ensure Student Success directly addresses the conundrum facing teachers. Already, they report they may have lost the allegiance of children. They feel it every day as they scramble to reel them in, to win their attention, to have them listen. As they ratchet up traditional methods, they see students drifting further away. Reaching students, however, remains *the* challenge, more than having to cope with overloaded curriculums and state and federal assessments.

At the same time, teachers cannot succumb to the relentless insistence of electronic media. If they do, they too will become conduits for content prepared by others, of Big Brother if you will. Teachers would then become clay in the hands of the media conglomerates, such as Disney's manipulation of princesses and fairies in the lives of little girls—and more recently, Disney XD, aimed at boys from ages six to fourteen. They also could become subject to the global surveillance of social media's Twitter.

Exciting Classrooms points out that teachers have an opportunity to make a significant impact on students and their families. They can begin by relinquishing strict classroom control from the front. When they let go of this delivery mode, they are able to interact better with students. They invite students to become more receptive. In deciding to meet them halfway—perhaps more than halfway—they make learning more possible.

They can shift from delivering knowledge and skills and concentrate instead on what students are learning *in* their classrooms. The intention of teaching, after all, is to cause learning. It's not what teachers *teach*—essential as it may seem—but what students *learn* that counts. When teachers make this shift, they mentally leave the front of the room to teach alongside students. They interact with them and enrich their thinking, creativity, assessment, and communication. They create exciting and engaged classrooms.

When teachers commit to this shift, students will learn how to teach themselves. Schools should listen to the oft-quoted wisdom of Albert Einstein: "We can't solve problems by using the same kind of thinking we used when we created them." Having an education today means to learn *and* to learn how to learn. Teachers are instrumental in this process. They make it possible for students not only to learn *from* them and but also to learn *with* them. Students play a key role in this process when their minds become engaged and committed to worthwhile pursuits. Otherwise, they will waste their time.

~ ~ ~

Exciting Classrooms is structured to meet the needs of readers, who include teachers, professors, administrators, and others interested in what happens in classrooms. Each chapter concludes with a "Reflection" in which Dan Hilliard offers relevant insights. It is followed by "Points to Pursue" to inspire readers' further thinking and discussion. Each chapter also stands alone, so readers can select the ones that interest them.

For example, if you want to examine the role of classroom lecturing, you could begin with chapter 1, "Implement 10-2 Thinking." Those of you who wish to explore issues facing teachers might begin with chapter 6, "See the Big Picture." If you want explore an issue that interferes with successful teaching, read chapter 10, "Abolish Tracking." Or, if you like a broader perspective, read chapter 19, "Invoke the Cosmos." And, if you want to begin with a personal story, read Coda, "Make a Difference." Reading the whole book, however, provides a rich perspective on teaching and life.

In addition, teachers and professors in particular are encouraged to examine the "Teaching Manifesto" in the Appendix before and/or after reading the book. The Teaching Manifesto provides guidelines for making classrooms exciting and engaging. Teachers are invited to sign the Manifesto to indicate their commitment to follow its principles. Other interested readers might want to read the Manifesto to gain perspective on what's possible to make learning happen *in* the classroom.

In essence, *Exciting Classrooms* serves as a friend, companion, and mentor. It nurtures true collegiality, through which the whole becomes greater than the sum of its parts. Teachers at all levels who read this book—especially with colleagues—will become better teachers. Because of its eclectic approach, administrators should make it a faculty read to encourage conversation about what matters in teaching.

Schools of Education will find it to be an engaging resource in a wide range of courses. Parents, superintendents, board members, and interested citizens who read it will be better able to help teachers—and future teachers—create exciting classrooms. Ultimately, everybody has a vested interest in education—and in this book.

NOTES

1. Scott Sampson, *How to Raise a Wild Child: The Art and Science of Falling in Love with Nature* (New York: Houghton Mifflin, 2015) speaking on "On Point with Tom Ashbrook," March 26, 2015.

2. Marc Prensky, "Digital Natives, Digital Immigrants." (2001). http://www.marc-prensky.com.

Part I

WHAT CAN WE DO IMMEDIATELY?

When teachers learn about specific, doable strategies, they modify their teaching skills and create exciting classrooms.

Part I offers five immediate strategies to improve students' learning.

Teachers have extraordinary skills. They instruct, organize, analyze, synthesize, create, articulate, observe, evaluate, write, initiate, study, plan, communicate, persuade, motivate, process, prioritize, problem-solve, meet deadlines, use technologies, negotiate, relate, listen, remember, reflect, adapt, diagnose, advise, counsel, coach, empathize, follow through. . . .

They call on any and all of these skills throughout the day. It is common knowledge that in the number of mental tasks teachers perform in a given day—up to three thousand—they are second only to air-traffic controllers. Teachers keep an eye on the big picture and pay attention to minute details at the same time. And, they do it for the most part alone.

No wonder, then, teachers balk when they are told to drop what they are doing—and may be doing well—and change to a new approach, or a new curriculum, or new method. The act of being told what to do and when to do it signals that they are inadequate decision-makers and builds resentment. A basic premise, then, of this book rests on respect for the hard work teachers do, and at the same time invites them to reconsider their practices in light of the needs and demands of today's students, culture, and global world.

Part I asks teachers to build on what they know that they already do well. It invites them to reframe, restructure, and reorient common practices in new directions to make their classrooms exciting. This shift will have a powerful effect on the motivation, involvement, and success of students—and will deepen the satisfaction of teachers and students alike.

Each chapter in Part I offers accessible and proven ways to teach well. These methods represent a small sample of what teachers can do immediately. Implementing them will bring the teachers closer to their students' minds and allow them have more success in today's rapidly changing world.

Chapter 1

Implement 10-2 Thinking

Dennis . . . Peter . . . Mary . . . Sebastian . . . José . . . OK, all here except Miranda and Natasha.

A reminder: Tomorrow I will review this week's material for the test you will take on Friday. Be sure to go over your notes and reread Chapter 12 in your textbook.

Which chapter, Ms. Bernardi?

Chapter 12, Ellie.

Now for today's lecture. We will continue discussing Lincoln's presidency prior to the outbreak of the Civil War. Yesterday, I spoke about the Lincoln–Douglas debates. Today, I will begin explaining the results of those seven debates. Please take out your notebooks and copy down the quotations I've put on the board.

We've all been here. As students, we quickly learn classroom routines. The longer we are in school, the more consistent they appear. When we become teachers, we continue the pattern. Taking attendance, collecting homework, setting the lesson, delivering material, winding down, assigning homework, dismissing the class. . . . We know the drill.

What keeps Allegra Bernardi lecturing in her American History class day after day? She began doing it in her first year, because she was nervous about letting her students interrupt her lessons with questions and comments. As a young teacher, she figured if she kept talking she would maintain better control. She would also keep pace with her colleagues. And, covering as much material as possible is essential if she is to meet the pressures of federal and state assessments.

After all, talking to students is the way teachers have always taught. Besides, her students are used to this approach. Parents also expect her to do it, as it is the approach they know. And, some of Allegra's colleagues have told her she might not keep her contract if she deviates from this embedded norm, since it is "the way teachers teach."

But, does Allegra recognize the impact of all her talking? Is she aware of what's happening in her students' minds when she delivers information class after class, day after day? What if she steps back for a moment to witness her students sitting at desks taking notes for the period? Then, visualize those same students repeating the same pattern in at least three other classes every day? Four classes a day, one hundred eighty minutes, over five hundred hours in a year!

Or, what about elementary children who sit at their desks listening to multiple series of instructions, followed by seatwork with workbooks and repetitive worksheets? What's happening in their minds? How are they processing their lessons? What values are they internalizing? What *are* they actually learning?

Unfortunately, Allegra and her colleagues rarely take time to find out—nor do they feel that they have the time. Yet, many complain that more and more of their students do not relate to lectures and whole-class lessons. Fewer of their students are willing to do homework and seem not to care about quizzes and tests. What, then, might encourage Allegra and her colleagues to stop talking so much? What might convince them to reframe their teaching and create more exciting classrooms?

- They could begin by visualizing themselves sitting at a student's desk—as Dan Hilliard did—and choosing to activate and engage students' minds instead of asking them to take notes.
- They could acknowledge that copying notes or filling out worksheets has hardly any relevance to digitally wired children who live in a globally connected world. Passive learning sends the wrong message.
- They could recall their teachers who deferred from talking to the whole class and instead invited the class to respond to provocative questions, creative ideas, and rigorous projects.

Evidence is building in research, journals, and literature for developing and implementing engaged teaching. One example, the Partnership for Twenty-first Century Skills—a leading coalition of teachers, industry, library groups, educational providers, and government groups—advocates skills that adults will need to succeed in the decades ahead:[1]

- Information and communication skills, including media literacy
- Thinking and problem-solving skills, including critical thinking; systems thinking; problem identification, formulation, and solution; creativity and intellectual curiosity
- Interpersonal and self-direction skills: collaboration, self-direction, accountability, adaptability, and social responsibility

- Global awareness
- Financial, economic, and business literacy; entrepreneurial skills to enhance workplace productivity and career options
- Civic literacy

None of these skills can be learned by sitting and listening. Instead, teachers might heed the words of the Spanish proverb, "What one does, one becomes," or the wisdom of the Buddha, "We are what we practice." If students practice sitting at desks half-listening, what will they become? How well will they know themselves? What will they care about? What skills will they have to prosper in the twenty-first century?

~ ~ ~

Where can teachers begin?

Vincent Roberts, now in his second year, has been struggling. He comes well prepared every day. He tries to make every class interesting. He works hard and cares for each and every one of his students and often leaves school exhausted. He believes—as some research confirms—teachers are the most important factor in student success. Yet, his sophomore History students often nod off during his lectures. How, then, can he make his classes more engaging?

One evening, he ponders, "How can I take advantage of my conversational skills and make learning exciting *in my classroom*? Maybe I could say less and listen more. Maybe I could allow students more time to talk and learn from what they are saying—and so they too may learn from each other."

For the next several weeks, Vincent makes this shift. He starts to discover a deeper satisfaction in his teaching as more students retain more. He enjoys this new energy. Suddenly, there is no turning back. "I no longer have to be stuck in my past practice. I no longer need to stay in what I now see as the trash heap of repetitive delivery."

If a teacher, like Vincent, is to complete this essential shift, he needs tools. One of the best and most accessible tools Vincent learned about at a Social Studies conference is 10-2, which Mary Budd Rowe developed over thirty years ago.[2] Rowe's 10-2 innovation provides a natural pathway for turning talking skills into student involvement and learning. For every ten minutes of delivering information, knowledge, or skills, 10-2 provides students two minutes to process.

Some examples of implementing and assessing the principle of 10-2 that Vincent learned about at the conference are:

- In math, after introducing improper fractions for about ten minutes, ask students to work alone or in pairs or in groups for two minutes to create problems using these fractions.

- In history, after taking ten minutes to discuss slavery as a cause of the Civil War, ask students to take two minutes to create a graphic organizer to demonstrate their understanding.
- In Language Arts, tell students not to take notes while giving a mini-lecture on the complexities of a Shakespearean plot. Then ask them to write down in two minutes what they understood.

Vincent is eager to try this approach. First, he takes time to familiarize himself with Rowe's idea. As students process during the two minutes, he will have to walk around the room and listen. When he lectures nonstop, he doesn't know what students are absorbing. He likes Rowe's idea to allow students five minutes to ask questions after the final ten minutes of his lecture. First, it provides an opportunity for them to review their understandings of the lesson, and second, it will give him feedback to indicate where to take the next lesson.

Instead of taking notes continuously, as Vincent's students usually do, the opportunity to process intermittently has them leaving class retaining more—much more—than when he lectures for the whole period. He assigns homework directly related to what his students are learning *in* class. "This is home-practice that makes sense!"

The choice to implement 10-2 Thinking is particularly important for those who lecture. The age-old format deriving from medieval times requires students to take notes throughout the period. But, when a teacher commits to 10-2 Thinking, he reshapes his lectures into ten-minute segments and plans for the two-minute activities. At first, he and his students find this shift challenging. But with persistence, as Vincent discovered, it works.

The most significant value of 10-2 Thinking is its focus on learning. Students participate, mirroring their interactive lives. When a teacher only lectures, he does not know whether or not students are learning until the test, which is way too late. When he uses 10-2 Thinking, on the other hand, each processing segment provides him immediate feedback. Any time his students are "not there," everyone is wasting time! In the words of Dylan Wiliam:

> If students left the classroom before teachers have made adjustments to their teaching on the basis of what they have learned about the students' achievement, then they are already playing catch-up. If teachers do not make adjustments before students come back the next day, it is probably too late.[3]

"These are profound words worth rereading," Vincent says to himself.

The principle of 10-2 Thinking also applies at the elementary level. Teachers often speak at some length when introducing a topic. It behooves them, then, to break up instructions into segments to allow students to process and ask questions. Teachers at all levels express concern that students will gossip if given time to talk with each other. On the contrary, the two minutes lets teachers listen in. Students welcome opportunities to talk with their peers rather than sit quietly all period.

When teachers claim that the 10-2 Thinking principle is irrelevant, they should heed the words of Sheila Webb, a kindergarten teacher in Athol, Massachusetts, who uses it consistently. "I love it! The students benefit so much from working with each other. The conversations are appropriate and relative to the lesson. Oftentimes, the reluctant students are right in the group talking about their own experiences or interpretations."

When teachers lecture, they often act as conduits. But when they choose 10-2 Thinking, they invoke the interactivity of language, the power of dialogue. Vincent also discovered at the conference that he could apply "wait time" to his lessons—another of Mary Budd Rowe's innovative ideas. After asking a question, allow time for students to think before speaking. As Rowe advocated more than thirty years ago, teachers should wait for three seconds before calling on students, instead of the 0.5 seconds that most do. By waiting three seconds, Vincent learned to

- invite students who usually hesitate to participate,
- encourage full-sentence answers rather than one or two words,
- invite higher-order thinking,
- and make it more likely for students to respond and comment on each other's answers.[4]

Vincent also learned to wait another four-to-five seconds after his students responded to indicate his respect for their thinking—an idea suggested by Laura Reasoner Jones.[5] No more quick responses. Instead, pauses invite deeper thinking to seek deeper answers. Sometimes, he assigns one-minute writing intervals to allow his students time to search for clarifications and understandings. He feels that he is beginning to create a community of learners rather than acting as a knowledge-dispensary center.

Many of his colleagues who lecture, however, argue that since some students do well lectures should work for the rest—if only they would put in more effort. But, Vincent is convinced that lectures reach fewer and fewer digitally wired students. And those with learning disabilities—such as ADD, ADHD, and autism—cannot listen and take notes at the same time. In years past, those students who did not do well in academics were considered less smart and steered into the workforce. Vincent understands that all students deserve every opportunity to succeed.

Yet some of his colleagues hesitate to cross this threshold. They fear that to implement 10-2 Thinking will take time away from coverage. In a forty-five minute lecture, Vincent tells them, 10-2 "costs" about ten minutes.

Those minutes, however, are crucial, as they provide students time to learn before they leave class.

However, one kind of lecture fascinates Vincent, one he uses occasionally. He's seen on YouTube popular professors (he had one in college) engage a lecture hall of three-hundred students. The professor takes about ten-to-fifteen minutes to set up a scenario, then steps in front of the lectern and with a microphone asks for students to offer their opinions about the situation he described. He listens closely, reframes the issue, and invites them to consider their own thinking before the next class.

"This is the perfect format for popular teachers," Vincent says to himself. "They're experts in their field and know how to engage students in a large lecture hall. I like that they present material much like I do in my class but they take a longer time to process it. Perhaps I should try that."

When teachers commit to 10-2 Thinking, they do not have to be wedded to its framework. They can vary the ratio, for example, 7-3, 15-3, and so on. It would depend upon the students, the context of the material, and purpose of the lesson. Whatever the ratio, Vincent is convinced that the 10-2 Thinking approach ensures that learning happens *in* class.

Eventually, Vincent discovers that his lessons are moving toward greater processing times. When learning becomes central, the ratio, for example, can shift from 10-2 to 2-10. Given the abundance of resources at their fingertips—including cellphones and tablets—students can seek information on their own in class and at home.

The research makes clear that depth is more important for learning than breadth. Delving into material opens learning potential more than rushing through it. Teaching for understanding activates the mind to think intelligently when confronting new concepts. Teaching for rote memory, on the other hand, can stymie long-term retention. By invoking 10-2 Thinking, as Vincent has, teachers step out from under the explanation umbrella and engage in conversation. As they teach for understanding, they talk less, students learn more—and so do they.

REFLECTION

Dan Hilliard and Allegra Bernardi often discuss the impact of lecturing. "Why do we do it when *we* were often bored listening to lectures day after day?" Dan shares his intention to move away from being the prime talker in his classroom. "I am trying Mary Budd Rowe's 10-2 to see if it improves chances for my students to learn. My students and I struggled with it at first but soon found it workable—and satisfying. In fact, 10-2 Thinking has changed my perspective on teaching. I now include frequent in-class processing and assessments. Checking in and listening has become essential."

"If every teacher who lectures or talks a lot uses 10-2 Thinking," Allegra replies, "what a difference it would make throughout the school! Each student would leave class having worked with the material—and would go home with something with which to practice!"

That evening Dan recalls the time he sat in Sam's seat. Instead of assigning homework that day he had asked his students how they planned to pursue their learning at home. "I will try to give them more opportunities to have input. Maybe I can flip the process and have them learn something new at home before coming to class. I wonder how that will work?"

The next day he finds Allegra in the faculty room. "Allegra, would you observe me and give me feedback about my use of 10-2 Thinking? I want to explore how I can increase the amount of time my students talk and I listen. I'm thinking about moving closer to 2-10 Thinking. I'm even thinking of flipping some of my lessons."

"I think you have some good ideas, Dan, but we must be careful not to become stuck in either-or thinking. Sometimes, as you well know, we can talk to students for as long as twenty or twenty-five minutes and have their full attention. These times, what I call engaged talking, sometimes happen by surprise. Students become eager to take in what we have to say. It's like they're hungry for our words and hang on to every one. I do not want to give up those times."

"Neither do I."

POINTS TO PURSUE

Use a Timer

Allegra Bernardi took Dan Hilliard's idea and decided to get a timer. She thought that it would help her become more disciplined with her talking. She determined a prescribed amount of time to talk on a topic—and set the timer. After a few times, she told her students why she was doing this—and asked them to participate more than they were used to in her class. Her teaching has become more efficient. If you want to become more efficient, try this timer strategy.

Try 10-2 Thinking

Vincent Rogers became a better teacher after he introduced 10-2 Thinking into his teaching. While he struggled at times, his persistence paid off. He knew that Mary Budd Rowe was right.

If you lecture (or talk a lot), assess the possibility of using 10-2 Thinking. Take time to introduce the process, as Vincent did, knowing that it will take time to convert you and your students to use it. Be patient. Be flexible setting the proportions between input and process. Pay attention to their reactions. It will be worth it.

Try Wait Time

When you feel compelled to cover material, you often teach quickly. Ask one question, collect an answer quickly, then on the next question. Take time, then, to examine the potential of Mary Budd Rowe's wait time. Try it for several weeks to see if the quality of student participation improves. Also, extend the time during which you wait to respond to students' comments, as Laura Reasoner Jones suggests. Be patient, as this process takes time to work.

See if students notice how you've changed your behavior. When they seem to know, take time to explain what you've done and why.

Reduce the Amount of Teacher Talk

If you know that you do most of the talking to students, consider ways to reduce that time. Invite students to make suggestions about how they may become more involved. If you are willing to try 10-2 Thinking, take your time to get to using it. It will be hard for your students—and you–to break old habits.

If you find successful ways to reduce your talking to increase time for learning, make a point to share it—or teach it—to colleagues. If you know of a colleague who has reduced the amount of talking in her teaching—she perhaps uses 10-2 Thinking—observe her to find out what she does.

Share 10-2 Thinking

Find a colleague who insists on lecturing every day. Invite her to observe you using 10-2 Thinking with a definite plan to meet and discuss her observations. If she is willing to try 10-2, agree to observe her and offer help. See if you can convince her to let go of lecturing. This could be a real challenge, as again, old habits are difficult to break.

NOTES

1. Richard Selfe and Cynthia Selfe, "'Convince Me!' Valuing Multimodal Literacies and Composing Public Service Announcements," *Theory Into Practice*, vol. 47, no. 2, Spring 2008, 83–92, in *Marshall Memo* 325, May 19, 2008, 5.

2. John Saphier and Robert Gower, *The Skillful Teacher: Building Your Teaching Skills*, 5th ed. (Carlisle, MA: Research for Better Teaching, Inc., 1997), 219.

3. Dylan Wiliam (2007), quoted by Kim Marshall at a Teachers21 Retreat, "Insights from Research and Practice," June 11, 2008.

4. John Saphier and Robert Gower, *The Skillful Teacher*, 309.

5. This application of wait time came from Laura Reasoner Jones in *Teacher Magazine*, September 3, 2008.

Chapter 2

Instill Skills

Can you believe it? When I ask students to highlight, some highlight a whole paragraph—and even a whole page! Where do they get that idea?

We remember how we fended for ourselves when learning how to do school. We figured out how to do homework, study for tests, take notes, write papers, complete projects, and organize, organize, organize. Those classmates who did these things well turned out to be the good students, which may have helped teachers sort us out into ability groups.

When we think about it, parents and pupils share a surprising similarity: Each learns how to do what he has to do on his own. We expect preparation for parenting to be uneven, as we have no parent-instruction institutions—and more families are living apart from one another. But schools are institutions with a defined structure, run by teachers and support staff who guide students for thirteen years or longer. Yet, results belie their effectiveness.

More than fifty years ago, Del Goodwin, Social Studies department chair at Hanover High School in New Hampshire, spent an extraordinary amount of time teaching students how to approach schoolwork: how to take effective lecture notes (not outlining), write essays (beyond only five paragraphs), and prepare research papers (analytical answers to questions). His "A Manual for the Writing of Research Papers"[1] was exemplary. In those prerubric, preformative–assessment days, he spent an inordinate amount of time defining skills and procedures and provided feedback to students as they were learning.

Today, the emphasis on testing has teachers prepping students on how to take them. But, as the comment on highlighting above indicates, teachers need to do more with everyday skills. As pupils move through school, teachers often assume they know how to do basic skills and procedures from previous teachers. Once students leave primary school, teachers spend less time on skills and procedures and more on content.

Since almost everyone assigns homework, teachers think students know how to do it. When asking them to read a chapter for homework, they assume students know how. After all, students have had years of reading already. And, surprisingly, when teachers say, "Take out your notebook," they may take it for granted that students know how to take notes. With so much content to cover, teachers want to focus on delivery, not process.

If teachers took time to interview students about their skills, they would discover different levels of competency. A student who does poor homework, for example, may not have a clue as to what to do, not because of his unwillingness to try. When a student takes poor notes, teachers sometimes think he doesn't try rather than he may not know how. Students often are unwilling to ask for help in class to for fear of appearing stupid. And, when teachers see them highlighting whole paragraphs and pages, they, too, ask "Can you believe it?"

Abraham Mezzo teaches, because he loves being with kids. Sometimes his sense of humor supersedes his teaching. He loves playing with his name. On different days he is "Mr. Mezzotint," or "Mr. Mezzonine," "Mr. Mezzosoprano," and even "Mr. Mezzotov." Each time he would stay in character as long as he could. He wants his students to know that despite his high standards and rigorous lessons, a sense of humor makes life more bearable. Needless to say, most of his students love his irreverence but some do not. He has to be careful.

Abraham cares about making school better for everyone. He remembers in the 1970s when highlighters started becoming commonplace. He noticed then that his seventh graders had them in their pencil cases. Instead of using pens or pencils, some of them—and he too—started using them in place of underlining. Of course, no one used highlighters in textbooks, as the books were owned by the school. None of his colleagues paid much attention to them either. Highlighters functioned in a manner similar to pens and pencils. Yet, when he noticed how poorly his Language Arts students were using them, he knew that he had to do something. He did.

Now, many years later, highlighters come in a myriad of styles—and are ubiquitous. They have even more potential to redefine how students access information—and their own understandings of material. Abraham asks his principal if he could lead the faculty on how they might use highlighters. He prepared the following handout for his presentation:

1. Create or find a thoughtful and provocative one-page piece of writing that will hook your students.

2. Give each student two highlighters, one *yellow* and one *blue*.
3. Put a question on the board and ask them to use the *yellow* highlighter to search for information that answers the question. Tell them to highlight only words or phrases and not sentences or paragraphs.
4. Have them take two minutes to compare their highlighting with a partner in preparation for a class conversation.
5. Process this exercise with the whole class. Allow students to ask questions and offer comments. Seek a consensus about what should have been highlighted.

Then, do the following:

6. Put a different question on the board and ask students to use the *blue* highlighter to underline words and phrases in the same article. When they highlight the same words as they did with *yellow* marker, those words will appear *green*, which will stimulate further conversation.[2]
7. An option at this point would be to have students meet in groups to discuss their underlining and write a common statement in response.
8. Another option is to have them compare their highlighting with that of a partner. Before reconvening the class, have partners meet with another pair and try to find agreement among the four as to what should have been highlighted.
9. Again, regather the class and answer questions. To check their understanding, you can have students write a paragraph on their understandings of how to use a highlighter.

Abraham then summarizes his presentation:

> A student who highlights whole paragraphs is wasting his time. He is making no attempt to sort out key ideas or terms. A teacher who takes time to teach students how to use this remarkable tool will not only stimulate interest in the material but will also improve their retention. After several repetitions of the process, students will have acquired a valuable skill that will improve their opportunities to retain what they read.

After the meeting, several colleagues came up to him to thank him for taking the time to share his ideas.

Later in the week, Abraham put the following information into faculty mailboxes:

> Here's another one-page exercise that uses two highlighters:

Ask students to use one color to mark what they think is important; use the other for what they find confusing. Again, you will be focusing on teaching how to use a highlighter as a specific tool. By having students work with highlighters in the classroom, you provide an effective tool for practicing literacy skills. Using highlighters well activates close, purposeful reading and rereading, improves thinking and conversation, and opens up opportunities to discuss and argue concepts using new-found evidence.

You can create similar exercises when introducing Post-it Notes and Flags. For example, ask your students to search through a textbook—which they are not allowed to mark—and Flag answers to specific questions. You can have them use a different color Flag to answer a different question.

Or ask you can ask students to search for particular examples, opinions, or ideas. Set up a scenario like the highlighter examples above. Have students either work alone, with a partner, or with the whole class. Invite them to use different colored Flags for different purposes. The goal is to teach students to use tools they find appealing to develop essential skills.

One final thought: those of you who use iPads in class can do the same exercises, except you cannot combine a *yellow* highlight with a *blue* highlight to get *green* (#6 in my handout). Maybe some day.

~ ~ ~

Whenever teachers, like Abraham, take time to teach students how to learn, they find satisfaction. Devoting time to teach skills, however, may appear to interfere with meeting the demands of ever-increasing amounts of curricula and outside testing. Yet, without the skills necessary to succeed in school, students will flounder. As carpenters need to learn how to use the tools of the trade, so, too, do students. Teachers have the obligation to teach them how to use these tools well.

REFLECTION

In his early years as a teacher, Dan Hilliard underlined books with pens and wrote notes in the margins. Now he uses highlighters, Post-it Notes, and Flags. He particularly likes having students use Flags to indicate key ideas and pages in textbooks. When he first saw that his students were not using highlighters properly, he created lessons to teach them how to use them. He also taught them to use Post-it Notes and Flags. Because his students use these tools to help them focus on their reading, they have become more curious. They retain more as well.

He shared his thinking with Allegra Bernardi, who also had been paying more attention to the use of these tools. Together, they brainstormed different

Instill Skills

approaches. When introducing these skills to their students, they have been sure to integrate good content. They want students to see the value of applying good skills to enable them to learn better.

POINTS TO PURSUE

Survey Students

Del Goodwin never took for granted the skill levels of his students. Instead, he made sure that they had the skills necessary for any project he assigned them to. If you want to know what your students know about how they learn, you will need to ask them.

Periodically survey your students' knowledge and understandings of how you conduct your classroom. For example, how they prepare for tests, do their homework, write their papers, take notes, use highlighters, etc. Chances are you will discover misconceptions that you can correct.

Try Two Highlighters

Abraham Mezzo may have his quirks, but he knew a good idea when he found it. His creative use of highlighters with his students is instructive.

If you've never approached your students about using highlighters, find a one-page topic that would appeal to them. Introduce Abraham's two-highlighter approach described in this chapter, or your own variation. Do the exercise several times until students understand how to use the technique well. Follow up with home-practice for reinforcement.

Try Post-Its and Flags

Do similar activities using Post-it Notes and Flags. Have students create their own Post-it Notes and Flags assignments.

Connect with Colleagues

Faculties become better when colleagues share good ideas. Instead of relying on administration to set the agendas for faculty meetings, take the initiative to bring up topics.

For example, ask your principal if you can introduce teaching students how to use highlighters, Post-it Notes, and Flags in classes. Take Abraham Mezzo's ideas from this chapter—or your own—about how to use these valuable tools. The school will be better off. Students will retain more.

NOTES

1. Delmar W. Goodwin, "A Manual for the Writing of Research Papers," Hanover Junior-Senior High School, Hanover, New Hampshire, 1964.

2. Thanks to Chuck Emery of Powder Mill Middle School, Southwick, MA, for suggesting the use of primary-color markers.

Chapter 3

Teach Literacy

Okay class, for tonight I want you to begin our study of organelles by reading sections 1 and 2 of chapter 15 in the textbook. Answer the first five questions at the end. I will collect them before class. See you tomorrow.

Children are taught to read during their first years in school. By the time they reach middle school, teachers assume they know how. On the surface, this appears true for most of them. If teachers assume children are able to read for meaning and understanding, they may have to think again.

Comprehending textbooks, for example, is a challenge for many. Part of this challenge is answering the questions at the end of chapters. Most students attempt to read the text first and then try to answer the assigned questions. Others turn immediately to the questions then look for the answers in the text. Some struggle with other ways, hoping they will get it right. And others simply give up.

If teachers expect students to dissect and comprehend a textbook—or any book—they should not simply assign pages; they should first be sure students know how to read it. It is common practice, for example, for Language Arts teachers to teach students how to read books in every genre. Poetry is not the only challenge.

Most teachers recognize that textbooks are especially difficult to read. They are constructed in a series of "mention sentences," that is, a series of disconnected sentences, each "correct" in themselves but not well-connected and coherent. They rarely express narrative. Jim Grant, founder of Staff Development for Educators, shared this point of view at a workshop. He based his conclusions on close analysis of textbooks and attributed their "cleaned-up" quality to the Texas textbook review committee.[1]

So, what can a teacher do with textbooks?

1. Commit as much time as necessary to teach your students how to be students of the text. Recognize that today's digitally oriented students may find reading textbooks particularly difficult. Make sure they understand that they will not only learn how to read the text but will also learn its content at the same time.
2. Use a jigsaw method: Assign a different section of a chapter to each student or to pairs. Each person/pair focuses on a small part of a chapter. Ask them to read their section closely; invite them to use Post-it Notes or Flags—only if they know how—and/or take brief notes. Provide questions to help them focus.
3. Group together—up to five in a group—those who have read the same section and have them discuss their findings. Once they agree on the content, have them write a common statement to indicate their understanding. Move about the room to check common statements to be sure they understand their section before they share it with classmates.
4. Place students into mixed groups to report findings to each other. Their common statements assure consistency and help them focus. By the time they finish sharing, everyone will have a good idea about what the textbook chapter was about—and will be able to answer the questions at the end of the chapter.
5. For reinforcement, assign a jigsaw for home-practice. Encourage them to use cellphones or instant messaging to help each other.
6. Repeat this practice—or its variations—until students understand how to read and learn from your textbook.

The net result of these in-class/home-practice efforts teaches students how to become more fluent both in reading and writing. Their newfound literacy skills will give them a better chance for future success. However, when teachers fail to take this time, reading the text becomes moot.

When schools neglect to incorporate the rigor of literacy—not only for textbooks—they deprive students of an important tool for the twenty-first century. Literacy skills are essential in fields that demand higher-order thinking. They are necessary for accessing thinking about what matters. Where else but in the classroom will students have opportunities to develop essential literacy skills of how to read with pen in hand, how to write and rewrite, and how to discuss and argue effectively with evidence?[2] Without these skills, they will fall prey to the sound-bite media that bombards them every day.

Isaiah Peterson agrees to observe his colleague Ron Schultz as he lectures to his sixth-grade students about the role of historians. Ron stands at front of the room, asks them to take notes, and answers questions toward the end of the class. He appears well-prepared and enjoys his students—and they appear to enjoy him. He has a gentle yet authoritative manner. At the end of his lesson, he assigns for homework a one-page sheet that describes Sherlock Holmes's detective skills. He wants his students to locate and highlight passages about Holmes's skills and relate those passages to the tools of historians.

After the students leave, Isaiah says, "Your connecting Sherlock Holmes to historians is clever. Why did you give it as a homework assignment?" Ron immediately admits, "I know that it will be way over their heads, but I decided to do it anyway." "So, Ron, again why did you give the assignment?" After some conversation, Ron realizes that the Holmes piece would have been better taught in class. For one, because they like Sherlock Holmes it would have engaged his students in the historical process. But, more importantly, because the assignment is challenging, Ron would have been available to work alongside them.

His conversation with Isaiah leads him to consider other ways he could use the Sherlock Holmes sheet in class. He could group students into pairs or triads and ask them to connect the relationship between Holmes's tools as a detective with the tools of historians. Once they made their connections, each group would share with the class in an attempt to reach a consensus.

In the process, he could encourage them to use their cellphones to text message other groups or to seek the advice and opinion of people beyond the classroom. He could list higher-order questions on the board to stimulate their thinking. The lesson might well have turned into one of those magical hubbub classes, full of energy, focused noise, and engagement, rather than one characterized by the restless behavior that often occurs during his lecture-style teaching.

Ron thinks of other options. He could ask students to create a play casting detectives as historians. Or have them to make pamphlets or posters connecting Holmes to historians. Or he could ask them to draft a letter to convince their textbook publisher to include Holmes in the section, "What is History?" And, he could ask them to write reflective essays and then take time to help them edit and rewrite in class. Eventually, the essays could be made into a class book, "The Historian as Detective."

Then he has another idea. Once his students master the material and complete the class book, he could invite them to create public service announcements (PSAs) to persuade other students in the school to appreciate studying the past as detectives. The level of technology to produce the PSA would depend on the sophistication of his students. It might include Microsoft Word, PowerPoint, iMovie and Movie Maker, and digital still cameras, digital video cameras or smartphones. "How exciting for my students to use 'their media' rather than exclusively paper and pencil! And, to use their newfound knowledge in a creative way!"

These examples demonstrate how Ron could implement a myriad of possibilities available to engage his students in literacy learning *in his classroom*. If, on the other hand, he assumes that his students have tools necessary for learning, he would miss the opportunity to develop all-important literacy skills, a necessary prerequisite for success in the future. And, he would miss engaging with their minds.

REFLECTION

Teachers have to be vigilant about the literacy levels of students. They can't assume how well students read and write at any grade level. While they may appear able to read proficiently, some may be sliding along, concealing that they are not real readers. Dan Hilliard was surprised to hear in his first year of teaching from a former good student that she "really learned to read" in her senior American Studies class from his veteran colleague, Marty Goodfellow!

When teachers do not assume about what skills students possess, they provide opportunities for them to demonstrate proficiencies. After introducing a literacy skill, they reinforce it throughout the year. In fact, teachers now have to teach traditional literacy *and* twenty-first-century skills (see chapter 1, "Implement 10-2 Thinking"). Dan has become aware of this imperative and spends increasing amounts of time putting both sets of skills at the center of his teaching. His students will become capable of teaching themselves, perhaps the most important gift he can give them.

POINTS TO PURSUE

Assess Your Students' Skills

Take time to learn what students know about reading and writing. Pre-assess by passing around a short, one-page, provocative reading material relevant to your subject or grade level. Ask students to study it and observe how they approach it. Do they simply read it? Do they use highlighters? Underline? Write in the margins? Ask clarifying questions? Seek help from classmates?

Allow time for them to "think-pair-share." Give them time to reflect alone, then discuss their perceptions with a partner, and then share with the whole class. This is a useful technique, as it involves everyone.

Take Time for Metacognitive Discussions

If you only plow through lesson after lesson, you miss opportunities to process student thinking. Take time, then, to have thinking-about-thinking discussions. Discuss with them about their mental processes and their awareness of how they think and use strategies. Discuss the importance of comprehension, as well as how to generate questions that lead to further learning.

Such metacognitive discussions can put teacher and students on the same page.

Include Narratives with Textbooks

After his conversation with Isaiah Peterson, Ron Schultz discovered many ways he could incorporate Sherlock Holmes's thinking into his students' assignments. Ron recognizes that textbooks are bereft of stories. He sees that the Sherlock Holmes piece can bring life to his lessons.

If you use a textbook, particularly in the humanities, make every effort to incorporate narrative material whenever possible. Use good questions to help students make connections and provoke evidentiary thinking.

Assess Twenty-First-Century Skills in Your Curriculum

Do you agree that the twenty-first century demands that schools teach twenty-first-century skills? Given the expanding requirements of the literacy curriculum, how would you justify teaching these skills so as not to water down the academic curriculum? How can you convince others that teaching these skills is every bit as important? These are vital questions.

Seek Colleagues Who Teach Both Literacy and Twenty-First-Century Skills

Take time to reassess your priorities. Do you teach both traditional literacy *and* twenty-first-century skills? How effective are you? Find other colleagues who claim that they do and agree to observe each other. Try each other's ideas and insist on feedback. You will learn from one another.

NOTES

1. See also "A Glossary of Banned Words, Usages, Stereotypes, and Topics" (thirty-five pages!), in Appendix 1 in Diane Ratvitch, *The Language Police: How Pressure Groups Restrict What Students Learn* (New York: Vintage, 2003, 2004).

2. Michael Schmoker, *Results Now: How We Can Achieve Unprecedented Improvement in Teaching and Learning* (Alexandria, VA: ASCD, 2006), for literacy; and Tony Wagner, *The Global Achievement Gap* (New York: Basic Books, 2008), for twenty-first century skills.

Chapter 4

Design Invitations

Steve Thomas's students arrive at his classroom door and find all the desks at the edge of the room. They hesitate . . .

Come on in and find a spot on the floor! I've put an intriguing problem on the board and large posters on the walls that are designed to raise your curiosity—and take you away from your desks. I wonder what you will discover!

You have the whole period to begin work on this problem. You can work alone or with anyone you'd like. You can use any resources from the bookshelf and computers in the room or in the library. You can ask me any questions.

Forty minutes later . . .

"For homework, I want you to explain to someone at home or in your neighborhood what you did today in class. Then come to class tomorrow prepared to discuss and write about what you did, how you shared it, and how you felt about the process.

No lecture. No notes. No roll call.

Steve had wanted to do this ever since a colleague suggested that he see *Dead Poets Society* over Christmas break. He became fascinated watching John Keating (played by Robin Williams) take his students to the trophy room on the first day of school. He was intrigued with Keating's ability to appeal to their intellect and emotions. Known for creating surprises in his classroom, Steve promised himself he would try something as radical with his middle school social studies students upon returning to school in the New Year.

Steve's yearning to intrigue his students illustrates a fundamental responsibility of teachers. As the digital universe surrounds their lives, students arrive in class with less interest in desk learning. Steve has heard colleagues complain, "These kids don't care"; "If parents cared, then our students would"; "Boys hide inside baggy clothes and girls dress as if they're going to a party"; "All they want to do is use their cellphones and iPods";

"Few of them do their homework." Steve hears colleagues claim that they are teaching in a different world, certainly different from when they grew up. He agrees with their sentiments but is open to the challenge.

Teachers are responsible for initiating learning *in* their classrooms. Unmotivated students are their responsibility. They cannot give up on any of them until they've done everything possible to engage their brains. Some students arrive already defeated, having given up hope, believing they are less than smart. They slink through the door and sit as far back as possible. When teachers give up on them, they put another nail in their coffin, instill yet another confirmation of their inadequacy, and add another step on their trip to the street. And, rather than appear stupid, these students often misbehave.

Every beginning—every lesson, every unit, every year—needs to be an invitation to learn. Invitations, despite claims to the contrary, are a teacher's most powerful tool. Threats and coercion have no effect on a student who is convinced that learning in school has no value.

In addition to the surprise of going to the trophy room on the first day, Keating chooses Robert Herrick's "To the Virgins, to Make Much of Time" as his text. Herrick's poem allows Keating to address the deeper lessons of life that he wants students to pursue in his literature class. He concludes by pointing to old photos of former students and says, "You, too, will soon be pushing up daisies. Carpe Diem, boys. Seize the day!"[1]

Keating's students want to return to class the next day, and the next, and the next. His invitations let them know of his commitment to them and to what they will learn. Steve's invitation after the holidays as well aims to stimulate his students. He wants them to see the value of open-ended creative problem solving and to trust their own initiative—two of his long-term goals. He invites them to search ancient eastern philosophies of Confucius, Lao Tzu, and the Buddha on their own and decide which is the most significant. Steve opens the door to weeks of stimulating research, conversation, and writing.

Teachers love John Keating's foray into the trophy room, but few emulate him. Invitations to learn, after all, take time and require creative juices. Given the pressures to cover material as fast as possible, invitations can cut into teaching time—and losing time creates anxiety. Bariyyah Lawrence, a veteran teacher devoted to her students, stopped teaching fourth grade because she could not escape the anxieties that she and her students were feeling every day about the MCAS (Massachusetts Comprehensive Assessment System), the state's high stakes test. She feels safer now that she's teaching first grade. So do her children.

Judging from research and classroom observations, most teachers prefer daily routines, which assures them of being able to cover required material. Yet, some take John Keating and Steve Thomas's path. They value novelty.

Steve's favorite metaphor to describe his view of novelty relates to perfume: the scent of perfume quickly recedes shortly after one senses its aroma. So, in school without novelty, boredom encroaches. When teachers vigorously engage students, their lessons often linger after the bell.

~ ~ ~

When teachers invite, they treat students as honored guests. They move away from acting as authorities who direct from the front of the room. They recall teachers who every day told them where to sit, what to do, when to do it, and how. Everyone complied because this was the way to do school. However, choosing the power of invitations, teachers no longer espouse compliance.

Viewing students as honored guests—despite having been assigned them—allows teachers to see them as who they are and who they can become. They become partners in learning *with* students rather than purveyors of knowledge *to* them. They act as hosts serving smorgasbords of ideas, questions, reflections, materials, skills, information, and understandings. Classes become acts of exchanging rather than one-way telling. "What can I do every day to invite students to learn *in* my classroom?"

The decision to extend invitations, however, is the first half of the equation. How students and families respond is the other half. Invitations, like gifts, only succeed when accepted. John Keating's invitation worked because his students accepted his challenge to seize the day. If an invitation fails, try another. Be willing, confident, and persistent.

Invitational classrooms respect learners with an agreement—an equation—in which teachers engage in a learning exchange with students and their families. When teachers talk and deliver, they distort the equation; what students "receive" requires them to regurgitate what they've "learned" if they are to get a passing grade, let alone get an "A." No opportunity to process, think, or choose. No opportunity to complete the equation.

It's no surprise, then, as students move into middle and high school they feel increasingly dissatisfied sitting detached in delivery classrooms. Fewer do homework or study for tests. Mary McGillis, a new, energetic ninth-grade Biology teacher, was astonished to learn from her colleagues that students in her school do not study for exams. They told her that unless she assigns a review project, none of the students will bother. Mary recalls that she and her classmates took exams seriously. As she thinks more about it, she realizes that despite her best efforts her science students are not willing to work as hard as she did.

When a teacher implements a balanced-equation classroom, she commits not only to bring material to students but also to bring students to the material.

Instead of handing information to her students as truth, she treats content as a lump of clay. She shapes opportunities to engage and invite her students to reform it in relationship to their understandings. Together, she and her students complete the shaping through a deeply creative process.

Not only does she develop an understanding of her teaching, but her students also develop understandings that they can take into future learnings. No more studying for tests, striving to pass them, and then forgetting everything the next day.

Creating a classroom culture centered on invitations takes patience, time, and persistence. When, for instance, choosing to apply discipline through consequences rather than punishments, a teacher builds trust and confidence. She lets students and parents know that her classroom is personal, active, and student-centered, not impersonal, inactive, and passive. When she teaches for learning, she is released from the tyranny of teaching-as-talking. Colleagues might put pressure on her to abandon such thinking by saying, "This is not how we do things around here." But once she commits to this process, she cannot turn back.

We all remember our great teachers. Whatever their teaching styles, we felt invited. Even when they lectured, we felt privy to their minds. We felt included in their world. We learned. We too know we've succeeded when we wake up at the end of class as if in a dream. "Where did the time go?" we ask. "Where *did* it go?" say our students.

REFLECTION

Unless we are willing to take responsibility for motivating students, we may not get much from them. Choosing not to motivate sets up a cycle. Students come to class each day less and less interested. We raise our voices, ratchet up our delivery, repeatedly call out for their attention—but to no avail. The cycle is set. Students see us as not caring; we see them as lazy and unwilling to learn.

If a teacher looks inward at her role and responsibility, she will recognize what she may need to change. She is the adult, after all. While she might consider John Keating's "carpe diem" or Steve Thomas's moving desks to the side as extreme, she certainly can begin by designing invitational lessons.

Dan Hilliard's first direct experience inviting his students to learn came on the day he sat in Sam's seat in the middle of the room. Later, when he saw *Dead Poets Society*, he vowed someday that he would take such a radical step with his students. But, he wants to be sure that he's not tempted to do it just for show. He wants his teaching to be integral to what he intends students to know, understand, and be able to do. Some day he will know the time when to try his "carpe diem."

POINTS TO PURSUE

Go for It!

Have you thought about trying something radically different with your students? Have you wanted to try a John Keating's trophy-room lesson or a Steve Thomas's emptying-the-desks lesson?

Devise your own radical step. Don't worry about its success, just give it your all. Whether it works or not, you will have a provocative, metacognitive discussion afterward. Who knows what it will lead to? Your willingness to take a risk will encourage your students to do the same.

Make Motivation Central to Your Teaching

Keating and Thomas took radical steps to motivate their students. How important do you think it is to motivate your students? What responsibility do you think students have for their own motivation? What is the balance point between the efforts of teacher and students? What can you do to reach this balance point? Should you involve parents?

Students As Honored Guests

Are you willing to see your students as honored guests? If you did, what differences do you think it would it make in your teaching? Take time to assess your attitude.

If you think that you'd like to shift your classroom toward a more respectful relationship between you and your students, how would you go about it? What would you do to let them know? How would your classroom be different?

Remake Old Lessons As Invitations

After learning about better techniques, sometimes teachers think that lessons designed the old way need to be thrown out. Before you do, take a close at all of the work you did to develop your old lessons. Pick one of them and use as much of it as you can when you decide to convert it into an invitation-to-learn lesson. Use the Taps Template for Teacher Planning (see chapter 5 "Make Meaning") to flesh it out.

When you reteach the lesson, pay attention to the differences you discover. Were you able to lure more students into wanting to work? Was it successful with all your students? What would you do differently?

Consult Colleagues

You know colleagues who have reputations for stimulating students. Some are flamboyant, others introversive. You often hear students talking about them. Ask if you can observe. If you like what she does, ask if you can try some of her ideas—and share yours. Through such exchanges, more students in your school will receive the benefits of innovative teaching.

Include Student Ideas

Students are great as a resource. They sit in class after class and know what they like and don't like. If you've never discussed with them about their impressions of your classroom, invite them to suggest ways to make it exciting. Listen. Try their ideas to let them know you are listening, and are willing to learn from them.

Move Your Desks

The physical arrangement of your room speaks volumes about you and your intentions. Desk in rows versus in a horseshoe each gives its own message. A room with desks, soft chairs, and couches sends yet another message.

Consider establishing different room arrangements to meet different learning expectations. With a stopwatch, teach your students how to move desks and chairs efficiently. Do it more than once. Be sure to have a worthwhile purpose for whatever arrangement you use.

NOTE

1. Peter Weir, *Dead Poets Society*, Touchstone Pictures, 1989.

Chapter 5

Make Meaning

Here's an index card for each of you. On one side please write three ideas you learned from our discussion today. On the other, please write a question we should pursue tomorrow to better understand what we are learning.

You do not need to put your name on the card. I will use them to assess what we accomplished and where we might take our work from here.

When a teacher shifts from talking *at* students to talking *with* them, they perk up. She keeps an open mind. She listens. She sees them engaged. She pays attention to what works. Her success leads to other strategies. She searches the Internet and studies educational publications. She read books. She rearranges her room. She asks colleagues for their ideas and practices.

Envision a piano teacher. She invites her pupil to play alongside her. She plays, then he plays. Back and forth. Back and forth. An interactive process. What if during the lesson she only shows him how the keys strike the soundboard, how to identify the notes she plays, points to the score, and so on? He would leave for home without having tried any of the techniques. How could he practice?

A teacher who emulates a piano teacher engages, connects, and supports. If, on the other hand, she only delivers information, she puts the onus of learning on her students. Some of students who are good at taking down notes might be able to learn at home. Others probably not. A teacher who lectures often feels satisfied. "If I present a well organized lecture, students should be able to learn. After all, I am responsible for covering the curriculum—and there's too much already!—so delivery is the most efficient way."

However, if a teacher wants to engage more students and improve their chances for success, that is, is willing to emulate the piano teacher, she can try the four strategies in this chapter. Each brings her closer to her students. Each brings her students closer to the material. And each helps to shut down the gap between teacher delivery and student sitting. *Exit Cards, Recap Cards*, and *Give One/Get One* are interactive and instructional. The fourth strategy, the *TAPS Template for Teacher Planning*, assures that lessons and units are designed within a coherent and sensible format.

EXIT CARDS

Every day, teachers face lots of students. Most of the time they are concerned with keeping pace with the curriculum. Secondary teachers set pacing goals with one another at department meetings. Elementary teachers feel pressure to cover the necessary material in all subjects within specific time frames. As a result, teachers spend less and less time assessing. And because they work alone and their schedules are full, they have little time to observe and provide feedback to one another. Many ask only for end-of-the-year evaluations from their pupils on the last day—too late to use to improve their teaching.

Exit Cards help teachers alleviate this lack of effective feedback. They are simple to use: near the end of class, pass around index cards, ask for comments or questions, and collect them as students leave. Exit cards can be used after a lesson, at the end of a unit of study, or even in the middle of a block period—any time that's appropriate.

Peter Macon has been teaching math to seventh graders for five years. He loves his job but worries that some of his students are falling behind. Learning math is a cumulative process. He's noticed, however, that at any one time up to a third of his students fail to keep up. At a math conference, he learned about Exit Cards and started to use them.

He tried different types of Exit Cards to determine which ones worked best. The first time he asked, "Please tell me what's bothering you about this class?" He received mixed messages, few of them very helpful. The next time, he tried a more direct approach. He wrote two phrases on the board, "I like . . .," "I wish . . ." He thought his students would provide clues as to what helped them during class and what else they would like from him. He was pleased. He then offered other pairs including "I want . . .," "I need . . .," and "I heard . . .," "I said . . ."

Later, he took a different approach. He framed two questions: "What worked for you today?" and "What question do you need an answer to?" He liked this approach, as the responses were specific and he could apply them to his next day's lesson. When he tried asking negative questions, such as "What didn't you like?" or "What didn't work for you?" he found answers less helpful. Positive questions generate better ideas both for him and for his students.

Later, he asked them a question pertaining to himself. "Is there anything I need to know to teach you better?" His students took the question seriously.

He tried several of their ideas. Other times, he asked direct content questions, such as "What do you think was the big idea of today's lesson?" and "What question do you have about what you learned?" He found that these types of questions also worked well. Occasionally, Peter asked students to sign their names, particularly when he wanted to know individual preferences.

Peter likes Exit Cards, because they're immediate and anonymous. They take little time away from his lessons, yet provide him with valuable information about his teaching and about what his students are learning. Without Exit Cards Peter could only ascertain their body language and guess the success of his teaching. Now that he has instant and valuable feedback, he is able to plan better, teach better—and, of course, assess better.

Once he became a committed user, Peter began to ascertain patterns as to what's working (do more of the same) and to what's troublesome (make changes), and used these patterns to gain insights (discover new ideas). Peter thought of organizing his Exit Cards, so he now uses a specific color for each class. Then, he has the proper context when reading them.

Being one of the more gregarious members of his faculty, Peter couldn't wait to share his epiphanies about Exit Cards. If others start to use them he would learn new ways to use them. He figures he is only at the tip of the iceberg as to their effectiveness. From a conversation with Megan Stoddard, a third-grade colleague, he learned that she not only uses Exit Cards but also uses a different color for each subject in her classroom.

Given that it takes about two minutes of class time for Peter's students to fill them out and not much longer to read, Exit Cards have been a wise investment. They make assessment a daily practice. No more waiting for quizzes and tests to tell Peter how his students have been doing.

RECAP CARDS

Exit Cards provide instant feedback. Peter later discovers Recap Cards, which give his students opportunities to test their knowledge, skills, and understanding during the last ten minutes of class.[1] Instead of him relying on "Thumbs up; thumbs down," or asking, "How many of you think you know . . .?" or calling on a few students for a quick assessment, Peter discovered that Recap Cards allow *every* student to process the day's lesson and receive immediate feedback.

Peter outlines his procedure for using Recap Cards as follows:[2]

1. With about ten minutes of class time remaining, I give each student in his cooperative learning group a standard-lined index card (4 × 6 inches, 5 × 8 inches).

2. I have them recap the most important points in the lesson or solve the assessment problem of the day. I make sure they put their name on the card.
3. After they have finished writing, I instruct students to pass the cards to a peer in their group. I ask peers to rate the recap according to a predetermined rubric for good communication (see below). Then, the reviewers place their initials against the rating. Later, I record the peer evaluation values.
4. The students return the reviewed recaps to their owners. One or two students who scored three stars (highest rating) from their peers share their responses. If time permits, we discuss the ratings and how the recaps can be made stronger. Periodically I post examples of excellent recaps or place them on an overhead next to the rubric.
5. I change the cooperative learning groups biweekly to ensure that each student receives a wide range of opinions.

The rubric Peter uses is as follows:[3]

- Three stars for a recap that is clear, accurate, grasps the main ideas of the lesson, and shows how the problem was solved.
- Two stars for the satisfactory job of getting the main idea, but the response is either unclear to the reader or has several errors. The response shows only a basic understanding of the ideas involved.
- One star for an attempt at the problem; response is hard to read, not very clear, or has several errors. It shows only a basic understanding of the ideas involved.
- Zero stars reflect major errors in understanding the ideas.

Peter uses Recap Cards to learn how well everyone has learned his lesson. The cards are comprehensive and provide immediate feedback both to him and his students. Peer assessment provides direct feedback and often solidifies the lesson.[4] Peter often sees students who struggle during his lesson begin to pick up the material during this review process. "Peers teaching peers works better sometimes than my teaching!"

~ ~ ~

Exit Cards and Recap Cards are invaluable. Simple to use, they provide teachers and students immediate feedback. These are only samples of summarizers that can provide valuable formative feedback. Among others are the following:

- *Envelope Please* and *Crumple and Toss*: These are similar to Exit Cards but with a twist. Ask students the same types of questions and either put the cards into an envelope or toss them into a basket. Using the Envelope, like we use Exit Cards, ask students to write questions about the lesson. After checking them over, teachers can pass the envelopes back randomly for peers to answer the questions the next day.
- *3-2-1*: An example of this would be, "Three big ideas about . . .," "Two problems you see," and "One question you want answered."[5]
- *The Important Thing*: Create a brochure applying evidence about a lesson, based on Margaret Wise Brown's *Important Book* (New York: Harper and Row, 1949).[6]
- *The One-Minute Paper*: This is a popular, higher-education tool used at the end of lectures, in which students answer, "What is the big point you learned in class today?" and "What is the main unanswered question for you from today's class?"[7]
- *Ticket to Leave*: Another term for Exit Card.

Peter Macon's experiments with Exit Cards and Recap Cards exemplify the workings of a teacher who wants an exciting classroom. To take the guesswork out of assessing of his teaching, he hears directly from his students. Once he discovered Recap Cards, he sees them as an invaluable tool to assess what his students learn—or not—on any given day.

Recently, Peter discovered a wonderful new tool that enables him to immediately assess what his math students are learning. As he teaches the concept that every quotient of integers is a rational number, most of students appear to grasp it quickly. He then assesses their answers using his new tool "Socrative."[8] His students were already logged in on their iPads. A box was open on their screens in which he puts a problem. The students' answers appeared by their names on his screen. Only five got it right!

He presented other problems, and after fifteen minutes all the students were able to derive correct answers. At the time his students were learning what he wanted them to. Sometimes as reinforcement, at the end of a "Socrative" lesson he uses Recap Cards. Most students score with three stars. He is beginning to like his teaching more every day! So many ways to reach students!

GIVE ONE/GET ONE

Give One/Get One—or as some teachers prefer, Seek One/Share One—offers an invaluable way to activate learning. For example, using the Give One/Get One form (Figure 5.1), a teacher can ask students to fill in the top three boxes

Give One/Get One		
What can you do to help all students be successful in your classroom—especially the most difficult and challenging students?		
I contact parents early in the year to tell them something good about their child.	I place students near where I can see them.	I set up a private signal to let John know when I can see that he is about to cause trouble for himself.
Set up a parent conference and include a guidance counselor.	Set up a parent conference and include a guidance counselor.	Provide physical space and room to move for Bill to help him focus. It usually works.
See Ross Greene's "Three Baskets" from his book The Explosive Child: sort out handling meltdowns; high priority behaviors we work out, and low priority ones we can remove from our radar screen.	Take time to discuss patterns of class behavior to teach and reinforce a respectful classroom; be willing to take time to do this, or nothing will be learned.	Assume that the student does not know how to do something rather than that he does not want to do it.

Figure 5.1 Sample Use of Give One/Get One.

with three ideas/facts/questions they know from what they've been studying. She then asks them to move around the room both to gather classmates' ideas and to share their own. Once they have filled the remaining six boxes, they return to their seats.

Give One/Get One provides students an enjoyable opportunity to share their thinking and pick up different information. They particularly like moving around—and need it! The process encourages community building, as it opens students to learn from one another. It also builds confidence, as they observe peers writing down their ideas. And, it builds collective responsibility for learning the material in question. Like all new procedures, teachers should take time to teach students how to interact using Give One/Get One.

Bob Mullen, a longtime teacher and now a consultant, uses Give/One Get One in his workshops with teachers to show them its effectiveness. In his sixth-grade language arts–social studies classroom, he had a reputation as one who tried new strategies. Hardly a week passed in which his students were not challenged to learn in a new way. No one was bored!

He selects topics he wants workshop participants to know more about. "Give One/Get One is one of the easiest and most effective activators of students' brains," he tells them. "It can be used for a variety of purposes from intriguing students to want to learn, to sharing with others about what they know. And, one of my favorites is using Give One/Get One for Review." (See Textbox 5.1.)

Textbox 5.1 Give One/Get One as Review

- ✓ Pass out a Give One/Get One sheet (designed in any way you'd like).
- ✓ Begin by asking students to fill in the three top blanks with what they think will be important to learn for the upcoming test.
- ✓ Have them leave their desks to gather ideas from their classmates.
- ✓ Whenever they find a peer having the same idea(s), they should put the peer's initials on their sheet in the corresponding box; peers should do the same on their sheets.
- ✓ When they find a new idea, they should put it in a blank box. Once they have all boxes filled in, they have to return to their seats.
- ✓ Ask the class first to share those items that have the most number of initials on their Give One/Get One sheets. Record these most common ideas on the board.
- ✓ Then ask students to share other ideas that they believe are important even though no one else may have listed the same idea. Put these on the board, unless it is obvious they should not be added.
- ✓ Add a couple of essentials of your own if they have not come from students.
- ✓ Make up—or modify—the test based on what's on the board! Why?
- • Students will be empowered because they will have a say in what they believe they've learned.
- • The teacher discovers what students have learned, which may or may not be what she had intended.
- ✓ Ultimately, as a teacher, you are acting like a coach, that is, using the material that will be used in the "game" (test). No more guessing games! You design a fair test. Students study what they need to study.

"This approach helps students review and prepare for a test," Bob confides. "You don't have to do that tedious review of material for students. Instead, you set up 'Give One/Get One as Review' to invite your students to review independently, with each other, and then as a class." After some discussion, participants become convinced that the opportunity to interact for review lets students *and* teacher know what they need to learn. Students do the work of the review. The teacher does not "go over" what will be on the test while students sit passively at their desks. A win-win situation, particularly as Bob noticed with his own classes when more of his students did better on tests.

Teachers can use Give One/Get One at any time during a lesson. Some use it to preassess students' knowledge, understandings, and skills. Others use it in the middle of a lesson to stimulate sharing of ideas or to answer questions. Some use it at the end as a summarizer. As with other interactive strategies, teachers use Give One/Get One in the context of what they want students to know, understand, and be able to do. Otherwise it becomes a gimmick. The TAPS Template that follows assures that teachers use ideas including Exit Cards, Recap Cards, and Give One/Get One meaningfully.

TAPS TEMPLATE FOR TEACHER PLANNING

This last strategy demonstrates the importance of aligning teaching and integrating interactive methods within a clear, well-defined context. The TAPS Template for Teacher Planning (Figure 5.2)[9] builds on Grant Wiggins and Jay McTighe's Backwards Design structure—with input from Chip and Dan Heath—and Carol Ann Tomlinson's Differentiated Instruction methods. In choosing this template, teachers commit to the fundamental elements of successful instruction. At the same time, they avoid teaching a series of disconnected lessons as can happen, for example, when they rely on textbook chapters as their curriculum.

The TAPS Template requires teachers to pay careful attention to every part of a lesson, unit, and course of study. For example, effective essential questions are crucial to drive the learning, such as these questions from the Math Forum at Drexel University: "What do you notice?" "What do you wonder?" for considering the implications of a solution to a problem.[10] Such questions emerge from a thorough understanding of the intended lesson or unit. The TAPS Template includes well-known elements of teaching and assures that a coherent structure will result. Building a template takes time, patience, collaboration—and hard work.

When planning with all of the *T, A, P,* and *S* elements of the template, teachers diversify their teaching to meet the flexible needs of students. They avoid relying on only one-size-fits-all, whole-class lessons. In both the

Make Meaning 39

How does this lesson/unit/course connect to core ideas? *What will students know, understand, or be able to do as a result of this lesson/unit/course?* *How does it connect to the previous and the next lesson/unit/course?*	
What essential questions might you ask to drive the thinking? For example, "What do you notice?" "What do you wonder?" "Why do people go to war?" and "What makes this novel great?"	
How will you activate lessons, excite students to want to learn? What mystery could you create? What surprise might you use? Is there a story you could relate...?	

Format	Used for
Total Class	• *Directions* • *10-2* • *Video viewing* • *Give One/Get One...*
Alone	• *Journal writing* • *Quizzes* • *Reflections...*
Pairs/Triads	• *Peer review* • *Think-pair-share* • *Clock partners...*
Small Groups	• *Tiered instruction* • *Interest groups* • *Give One/Get One* • *Anchoring activities...*

How will you and your students know what they are learning?
How will students summarize the learning, e.g., using Exit and Recap Cards?
What homework—home-practice—will you give to connect and excite students?

Figure 5.2 TAPS Template for Teacher Planning.

planning process and when teaching the TAPS Template, teachers keep in mind two questions:

"Who's not going to get it?"

"Who will get it quickly or already know it?"

Once these questions become embedded, teachers no longer assume that all students learn in the same way at the same pace. Both questions remind them to pay attention to individual students—in planning and execution.

Implementing the TAPS Template for Teacher Planning assures that students learn coherent, aligned, and relevant material. It assures, as well, along with pedagogies such as Exit Cards, Recap Cards, and Give One/Get One, it will make for purposeful learning. Students understand the context of what they are asked to learn, and are able to connect the various pieces. They do well when teachers offer diverse approaches both in their teaching and in asking for feedback. The four strategies offered in this chapter allow teachers to use their known skills in new and rich ways that benefit their students—and them.

REFLECTION

After Dan Hilliard learned about these four strategies, he was dumbfounded about why he had not heard of them before. Then he remembered that it often takes about thirty years for good ideas to become common practice. For example, it took thirty years after the Wright Brothers developed the first successful airplane to implement commercial flying.

Ever since Dan heard the metaphor linking the piano teacher to the classroom teacher, he has paid more attention to what his students do in his classroom. Using Exit Cards, Recap Cards, and Give One/Get One improved his ability to assess and to redesign his teaching. Because he likes these processes, he invites colleagues to his room on the third Thursday of the month to have conversations about best practices. So far, five of his colleagues have joined and others have expressed interest. For the first meeting, he introduced the Taps Template for Teaching as a framework for thinking about best practices.

Good teachers become alert to new and better ways to teach and learn. Implementing the strategies such as those in this chapter enriches their repertoires. More importantly, they let go of traditional practices that no longer work; new habits of teaching replace the old.

POINTS TO PURSUE

Use Exit Cards and Recap Cards

Follow Peter Macon's lead in this chapter. Take advantage of students' feedback as he did, by using Exit Cards. Make it a practice to use them often. Don't wait until the end of a unit—or the year.

Try Recap Cards. Take your time to introduce this process. Don't worry if students do not take them seriously at first. If you persist, they will see their value.

Share Your Use of Exit and Recap Cards

Asking fellow teachers to take a whole planning period to observe your classroom can be time consuming. If, instead, you invite a colleague to drop in at the end of a lesson when you intend to use Recap Cards, they'll be more likely to accept your invitation. After your demonstration, ask for feedback. Perhaps you will start making colleague feedback a habit in your school.

Try Multiple Give One/Get One Approaches

Take a lead from Bob Mullen and design Give One/Get One exercises to activate your students' learning before, during, or at the end of a unit. Give One/Get One is an effective way to engage students to learn in class.

Take your time to integrate this process into the habits of your classroom. Provide plenty of time for students to learn how to use each form of Give One/Get One that you introduce. Once this concept is internalized, students will be grateful, as they will retain more.

Commit to Using the TAPS Template for Teacher Planning

When using the TAPS Template, you establish clear intentions for your students and for you. Take time to assess how using the template engages more students than your old planning system. Determine what differences it makes to you. Share your work using the template with colleagues to generate valuable discussion about what's important in teaching.

Design a Seminar for Colleagues

Because everyday pressures keep teachers overbusy, propose establishing a bimonthly seminar—like Dan Hilliard's best practices' Thursdays. Make the focus on improving practice. Begin by discussing and agreeing to try the ideas in this chapter, and all the other ideas and practices in part I. You will become better teachers.

NOTES

1. John Quinn, Brian Kavanagh, Norma Boakes, and Ronald Caro, "Two Thumbs Way, Way Up: Index Card Recap and Review," *Teaching Children Mathematics*, December 2008/January 2009. The National Council of Teachers of Mathematics, 295–303. Thanks to Ginny Tang who led me to this source.
2. Ibid., 300, adapted.
3. Ibid., 297, adapted.

4. Ibid., 303. The authors claim Recap Cards to be one of the more innovative approaches, alongside implementing NCTM standards. The results were impressive: 100 percent of the students in the class described in the article passed New Jersey's fourth-grade mathematics assessment, with 73 percent falling within the category "advanced proficient."

5. From Jon Saphier and Mary Ann Haley, *Summarizers: Activity Structures to Support Integration and Retention of New Learning* (Carlisle, MA: Research for Better Teaching, 1993). Along with *Activators: Activity Structures to Engage Student's Thinking Before Instruction* (Research for Better Teaching, 1993), are invaluable reproducible resources for mobilizing learning at both ends of a lesson.

6. Ibid.

7. Ibid.

8. "5 Fantastic, Fast, Formative Assessment Tools" by Vicki Davis in *Edutopia*, January 15, 2015, http://bit.ly/1xUUm0J found in *Marshall Memo* 579, March 23, 2015.

9. The TAPS Template for Teacher Planning was developed with my colleagues at Teachers21, Wellesley MA.

10. With thanks to Barbara Delaney, Bellingham Middle School, Massachusetts, who found these wonderful questions at a Drexel Math workshop. Google essential questions to find a plethora of them.

Part II

HOW CAN WE EXPAND OUR TEACHING PRACTICE?

By taking the longer view, teachers discover the strength of seeking wisdom both old and new to resolve difficult questions.

Part II invites teachers to expand their practice and seek answers.

Once teachers shift practices toward creating exciting classrooms, they think differently. They reflect more and consider broader perspectives. When they see students respond favorably to new practices, it encourages them to try other new approaches. Being willing to look within themselves *and* beyond the world of the classroom world, they discover new ways to nurture learning.

Part II invites teachers to step back and assess the big picture. Despite the fact that their work takes place in isolated classrooms, good teachers see their thought processes as they mature in their teaching. They see the larger factors governing the world and causing rapid change. And, they seek ways to stay abreast of current innovative thinking.

Ultimately, creative teachers examine the full range of their practice. They ask hard questions, questions that help them meet the needs and demands of students, their families, and the global world. As they expand their teaching, they find answers and discover new questions—an endless process.

Chapter 6

See the Big Picture

Whether we want to admit it or not, we are in the midst of a huge cultural shift in our society. Some have called these times as significant as the Renaissance—and others say more so!

Teachers tend to teach by osmosis. From their earliest days as pupils, they absorb the habits and practices of their teachers, who stand at the front of the room, take attendance, deliver one-size-fits-all whole-class lessons, use textbooks, fill out plan books, average grades, assign homework, and keep kids after school—and do it alone.

As pupils they internalize beliefs about teaching. For instance, a history teacher develops the notion that he needs to anticipate answers to every student question, when in fact he might better stimulate thinking by conjuring "unanswerable" questions. Or, he may believe that his students must take notes every day to digest what he tells them, rather than asking them to seek answers to authentic, worthwhile questions—thus inviting thinking into his classroom.

Or, a math teacher who has internalized one way of encountering math as a pupil repeats the same pattern with her students. She begins every class having them put homework on the board, corrects their examples, and collects the homework. She then teaches a new concept, and if time allows she lets them do the homework assignment until the bell rings. Had her math teachers allowed time in class for her and her peers to invent solutions to problems and present them to the class for scrutiny, she might have become a different—and better—math teacher.

Habitual practices often constrict imagining other possibilities. Many teachers employ a weekly approach to lesson planning. Friday is test day for material delivered Monday through Wednesday, with Thursday for review. This routine, logical on the surface, tends to fragment thinking and learning because it does not allow for flexibility and in-depth exploration. However, it is the perfect methodology for coverage.

When teachers pay attention to the ill effects of established practices, they begin to notice their impact. For example, instead of blaming students for their failure to do homework, teachers might see their part in this failure. They might consider reconfiguring the role of homework as follows:

- Redefine "homework" as "home-practice" to inform students of its true purpose.
- Offer options, such as allowing students to pick six of ten questions/examples they think will help them learn best.
- Ask students to create their own questions and answers.
- Instead of writing, invite them to create a graphic organizer to illustrate what they know.
- Finally, and perhaps most intriguing, ask them to choose what they will do for home-practice. See what arrives the next day.

Why should teachers take time to reexamine habitual practices, particularly if they think they are working well? Unlike generations before them, today's schools are heading into an unknown cultural future. Given the quickening pace of the doubling of knowledge, the plethora of new technologies, and the ubiquitous access to the Internet, teachers cannot act as if the world is what it was for them.

Responsive teachers are open to the present media-driven culture. Those who cling to teaching habits of old may soon face obsolescence, as students prefer to learn from the media's multiple resources. The more students become bored in the classroom, the more they will immerse themselves into technology's instant capacity to connect them with whatever they see—or want to see. Teachers will be shut out of their lives.

Given present uncertainties, teachers can look to discover new possibilities to excite students. They can steer them toward engaged tasks that invite inquiry and—perhaps most important—require struggle to find resolution. Once students experience the joy of using their minds to solve intriguing scenarios and problems—no easy task!—they may be less tempted to stay inside the instant nonthinking of texting and Googling.

Teaching students to live in the questions rather than jump to quick answers requires a new paradigm. Teachers have to let go of outmoded teaching comforts and routines. They reexamine the contexts in which they teach and determine how to make them more engaging. They collaborate with colleagues. They delight in the struggle to discover new perspectives. The three ideas in this chapter offer ways for educators to evaluate the implications of today's fast-changing culture.

THE BIG SHIFT

Given the incessant demands of working in schools, teachers rarely take the opportunity to view their teaching from a broad perspective. Francis Jordan in his first year in the classroom was surprised to discover the complexity of teaching his sixth graders in what he thought was a good school. He and his colleagues were being asked to do far more than they bargained for. At a faculty meeting he asked, "How can I even think about the broader issues facing our society when I have so many children who need my attention? I have kids with autism, who come from single-parent homes, who live in dire poverty, who bully other kids. It's endless really—and, I do it alone."

As he thought about his conundrum, Francis knew he should immerse himself into the lives of his students. Not to become immersed, he would distance himself from them—and they would know it. However, when he took time to see the big picture inside and beyond the classroom, it gave Francis perspective—and solace. Being willing to look further down the road allowed the freneticism of the moment to reside within a greater context, and allowed him to arrive at a better sense of where everyone—he and his students—was headed.

He liked tackling matters of consequence. The more he brought up intriguing problems, controversial issues, and big perspectives, the more his sixth graders became excited and engaged. They thought him quirky at times but liked his energy and humor that kept them involved. Hardly a dull moment. He began to love his teaching.

After teaching for nearly forty years, Francis left the classroom. He spent his last twelve years serving as a consultant. He wanted to bring his big-picture perspective to his teacher workshops. As part of his packets he included a one-page commentary that he titled "The Big Shift" (Textbox 6.1). After having someone read it aloud, he asked participants to meet with one or two others who they did not know and discuss three questions:

1. What do you observe that's different about today's students?
2. How have you had to change your teaching in response?
3. As a result of discussing The Big Shift, what might you consider doing differently?

After ten to fifteen minutes, Francis invited pairs/triads to join another pair/triad to select what big idea they should bring back to their table group.

Textbox 6.1 The Big Shift. (*Quote from: Marc Prensky, "Digital Natives, Digital Immigrants.")

> Whether we want to admit it or not, we are in the midst of a huge cultural shift in our society. Some have called these times as significant as the Renaissance—and others say more so!
>
> This shift is evident in the exponential expansion of the media both in content and technologies. These effects are most obvious in the children we are now being asked to teach.
>
> We are at the vortex of this radical shift in our culture. Unless we respond with intelligence, creativity, and commitment, our students will zoom past us ignoring our outmoded methods and approaches. They will find ways to educate themselves, as do all pioneers who invent solutions to newfound problems.
>
> "Our students have changed radically," says Marc Prensky. "Today's students are no longer the people our educational system was designed to teach."
>
> We need to examine our current purposes and practices in light of the information-age culture. We cannot remain in isolated classrooms. Students cannot be expected to work in isolation either. Instead, as we move toward collaboration and cooperation, our students will need to be encouraged and supported in working together to learn. Already, they are sending instant messages of homework—and some with their teachers! Individual accountability will remain, yes, but it will come to mean something different. What, we are not sure.
>
> We will need to collaborate and to create ways for meeting today's students where they are and nurture them to become good students, good citizens, and good people. This is not about indulging them. We have much to offer—and can decide just what that is.

After ten minutes, each group shared its conclusions. Francis was never sure that these conversations had much impact, but he felt satisfied that he at least broached this key issue.

"Maybe," he thought, "teachers don't really see themselves considering bigger issues. They are too busy entangled in every-day challenges. Somebody else would have to deal with such matters." Yet, as he wrote in "The Big Shift," teachers "have much to offer—and can decide just what that is."

To bring his point home, Francis cites an idea of Richard Lavoie from a speech he gave in Fitchburg, Massachusetts.[1] Lavoie used three words to define the way we now live: "Unlearn, Learn, Relearn." Using the example of the telephone, Lavoie traced our society's relationship from the rotary phone to the cellphone.

In nearly all aspects of today's culture, Lavoie reminded his audience of the need to unlearn what they learned in order to learn anew just to keep up. He cited cellphones, computers, GPS, TiVo/DVR, and Amazon's Kindle. "Once we've finally learned how to use one of these, a new model appears. Unless we update, the old model soon becomes obsolete." He let the audience know that this way of living is natural for the young, but is often is a struggle for teachers. Many nodded their heads in agreement.

HOW PEOPLE LEARN

Another handout invites participants to examine their teaching practices in light of a well-known graphic, "How People Learn" (Textbox 6.2). Most of them have seen this information in one form or another and usually nod their heads in quick agreement and are ready to move on.

When Francis used an earlier version of the graphic, he hoped to demonstrate that students learn better when actively engaged. However, he did not get much reaction. Later, he added a line between "See and Hear" and "Say." He asked them to discuss the implications of teaching "above the line" and "below the line." He put them either in pairs or triads and sometimes regrouped them into fours or sixes (as he did with The Big Shift).

Textbox 6.2   How People Learn. A common chart or pyramid that teachers hear about in education courses looks something like this one

People learn...

- 10% of what they READ
- 20% of what they HEAR
- 30% of what they SEE
- 50% of what they both SEE and HEAR

- 70% of what they SAY
- 80% of what they EXPERIENCE
- 90% of what they SAY and DO
- 95% of what they TEACH

Source: This particular chart has been adapted from charts by Edgar Dale, Eldon Ekwall, and James L. Shanker, William Glasser, and David Sousa. While the original source of the research is unclear, it provides for stimulating conversation when including the middle line.

To stimulate conversations, Francis includes the following questions:

- How does this chart relate to how you distribute your instructional practice both above and below the line?
- Is below-the-line teaching "better" than above-the-line teaching?
- Can you teach effectively only from either above the line or below the line? Should you?
- How accurate do you think are the percents as stated in the chart? Are they accurate for you?
- What other questions does the chart raise?

The revised chart compels participants to focus on learning. They often agree that the percentages do not apply equally to all people. Yet, the chart shows teachers that they should not remain stuck in the delivery mode. When they teach only from above the line, they see themselves doing all the talking. However, when they project themselves teaching below the line, they engage and interact with their students.

Sometimes participants admit to Francis they would like to teach below the line, but the challenges of covering overburdened curriculums necessitate that they remain above it. He points out, however, that staying above the line assumes that students learn when the teacher explains. When participants reflect about their time as pupils, they remember how little they learned from just having to listen.

The last line of the chart, however, raises a common concern: "How can we monitor all of our students when they are teaching one another?" Francis recounts his own experience of how this activity benefited both his students and him. Before he had his students teach one another, he required them to write what they would share. This way he could assess their thinking—and writing skills—before they taught. This process took more time but proved effective.

ENTITY THEORY VERSUS INCREMENTAL LEARNING

The third big idea that Francis offers participants asks them to rethink how they perceive student learning potential. He includes a chart in the packet from John Saphier that was derived from the work of Jeff Howard. The chart emphasizes Howard's understanding of the distinction between fixed and fluid intelligence, between "Entity Theory," the bell curve based on IQ that determines fixed intelligence levels of students, and "Incremental Theory," which is based on Howard's fluid concept of "Effective Effort" to enable students to "get smarter" (Figure 6.1).

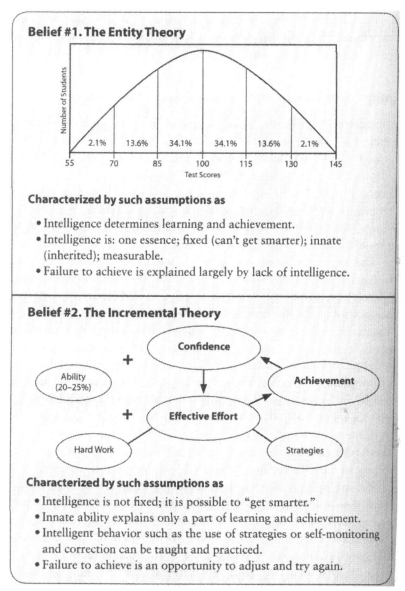

Figure 6.1 Two Beliefs about Intelligence and Achievement. (Adapted from the work of Jeff Howard, Founder and President of the Efficacy Institute, and John Saphier, President of Research for Better Teaching.)

The concept of fixed intelligence is based on the bell curve that formed the basis for the factory-model schools of the past century. Young children were put in grade-level classes and sorted out by IQ. Researchers now understand that natural intelligence indicates a small fraction of future success. Daniel H. Pink concludes that IQ counts for the entry point in high-level fields but connotes only a 4–10 percent effect on success.[2] Jonah Lehrer makes a compelling argument that self-control has a greater effect on academic success than IQ.[3]

The mantra of Jeff Howard's Efficacy Institute, "Smart is not something you are. Smart is something you get," is a prime example of the Incremental Theory in practice.[4] Teachers would be wise not to assume the entity level of anyone's intelligence but instead teach keeping in mind Incremental Theory. Nothing less should be acceptable.

To build confidence in students teachers can use errors as feedback rather than as indicators of low intelligence. Having this frame of mind, they suspend prejudgments about students who have been grouped or tracked. Instead, they concentrate on each student's potential and provide multiple pathways for getting smarter.[5] They can guide him to "exceed expectations"[6] by invoking Saphier's dictum:

"This is important."
"You can do it."
"I will not give up on you."[7]

Without a doubt, invoking the Incremental Theory frees the potential of teacher and students alike. If, on the other hand, teachers apply the Entity Theory, they deprive students of realizing their dreams. If they appear to lock into a student's limitations, they send a message—unwittingly or not—that he is less than he might be. When schools are organized around "ability levels," they invoke either false assumptions about brightness of "high-level" students, or perhaps, more insidious, inferiorities of "low-level" students. (See chapter 10, "Abolish Tracking" for an extensive discussion of this issue.)

When educators keep in mind The Big Shift perspective, when they understand How People Learn, and when they adopt the Incremental Theory mindset, they become open to seeing *every* student as capable of reaching the stars—every student.

REFLECTION

Taking the longer view and exploring the big picture requires time and effort. Unless educators are willing to take this step, they may find themselves becoming obsolete inside a rapidly changing culture. Students wired for digital thinking may reject teachers' old ways of dispensing knowledge and skills. Instead, teachers have to find their bearings in this new world and bring intelligence, skills, and wisdom into the classroom.

Dan Hilliard has the insatiable curiosity of Rudyard Kipling's elephant's child. At home, he asked more questions than anyone in his family. Sometimes, he would ask a second question without waiting to hear the answer to the first. As a teacher, he's discovered that his curiosity leads him to try new ideas and take risks.

Sometimes, he gets into trouble. Early in his career on the first day of school he told his tracked "top" section that they will have an "A" for the year. "Because you are the best students in your class, you will most likely get A's anyway, so I don't want you to worry. We are here to learn." He stuck to his commitment despite the chagrin of the guidance counselor.

Dan has become fascinated by today's fast-changing culture, particularly as it affects his students. He tries to imagine how he would grow up in their culture instead of staying fixed on the relatively fixed world of his youth.

POINTS TO PURSUE

Finding Empathy with Students

Teachers have the enviable task (some would say) of instructing the young. Yet, children who enter your classroom appear different. Where you were much like your parents when you were young, today's students are growing up in a new milieu.

How can you celebrate the young as they are? How can you see yourself growing up inside their world, inside The Big Shift? How can you help them become thoughtful, creative, and civil citizens amidst media pressures to emulate celebrities, watch frivolous television, and listen to misogynous popular music, among other incongruous phenomena?

Moving Away from Delivery to Invoke Learning

Francis Jordan found that when he put a line dividing the top from the bottom in the How People Learn chart it stimulated participants to think more about their teaching habits. He often wondered, however, just how much difference this chart made in practice.

How can you free yourself from hamster-wheel teaching in which you feel you are going nowhere? While you are feeling pressure to cover material, are you willing to support students to teach each other along the way? How can you let your students into the process of completing the equation of teaching and learning?

Using Entity Theory to See Students as They Are

Jeff Howard advocates the key value of getting smarter. The principles behind his Efficacy Institute separate fixed intelligence from incremental intelligence. Teachers can choose to see their students—and themselves—as either fixed or as having growth potential.

How do you relate to the Entity Theory/Incremental Theory continuum? Have you thought of yourself as a "fixed" teacher or a "fluid" teacher? Try this test: Do you see some students as "naturally bright," because of their demeanor? Do others appear "slow" when it may be far from the truth? How can you move beyond these biases?

Help Students Find Their Brightness in an Ability-Group System

If you work in a school that schedules students based on levels, how can you overcome its impact on student self-perceptions? Except for courses in which students earn the right to take—such as Algebra II—how might you convince your school to value more heterogeneous grouping?

Once you acknowledge obvious differences among students, how can you find ways to drop such terms as "slow learner," and "low-level learners"? How would this change affect you and your school?

NOTES

1. Richard Lavoie, "It's So Much Work Being Your Friend: Helping the Child with Learning Disabilities Find Social Success," Speech at Fitchburg State, March 9, 2009.

2. Daniel H. Pink, *A Whole New Mind: Why Right Brainers Will Rule the Future* (New York: Penguin, 2005, 2006), 57–59.

3. Jonah Lehrer, "Don't: The Secret of Self-control," *The New Yorker*, May 18, 2009.

4. The Efficacy Institute, Inc., http://www.efficacy.org/.

5. Jon Saphier and Robert Gower, *The Skillful Teacher*, 319–20.

6. Ibid., 334.

7. Ibid., 296.

Chapter 7

Search for Wisdom

Have you ever thought about Winnie the Pooh as a Taoist?

The mystics see from universal space. The Vedas speak of looking from behind the eyes. The Taoists say the Tao is unnamed, the source from which all emanates. Rumi invites us to sell our cleverness and purchase bewilderment. Eckhart Tolle speaks of the Now as the only reality. And, Robert Frost in "The Road Not Taken" voices the teacher–mystic in all of us. Oh, how we chose knowing we might have chosen differently! How we promise ourselves to return but keep on! How we look back and see our path as the better choice—and we think what a difference that's made!

Sarah Robinson fell in love with Frost's poem when she first heard it in her freshman year in college. After her first weeks as a middle school Social Studies teacher, she understands that she has chosen a road less taken. Despite the chaos, she is in the right place. She loves her classes. One day she shares "The Road Not Taken" with her students. As she is about to tell them that she chose the road that brought her to them, she has an epiphany.

> Frost meant that we *think* we choose the right road before us when in fact we only *believe* we do. We rationalize our having taken a unique path when we have no sense of it at the time. Frost lets us see our path—our teaching—for what it is rather than for what we think it has been. "The Road Not Taken" lets us know we've chosen such paths many times before and since.

Successful teachers recognize and accept reality. We may think that we've taken a special path, but we become wiser after we reflect on the meaning of the ones we found. We access the deeper meaning of our work. Knowing ourselves, knowing our preferences, after all, informs us of *our* adventure, one of our own making—and that makes all the difference.

~ ~ ~

Sarah immerses herself as she copes with a myriad of overwhelming tasks. She does her best to keep up with the expected and unexpected. She applies her sense of teaching to everything she presents and experiments with new ideas. But, it is not until years later that she allows larger perspectives into her life and teaching. She discovers not only the joy of learning the wisdom of the "greats" but also the gifts they bring. She explores texts from Lao Tzu, Confucius, the Buddha, Jesus, and writings by Thich Nhat Hanh, the Dalai Lama, Jon Kabat-Zinn, Wendell Berry, Rumi, and Hafiz, among many others. Some become seminal influences and forever change her practice.

Sarah cannot count the times their teachings energize her classroom. They help her cope with increasing pressures from an expanding media-centered culture, encroaching state and board authorities, and unrealistic expectations of parents. She understands her primary responsibility is to teach to the interior landscape of each and every child. She should meet their longing to understand themselves and their place in the universe—the place where the ancient sages dwelled.

After her department head asks her to teach Ancient History, she discovers the depth of this truth. Rather than relying on the textbook's inadequate narrative on ancient China, she incorporates primary sources on the analects of Confucius, chapters of the *Tao Te Ching*, and sutras of the Buddha. In addition, she has her students read Benjamin Hoff's *The Tao of Pooh* and selected readings from the Dalai Lama.

After thoughtful conversations with her students over several weeks, she borrows an idea from a colleague and asks her students to take an imaginary journey to China. This assignment has them seek the wisdom of the ancients to save a failing community in America. They are to write an essay reflecting their thoughts on one of the following questions:

How am I to understand and better myself?
How am I to live within my family so peace and harmony prevail?
How am I to relate to others so goodness prevails?
How am I to live well within nature and the environment?

Sarah wants her students to discover their own understandings of the wisdom of the ancients. She asks that they dwell within themselves to discover their own truths. She takes the advice of her colleague and does not ask them to seek out additional sources but to reexamine and explore those they explored and discussed in class. Sarah's not worried about parents helping, as they likely do not know nearly as much as their children do about this topic.

By the time students complete their journey and report their findings, they see themselves in a new light, often with astonishment. They sense the generosity of the assignment. One girl wrote, "I thought I knew myself before writing this paper, but now I understand myself differently and more clearly. Thank you, Ms Robinson."

Her assignment succeeded because of the following factors:

- It taps into core human concerns.
- It evokes a passion for seeking wisdom and relating it to her students' lives.
- It puts fundamental human qualities at the forefront, including civility, kindness, generosity, thankfulness, helpfulness, self-awareness, competence, hope, truth, wisdom, engagement, respect, responsibility, care, compassion, communication, and empathy—qualities that she emphasizes in her classroom.
- It demands probing discussions, rigorous reading and rereading, writing and rewriting. Each evening, she was able to assess their drafts on her computer and return them to their files on the school's network. This provided them with immediate feedback and encouraged them to stay involved—and the process used less paper, because no one printed out their drafts.

When she looks back at this assignment, Sarah knows it hit a "sweet spot." Being invited to seek to get in touch with their inner selves, all the students worked hard and wrote as well as they could. Each found his or her own path in seeking the universal truths inherent in the questions. While some struggled to grasp the implications of their newfound knowledge, all of them pushed their own envelopes. Sarah is grateful that she asked them to take that trip.

Teaching with wisdom in mind emerges slowly—and only when we become open to it. Most likely, it comes to us rather than our moving toward it. One of Sarah's earliest encounters happened at her local cinema as she watched Richard Attenborough's *Gandhi* with her middle schoolers. Observing Ben Kingsley's Gandhi, she feels the power of his presence; she sees herself needing to change how she approaches the world and her classroom. She now perceives herself more as who she is and how she behaves rather than in what she says. She's become more observant of herself both as a teacher and a person.

~ ~ ~

Sarah's colleague, Mike Lehman, loves ancient wisdom, too. In his Language Arts classes, he includes the ancients as often as possible. He has been in the school longer than Sarah. Everyone respects his wit, wisdom, and creativity. Learning about her trip-to-China assignment, he is impressed with its unusual format and really likes the four questions. "They are like essential questions, ones that have no right answers built-in. All of them demand higher-order thinking designed to provoke student interest. All those questions do that. I wonder if you realize that."[1]

"No, I don't," Sarah responds. "But each student wrote a distinct essay. No one came up with 'right' answers, as there weren't any. Thanks for the feedback."

Mike's interest in eastern thinking began when he first read Shunryu Suzuki's *Zen Mind, Beginner's Mind*. He was struck with the phrase in the prologue, "In the beginner's mind there are many possibilities, but in the expert's there are few."[2] Suzuki's words were counterintuitive to Mike's drive to become the expert teacher. He entered the profession wanting to drive to the top and be seen as the best.

Suzuki's words let him know that he can never become that expert. Now at every moment he remains open to possibilities. He no longer clings to his beliefs. Mike delights in others' insights, including those of his students and colleagues. Later, he hears about Thich Nhat Hanh's "There are two ways to wash the dishes. The first is to wash the dishes in order to have clean dishes and the second is to wash the dishes to wash the dishes."[3] These words open him to the true meaning of being in the moment.

His life as a teacher up to then had been an endless chain of completing one task after the other, after the other. Invoking Hanh's mantra "wash the dishes to wash the dishes" allows him to remain present to the task before him. Whenever he strays from this peaceful place, Mike recalls Hanh's words often simply by taking a breath. He introduced this idea at a middle school in a talk in which he invited students "to do your homework to do your homework." Paraphrasing Hahn,

> The fact that I am sitting here and doing my homework is a wondrous reality. I am being completely myself, following my breath, conscious of my presence, and conscious of my thoughts and actions. There is no way that I can be tossed around mindlessly, hating what I am doing and wanting to be somewhere else. I am here doing my homework, simply doing my homework. It is a miracle. It's awesome![4]

He put these words on pink index cards for anyone who wanted one. They disappeared.

Teachers tend to develop consistencies in their practice. They act as they believe. For instance, a teacher who is content driven strives to portray exciting information. He uses dynamic, interactive lectures, clever visuals, and intriguing handouts. Another teacher who believes students should feel good in his class aims to include emotion in his content. He does feel-good exercises at least once a week.

Reflecting on his earlier years, Mike realizes that he focused on rigor. He required his eighth graders to master considerable content. He also evoked lively discussions. Not until he came across Rainer Maria Rilke's famous wisdom "to love the questions themselves," however, did he balance the content of his teaching with a pursuit of inquiry.

When teachers are open to what comes their way, as Mike and Sarah demonstrate, they discover new paths, new outlooks, and new investigations. To love the questions means to become willing to ask before telling, to invite thoughts in rather than to stuff minds, and to pursue further questions rather than to anticipate correct answers. To live in the questions means to remain patient as students struggle to understand. Every day teaching is redefined.

~ ~ ~

Sarah shares with Mike her experience when first teaching *the Tao Te Ching*. Because she has always been eager to engage her students, she hoped to intrigue them with direct translations of chapters from the *Tao*. She also chose *The Tao of Pooh*, which she thought would engage and provoke. She had barely a week before she would begin teaching the *Tao*. Unbeknownst to her, she was heeding Mike's acceptance of the wisdom of Shunryu Suzuki's "in the beginner's mind there are many possibilities." She plunged in.

> The next six weeks proved to be among the most exciting of my teaching, Mike. My students and I pondered the wisdom of chapters from the *Tao Te Ching* and the freshness of Winnie the Pooh as a Taoist. We had the same excitement exploring the analects of Confucius and the sutras of the Buddha. At the end as you know, I gave them the assignment of the trip to China, which was one of the best I've ever put together!
>
> Recently, I have found that Zen stories, Hasidic tales, and Native American wisdom feed my teaching. These writings create great moments of insight. Among the most interesting is "The Rabbi's Gift" from Scott Peck who was not sure of its source.

Sarah then tells Mike a brief version:

> It is the story of a monastery fallen on hard times with only four monks and the abbot. In desperation, the abbot seeks the advice of a rabbi who lived in the nearby woods. After commiserating and reading the Torah together, the rabbi offers no advice to the abbot except his mysterious "the Messiah is one of you."

The Abbot returned to his monks with the cryptic message. The monks, suspecting truth in the rabbi's words, "began to treat each other with extraordinary respect on the chance that one among them might be the Messiah. And they began to treat themselves with extraordinary respect."

Soon, more people came to picnic and young men began to inquire and then joined. "So within a few years the monastery had once again become a thriving order, and thanks to the rabbi's gift, a vibrant center of light and spirituality in the realm."[5]

"How amazing to imagine each student as the Messiah, and how much more of a challenge to think of my colleagues—or me!—as the Messiah. This story encourages me to let go of assumptions, to see the gifts in everyone, including myself. And to live in the present. While I may not succeed, the gift of this story assures me that I will try."

Mike nods, "I can imagine classrooms where teachers and students treat each other with extraordinary respect—and treat themselves with extraordinary respect. What a difference that would make!"

"God blooms from the shoulder of the Elephant who becomes courteous to the Ant." Hafiz says it all.

REFLECTION

Paying attention to wisdom guides our lives and enriches our teaching. When we invite our accumulated wisdom into our classrooms, we deepen our commitment and understanding about why we teach. We become receptive to the lives and spirit of our students. When we deny the presence of our deeper selves, we curtail opportunities to see the deeper selves of our students.

Dan Hilliard grew up in a socially religious home; his family joined a church when he was twelve years old, so his father could improve his position in the community. In his early years of teaching, he did not find a church, but after a workshop at a Quaker School, he discovered that he liked the contemplativeness of Quaker Meeting. Since then, he's learned about eastern philosophy, astrology, past-life regression, and other alternative spiritual philosophies.

He began to fit "alternative" ideas into his lessons. His students like this aspect of his teaching, as they feel challenged. They're eager to understand themselves in the world. The whirl of social media, in which they strive to keep up, is often confusing. They like Mr. Hilliard, because he respects them—and because he gives them time to think and process.

POINTS TO PURSUE

What Feeds Your Teaching?

Sarah Robinson is grateful for having found Robert Frost's "The Road Not Taken." The poem helps her understand who she is as a teacher. What seminal poem, book, reading, essay, or film feeds your teaching? Why makes it special? How does it speak to your calling? Have you shared it with your students? With your colleagues?

What Is the Best Assignment You Have Given?

When reading about Sarah Robinson's ancient-wisdom assignment, does it remind you of the "deepest" assignment you've ever given? Did that assignment push the envelope of your students' minds and hearts? What unexpected results did it bring? To you? To your students? Were you ready for what happened?

If you've never ventured beyond conventional assignments, consider doing one along the lines of Sarah's sending kids to ancient China. Having instant media available with computers, tablets, and smartphones, student research would become intriguing.

How Can You Make Questions the Center of Your Teaching?

Essential questions have become an important tool in this age of Google. Searching an EQ will not bring easy answers. These questions require thinking, speculating, and time.

How can you bring questions into the heart of your teaching, especially if you perceive your need to teach as much as you can as quickly as you can? How can you get your students to love pursuing questions rather than wanting to give you right answers? How can you use questioning to help students probe their ideas about the uncertain future ahead of them?

Can You Find Ways to Successfully Teach an Unfamiliar Subject?

Teaching demands being flexible. As much as you'd like to keep things as they are, you sometimes are thrust into a new subject or a new grade level.

What will allow you, then, to accept the risk of teaching a subject with which you are not familiar? How can you let go of thinking that you have to be the expert? Can you trust that you will learn alongside your students? Can you invite them to openly explore with you?

See Your Students, Your Colleagues— and Yourself—as the Messiah

What if you took "The Rabbi's Gift" to heart and saw every student, every parent, every colleague, your principal—and possibly yourself—as the Messiah? Is this even possible in your mind? Anyone's mind? What difference would it make if you believed it? If your colleagues believed it? If your students did?

Would more students and colleagues choose to picnic in your room at lunch time?

NOTES

1. Google Grant Wiggins essential questions for an excellent foray into this important teaching skill.
2. Shunryu Suzuki, *Zen Mind, Beginner's Mind* (New York: Weatherhill, 1970), 21.
3. Thich Nhat Hanh, *The Miracle of Mindfulness* (Boston, MA: Beacon Press, 1975), 4.
4. Ibid., 4, adapted.
5. Adapted from Scott Peck, *The Different Drum* (New York: Simon and Schuster, 1987), 13–15. Also the full story can be found at http://www.community4me.com/rabbisgift.html, with a link to shortened version.

Chapter 8

Stay Current

If you consider yourself an average teacher, think of becoming better, one step at a time.

Josh Wilson takes his teaching seriously. From the moment he stepped into his first classroom, he knew he belonged. Everything felt right. The school, the kids, the community. By the end of his first year, he was convinced that he needed to be flexible. The way he learned to teach—sitting and observing as a pupil and from his teacher preparation program—was not adequate. He would forge his own path to reach his students and their families.

Josh struggles, however, to understand why change is so difficult for many of his colleagues. He notices when attending conferences, everyone comes back to school liking new ideas. Yet, he sees that few of them gain traction, as his colleagues continue to teach as they always have.

It reminds him of what happened to him after seeing Frederick Wiseman's documentary *Meat* in the mid-1970s. As Wiseman portrayed the process of stockyard cattle being dismembered in the slaughterhouse to the supermarket meat counter, Josh declared never to eat meat again. His resolve, however, lasted about two weeks, maybe three. He still can recall Wiseman's disturbing black-and-white images but continues to enjoy his barbecued burgers.

Recently, Josh discovered Jonathan Haidt's remarkable concept of the rider (mind) and the elephant (body) in his book *The Happiness Hypothesis*. The elephant in us enacts habitual practices we've learned to sustain our daily lives. The rider, on the other hand, represents our mind that looks around and ahead, wondering, speculating, and conjuring alternatives.

The rider is the viewer of Wiseman's documentary who commits to becoming a vegetarian. He is also is the teacher who attends a statewide workshop on brain research, is excited to bring back new ideas for revamping lessons, and shares his enthusiasm with colleagues. Yet, three weeks later, he is practicing as he always has, the ideas from the workshop having receded into the background.

"Why does this happen?" Josh asks himself. "Perhaps, if I share Haidt's rider and elephant metaphor it will help." Sometimes, people make radical changes in their lives on their own—changes that retrain their elephant. Some quit smoking one day never to smoke again. Others quit sweets and desserts to maintain low blood sugar. And some commit to exercise for health and fitness and stick to it. Still, as Haidt's book makes clear to Josh, change in teaching—perhaps in any profession—tends to be slow, as the continued persistence of teachers standing at the front of the room and delivering lessons testifies.

Perhaps it's because we teach alone. Teachers next door to us teach alone, too. To make changes, we need support and encouragement. Sometimes when we try something different, we do not have enough time to work it out, as we think we must keep up covering the curriculum and meet other external demands. Other times, our students have difficulty adapting to a new approach, so we back off and pledge, perhaps, to try it again next year. We find it easier and less stressful to let the elephant continue to do its thing. Besides, Josh says to himself, "My colleagues and I have no incentive to change—and no one to hold us accountable."

Josh decided to encourage his colleagues to stay current with the latest research. If they were to become more interested in new ideas and methods, it would improve their students' chances to learn. He would begin by sharing his ideas on the impact of Google. He's convinced that his students' apparent lack of attention stems from the instant responses Google offers.

He thinks back to the time with his eighth graders when he shared Carl Duncker's monk-on-the-mountain problem made famous by Arthur Koestler. This problem was a staple for him at his former school in the mid-1990s. It became part of the elephant of his teaching. After presenting the problem on the first day of school, his students would leave perplexed and likely generate discussion at the dinner table—even in busy households.

> One morning, exactly at sunrise, a Buddhist monk began to climb a tall mountain. The narrow path, no more than a foot or two wide, spiraled around the mountain to a glittering temple at the summit.
> The monk ascended the path at varying rates of speed, stopping many times along the way to rest and to eat the dried fruit he carried. He reached the temple shortly before sunset. After several days of fasting and meditation, he began his journey back along the same path, starting at sunrise and again walking at

variable speeds, taking many pauses along the way. His average speed descending was, of course, greater than his average climbing speed.

Prove there is a single spot along the path the monk will occupy on both trips at precisely the same time of day.[1]

The problem baffled most of his students and their families. Even when some of them solved the problem, others remained confused. He hoped that from this experience they would understand that his classroom was a safe place not to know and where they could persevere to find out. He wanted students to understand that learning was, first and foremost, about creative and critical thinking, seeking meaning, and solving mysteries. Questions were more important than answers.

With the good graces of his principal, Mark Johansen, who liked his faculty to take initiative, Josh recounts this story at a faculty meeting. "As you can see from trying to solve this problem, it offers a challenge. Only a couple of you have come up with a possible answer. Perhaps had we more time, you would. I remember the time I first tried to solve it, I suddenly found the solution without realizing it. Because it required that my thinking to be different, I thought it would be good to offer it to my students.

"But let's step back for a moment. Why do you think I don't use this problem any more?" The room becomes quiet. "Is it because of Google?" asks Marie Simmons, one of the most curious members of the faculty.

"Yes, exactly, that's what I think. Today students would surely leave class and open their phones or computer and Google 'monk-on-the-mountain.'" Voila! They would find the solution. No need to figure it out. No need to be baffled. No need to struggle. No need to use their minds. That is my concern about Google. On the one hand, it is a fantastic resource. On the other hand, it takes away opportunities to become perplexed, to wonder, because it enables us to find out almost immediately what we want to know.

"Before the Google era (BGE), we had the freedom to intrigue, to surprise, and often to be the first to bring new ideas to students. Early in my teaching, I could count on exposing students to something new and take time to explore its implications. As the years passed, I observed them coming into my classroom having more and more information, until in my later years, I rarely was able to surprise them.

"After Google (AGE), the paradigm has shifted. We can find almost anything, immediately—and information even finds us! People are satisfied when they can have information quickly. 'Why bother,' some ask, 'to make the effort to figure anything out?'"

"I know how we can get around Google," Marie replies. "We can create ways to say things that Google doesn't know. For example, you could change the monk-on-the-mountain to the rabbi-in-the-canyon problem. Use the same type of language to set it up. The students would be just as perplexed—and would have to stay with their thinking. Google would not know what to say. It would be a great opportunity for them to work with each other. I imagine the room would become noisy, a good kind of noise. And, surprise, surprise, they might even ask their parents for help—if they are home."

"I like that idea, Marie, I will try it."

The faculty spent the next half-hour discussing the impact of Google. By the end of the meeting, most of them realize that they need to pay attention not only to it and other search engines but also to the intricacies of the digital culture surrounding them. They agree to have further discussions both at faculty and department meetings.

Josh has thought a lot about using laptops but finds them wanting. He imagines that his students would surf while feigning to take notes, or perhaps fact-check his teaching, or more likely chat with friends. Opportunities for face-to-face interactions would decrease. There would be fewer threaded conversations in which he and his students look and listen to one another, observe facial expressions, and attend to intonations. He noticed when he observed a colleague who uses laptops that his students only spoke with him and not with each other. No one seemed to be paying attention to one another.[2]

He imagines if his students were to have laptops they would tether to their flat screens, randomly engage and disengage from the intended learning, and never become a community of learners. He's not willing to take the risk of losing opportunities to interact face to face. It would be like losing a language—a fundamental human language at that! However, students should have their own mobile devices, such as iPads or cellphones, with access to Web 2.0 tools and the Cloud for storage. Teachers and students should take advantage of the communication, information sharing, interoperability, and collaboration that these devices provide.

In this paradigm, Josh figures, much of the time teachers would work in a hybrid flipped-classroom model. During class students would do face-to-face project work/practice, as well as group exploration/problem solving. At home, they would use their mobile devices to review the previous night's lesson and dig for information that might help them support/solve problems. They could also encounter new material and bring their thinking and questions into class. The potential is endless—and will be more so as new devices become available.[3]

Whenever possible, Josh tells colleagues about new ideas or methods. One of his favorites is David Sousa's *Primacy–Recency* (Figure 8.1). Sousa bases his thinking on how the brain learns best. He advocates placing the major input portion of a lesson at the front of a learning episode (primacy); providing time

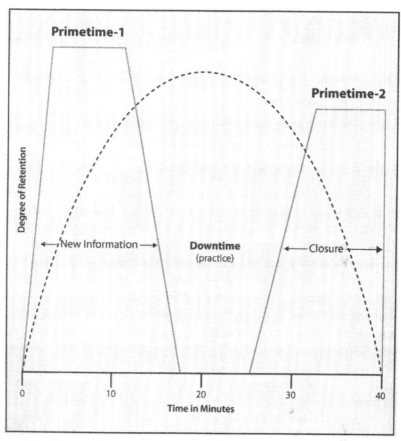

Figure 8.1 Primacy–Recency—Retention During a Learning Episode. (Adapted from David Sousa, *How the Mind Learns: A Classroom Teacher's Guide*. Revised Edition. [Thousand Oaks, CA: Corwin Press, 2001], 90. Used by permission of the publisher.)

in the middle to process; and concluding with active summarizers to cement the learning (recency). However, nearly all of his colleagues do most of their teaching during the middle of the period, a traditional routine embedded in classroom teaching.

Before showing Sousa's chart to the faculty, Josh inserts a curved line to indicate the difference between Sousa's approach and the traditional. He presents his version to encourage colleagues to pay attention to how most of them run their classrooms.

At the start of each period they usually collect homework, take attendance, give announcements, and handle other noninstructional matters; in the middle, they deliver their lesson; and at the end, they have students begin homework or relax until the bell. Josh concludes, "To be honest, at first my students struggled with Primacy–Recency, as it is contrary to what they've been practicing for years. But, it's been well worth it. Now they are learning more than ever! I hope you'll consider using it."

Josh particularly likes some of the findings from brain research over the past twenty years. MRIs, fMRIs, and PET scans have been able to observe the brain at work. Among the most significant ideas—some well-known, some not so—that he pays attention to are the following:

- Mihaly Csikszentmihalyi's Flow
- Howard Gardner's Multiple Intelligences
- The difference between short-term and long-term memory learning
- Down-shifting (shutting down emotionally) that limits thinking under stress
- Eustress (positive stress; just enough to stimulate) that differs from distress
- When people talk they learn
- The brain's natural inclination is to seek patterns
- Feedback plays an essential role in learning
- Exercise is crucial for improving learning

Despite his efforts to encourage his colleagues to change, sometimes he feels he's becoming a broken record. Some try a new method, perhaps just to please him, but often they give up. Apparently it is easier to do what they know.

Then, Josh discovered the *Marshall Memo*[4] that debuted in August 2003. Publisher and educator Kim Marshall acts as a "designated teacher's reader." He subscribes to sixty-four mainstay journals, magazines, and newspapers and many others. He writes cogent synopses of important and relevant articles that he emails to subscribers on Monday evenings. Josh is impressed with Marshall's writing style. After subscribing for several months, Josh believes his faculty should subscribe too as it is the perfect tool for staying current.

He convinces Principal Mark Johansen to take out a subscription for the school. Because the *Memo* comes to each faculty member's inbox, the cost is $12 per year per person, much less than the $50 he spent for his own subscription. He couldn't wait to see its impact. Mark agrees to devote time at each faculty meeting to discuss selected content from the *Memo*. Josh refers to it at department meetings whenever he can. He wants the *Marshall Memo* to become like Jonathan Haidt's rider who reassesses our everyday practice—and eventually leads us to retraining our elephants.

While at a conference, Josh hears about *The Main Idea*,[5] an email publication that offers elegant summaries and/or reviews of eight to ten current educational books a year. Jenn David-Lang, founder and scribe, captures big ideas in a readable and useful format. Norman Atkins, CEO of Uncommon Schools and Cofounder, North Star Academy Charter School, writes on *The Main Idea*'s website that "[Jenn] has the heart of a teacher, the brain of a think tank, and the patience of a librarian."

Jenn has summarized notable books by well-respected authors including Michael Fullan, Richard Dufour, Heidi Hayes Jacobs, Richard Stiggins, John Saphier, Tony Wagner, Ross Greene, and Robert J. Marzano. She also designs workshops for subscribers. For example, she put together a classroom management workshop with handouts based on the immensely popular Harry K. and Rosemary T. Wong's *The First Days of School*.[6] Josh convinces Mark to encourage his faculty to subscribe to *The Main Idea*. If twenty-five teachers were to subscribe, the cost would be $29 per year rather than $49 per individual.

~ ~ ~

Staying current with the latest research and methodologies is essential if teachers are to align themselves to best practices. Not to do so deprives students of what they deserve. Global demands, technologies, and social media are forcing schools and classrooms to reassess their practices. Paying attention to new knowledge, understandings, and pedagogies keeps them relevant in educating the young. *Exciting Classrooms* invites teachers to look for significant ideas and practices to enable them to teach effectively.

Teachers as riders can search for better ways to teach in order to engage today's learners. They can find ways to retrain their teaching habits and approaches—their elephants. Sometimes, it may mean separating the young from their electronic devices to challenge their minds to think, create, and resolve. Other times, it may mean integrating these devices into the classroom. Teachers can decide when and how.

REFLECTION

When Dan Hilliard first learns about the rider-and-the-elephant metaphor, he understands his difficulty in changing his deep-seated practices. He's already given up making New Year's resolutions. Dan sees his "New-Year's-resolution rider" like the viewer of Wiseman's *Meat*. Much personal hype without substance.

He recognizes, too, that he has done many of his teaching practices without thinking. He usually collects homework at the beginning of class; then passes out quizzes, tests, and papers if he has them; sometimes he takes excessive time on noninstructional matters; he often calls on the first hands raised; he grades papers with names on them; and for years he's kept his student desks in rows.

Dan surmises about how he might better inform his rider, so he could have more ways to consider retraining his elephant. He plans to observe colleagues during his planning periods. Perhaps he will discover better ways to interact with students. He's also heard about a neighboring school renowned for its alternative approaches to teaching and learning. He asks his principal if he can go visit and come back and report to the rest of the faculty. It's there that he learns about the *Marshall Memo* and *The Main Idea*.

POINTS TO PURSUE

Take an Inventory of Your Practices

How can you become more honest about your teaching? You can begin by making a list of common practices that you use in your classroom. Indicate on a scale from 1 to 4 the effectiveness of these practices. Eliminate the less effective ones and explore alternatives. Show your list to colleagues to seek their input—and encourage them to do the same. Set up weekly best-practices conversations.

Assess the Rider and the Elephant in Your Teaching

Josh Wilson's experience with Fred Wiseman's documentary on meat packing reminds him to remain diligent. He knows how often his rider has wanted to try something new, but the idea soon slipped away. His elephant persists.

How difficult has it been for you to integrate new ideas and practices in your teaching? Have you tried to connect with colleagues when implementing a new practice? When have you been successful in retraining your elephant? Under what conditions? Who helped you?

Try Primacy–Recency

Like Josh Wilson, if you choose to commit to implementing David Sousa's *Primacy–Recency*, stick to it no matter how challenging it is. Do it quietly, without fanfare. If it fails, give yourself credit for your effort—and either try again or try another brain-research strategy. David Sousa, John Medina, and Eric Jensen among others have many! Google any one of them for ideas.

Explore the *Marshall Memo*

If you want to enrich your teaching, keep a lookout for new ideas. They seem to come out nearly every day. For starters, visit Kim Marshall's website to explore the potential of the *Marshall Memo* for you and for your school. His *Memo* provides new ideas every week.

If you can't convince others to subscribe, subscribe yourself. You then can build a stronger case for having everyone subscribe—or at least in your department or grade level.

Explore *The Main Idea*

For another enrichment possibility, subscribe to Jenn David-Lang's *The Main Idea* to develop the habit of paying attention to new and significant literature in the field. Share her website with colleagues to encourage them to subscribe.

Establish a Book/Film Club in Your School

Form a teachers' book/film club with interested colleagues in your district. Commit to reading books and seeing films from both inside and outside the field. Your teaching will be the better for it, particularly if teachers from different grade levels and subject areas attend.

Faculties that read books and view films together enrich the conversation about teaching.

NOTES

1. Arthur Koestler, *The Act of Creation* (London: Hutchinson, 1964), 183–84. Koestler refers to the June 1961 issue of *Scientific American* as his source, but he remarks that the problem originates with the psychologist Carl Duncker.

2. Josh found support for this idea from Loren Noren, adjunct professor at the Stern School of Business at NYU who spoke against laptops in the classroom on "The Takeaway," April 6, 2015.

3. Bud Brooks, retired Director of Technology at Bancroft School, Worcester, Massachusetts, shared some of these ideas in a personal communication.

4. See *Marshall Memo*, http://www.marshallmemo.com.

5. See *The Main Idea*, http://themainidea.net/index.htm.

6. Harry K. and Rosemary T. Wong, *The First Days of School: How to Be an Effective Teacher* (Harry K. Wong Publications, Inc., 2004).

Chapter 9

Seek the Higher Road

Taking the higher road brings new horizons and invites educators to reform their practice.

When Jesse Wilcox stepped into his first classroom more than forty years ago, he found desks and chairs in rows facing the teacher's desk and a blackboard. He saw a similar pattern in every room. It had been the same when he sat in his classrooms as a child. Today, he sees that same pattern echoing throughout his school's corridors. Most of his colleagues still stand at the front of their students sitting in rows—and do most of the talking.

One evening Jesse returns home after yet another unproductive faculty meeting. This time his colleagues have resisted the effort of his Curriculum Committee to revamp the freshman year. The committee proposed a new house system that would put teachers into smaller teams so they could know students better. Few faculty agreed, however, as most of them saw the present system as "Just fine, so why mess with it? We are already a good school. We have a good reputation."

Like most of his colleagues, Jesse began as a stand-up teacher in his first year. He tended, however, to turn his lectures into discussions. He liked interacting with his sophomore history students more than talking at them. He found he could invoke his sense of humor to engage them, often using puns. Despite his choice to wear a coat and tie, he preferred running an informal classroom, a reflection of his personality.

An average student himself, he worked hard to push his students to become excellent. A tough grader, he insisted on rigor, sometimes asking more of his students than he probably should have. Because of his slanted bell curve (more D's than B's), he found himself having to defend his position in the Guidance Counselor's office.

Today, he is a different teacher. He's revamped his room. He began by painting his desks different colors. Students could choose which color suited them any given day. Now a few of those desks are scattered among several comfortable chairs, a couple of couches, lots of plants, and colorful displays.

His desk resides in the far corner. His teaching place could be anywhere. His students often arrive having been exposed to new material at home the night before rather than bringing in homework—or home-practice as he likes to call it. He finds his classes eager to discuss what they've discovered. He prefers to explore their thinking rather than dispense knowledge. Jesse is comfortable with his students whether they excel or not.

That night after the faculty meeting, he takes out his journal, as he usually does, and asks:

> Why do so many of us resist when hearing about a new proposal rather than to take the time to consider its full implications?
> Why do most of us in the district insist on maintaining our grip on teaching from the front of our rooms?
> Why do we continue to talk more than listen?
> Why do we still think that giving information is more important than processing it?
> Why do we persist in teaching the same material to all students at the same time?
> What holds so many of us back from taking the higher road of creative, challenging, interactive, and provocative teaching for ourselves—and for the school?

Teachers work in a profession that prides itself on consistency. Invoking tradition provides an anchor in the storm of change. Such consistency, however, often serves a teacher's needs rather than the needs of her digitally wired students. She sees *them* as unable to stay on task during her lessons; they see *her* as taking too long to make her point.

Teachers often view their responsibility as information bearers. They establish and maintain authority from the front by directing their students' eyes toward them. From the first grade, children see the teacher taking charge. They learn to do school well, and by middle school, they know the drill. It becomes second nature. Ironically, this paradigm remains second nature for the new teacher when she takes her place on the other side of the desk in her first classroom.

Unlike professionals in medicine, law, and business, teachers know from the beginning—or think they know—how to teach. They have been observing teachers since kindergarten. While other professions require internships, residencies, and apprenticeships, aspiring teacher candidates teach for a brief time, sometimes as little as six weeks. From their first day of school they are assigned to their own classroom. They teach alone. They receive little or no feedback. They are given no impetus to change.

Today, teachers feel they have more reasons to resist change, as increasing pressures from federal and state governments demand adequate yearly progress on tests scores. They are required to cover more and more material to meet this demand—and to do it faster. So, they find it easier to tell students what they want them to know.

Yet, they know that they are reaching fewer students. The effort to condense education into a narrow paradigm of clerical-level learning to meet test standards is forcing more students onto independent educational plans (IEPs). As society identifies more learning disabilities, special education becomes larger. Schools establish more inclusion classes to mainstream the learning disabled. Yet, teachers persist with old methods in the hope that somehow all will learn. Teachers do what they know.

In the end, perhaps it's simply easier for teachers to remain at the front of their students. Perhaps they do what they know because it creates less stress and more peace of mind as they confront the multiple complexities of everyday teaching. At least it appears that way.

Jesse Wilcox wonders about this. Maybe for many of his colleagues to make changes and implement new strategies is simply too demanding. School is already complicated enough. So is home. He returns to his journal and writes:

Perhaps it's easier:

- To tell students what to learn rather than to take time to empower them to participate in designing their learning
- To call on the first hands raised, repeat each answer, and then elaborate to complete the lesson rather than to partner with students in serious dialogue
- To give true–false, short-answer, multiple-choice tests (particularly ones written by publishers) rather than to design authentic performance assessments
- To teach from textbooks rather than to take time to design and implement innovative programs using the textbook only as a resource
- To teach all the kids the same material at the same time rather than to provide relevant materials based on student readiness, interest, or learning style
- To teach in one's preferred style rather than to adjust to the different learning styles of students
- To teach lessons from old notes year after year, and give the same quizzes and tests rather than to rework, redesign, and make relevant what students need to know, understand, and are able to do
- To assign reading and writing as homework rather than to teach these literacy skills in class
- To give the same homework assignments rather than to provide choice, alternatives, or to let students create their own

- To leave at the close of school and take care of personal business rather than to stay after school to collaborate with colleagues
- To watch a favorite television show at the end of the day rather than to read a journal or professional book; after all, school is tiring.

If Jesse shared this list at a faculty meeting he would offend many of his colleagues and the administration. At the same time, he realizes he's on to something. During his forty years, he has seen countless teachers replicate these methods and refuse to change. Fortunately, others treat teaching as a profession and stay current with research, new methods, and new materials. He decides to share his thoughts with Angela Scortino and Carlos Sanderos, two of the most innovative teachers in his department.

Angela has only been at the school for three years, but her students already know her as a dynamo. She is not afraid to risk a new approach or consider radical ideas. Carlos, on the other hand, has been a teacher for nearly twenty years. His progress toward freeing himself from the tyranny of lecturing, however, has taken him several years. He has become an excellent discussion leader and innovative curriculum designer. His students rarely leave without arguing with each other about what they were discussing in class.

Angela and Carlos agree with Jesse that many veterans do teach the "easier" way. His list may appear insulting, but it is true. These veterans work in the paradigm of whole-class lessons in which the "smartest" students received As, and the "less able" received lower grades. They act as independent agents and pursue teaching as it suits them. After all, they believe it's worked that way for years, so why change.

Jesse, Angela, and Carlos know these methods are failing students. Lectures, which may have worked for academic-oriented students, are putting more students to sleep. Fewer do their homework. Fewer care about tests and exams. They agree that traditional education is becoming increasingly out of sync with today's digitally driven students.

They want to find a way to encourage colleagues to take a higher road, one that respects students and responds to the demands of today's global, technical world. Jesse cautions them not to place blame. Instead, they should advocate for the teaching profession to stay current, just as people expect doctors and dentists to use only the latest instruments, techniques, and medicines. Then, add that the same principle holds true for lawyers, auto technicians, shoe salesmen, beauticians, restaurateurs, roofers, and cleaning services to name a few. Teachers should not be exempt from this responsibility.

Angela suggests that they begin by making a list of "higher-road" principles that will encourage teachers to move away from the "easier" path. The list should be eclectic and open-ended, so people will find some ideas they could latch onto. Carlos adds that they should ask the principal if they can present their list at a faculty meeting. It would be a risk, but worth it. They brainstorm and come up with their initial list; this list contains the following recommendations:

- Hold high expectations for all students—and encourage them to succeed beyond all expectations
- Challenge all students, acknowledge their different learning styles, and make sure each one learns before moving on
- Persist in taking risks to find better ways for students to learn
- Create or join study groups to examine best practices, lessons, and student work
- Meet regularly with colleagues using clear agendas that are designed to improve instruction
- Mentor and nurture new colleagues by offering support, ideas, and compassion
- Stay after school if necessary to prepare and meet with colleagues
- Attend students' games and performances.

They wonder, however, if they should share Jesse's "Perhaps it is easier" list.

~ ~ ~

Choosing to teach unconventionally takes courage and relentless effort. Doing it the "easier" way by not rocking the boat while keeping students and parents quiet and happy—or apparently happy—allows teachers to become comfortable. They feel safe, right, and normal. However, when a teacher teaches differently, he takes on the role of the underdog. He becomes a David in a world of Goliaths.[1] He gives up and lets go of practices that no longer work. He puts in untiring effort, hard work, and persistence, persistence, persistence—nothing less satisfies.

When teachers pursue the "easier" path, students do not learn. Teachers fool themselves when they think they are teaching well just because some students are willing to sit and listen, take notes, study, and ace tests. If others were to try harder, they surmise, those students would also get good grades. However, when they to look back to their own school days and remember how few of *their* classmates earned A's, they might reconsider these traditional practices.

Every school district has pockets of "Davids" who abandon the "easier" path and respond to the challenges schools and families are facing. These are the great teachers. Everyone knows who they are. They have taken the higher road. They have signed the Teaching Manifesto. (See Appendix, "Teaching Manifesto.")

REFLECTION

Dan Hilliard cringes when he hears blanket criticisms of his fellow teachers. However, many of them do stand at the front of the room most of the time. Yet, they are not necessarily poor teachers. His colleague, Jared Wilmot, enthralls his Language Arts students by sharing lively stories and insights into the novels he teaches. He talks a lot of the time, tells poignant stories, provides lively visuals, raises provocative questions—and allows time for them to interact. They can't wait for his next class. They love his friendly demeanor and carry new ideas out of his room almost every day.

As Dan has tried new methodologies, he pays attention to their impact. When he holds high expectations, most students step up to meet the challenge. Implementing 10-2 Thinking and Primacy–Recency has brought relevance to his lessons. Adopting the piano teacher metaphor has enlivened interactions with his students. The TAPS Template for Teacher Planning has generated energy and coherence to his lessons and units. And, he enjoys his best-practices Thursday discussion with colleagues.

But, too many teachers treat teaching as telling and fail to intrigue students. Dan often wishes he could share more of his ideas, but he hesitates. A few of his colleagues appear open to publicly assessing their teaching. It's just not done throughout his school. He hopes, however, that he will find a way.

POINTS TO PURSUE

What Would Rip Van Winkle Observe in Your Classroom?

Undoubtedly, all fields have practitioners who prefer "the old ways." Teachers are no exception. The Internet story of Rip Van Winkle's awakening one hundred years later where he finds an unrecognizable world except for the classroom contains much truth.

Have you wondered why so many teachers persist in teaching as their teachers taught them? Do you know why you loved your favorite teachers? What of their qualities would you like to emulate? Would Rip Van Winkle recognize what you are doing with your kids?

What Is Your Role in Being a Bearer of Information?

The earliest schools served primarily as information bearers. School was where you found out stuff. You could come home with information not even your parents knew. Today, information is everywhere.

Given teachers' historic role, how has the Internet affected what you decide to share? What information should you convey to your students? What information should you discover together? What can they learn from you that they will not find on Google? What do you want them to learn?

What Will Convince Teachers to Let Go of "Easier" Practices?

Jesse Wilcox comes up with long list of what teachers do to make their practice "easier." He is not sure, however, what to do with it. With his colleagues Angela Scortino and Carlos Sanderos, they decide to approach the faculty with a list of approaches teachers can use that are not "easier."

However, what keeps some teachers practicing the "easier" methods? Is it because no one observes them? If you practice "easier" methods, what will convince you to change? Would you even be willing to take the extra time needed, knowing you will not be paid for it?

Would you be willing to share Jesse's "Perhaps it's easier" list with colleagues?

Take the Higher Road

Jesse, Angela, and Carlos have chosen the higher road to teaching. Taking this road evokes one's true calling. Taking this road exudes enthusiasm. Nothing gets in the way of what you want to accomplish. In tough circumstances, you find the silver linings and move forward.

If you've hesitated to commit yourself to this level of teaching—to leave the "easier" path—what holds you back? If you decide to deepen your commitment, don't hesitate to ask for help from a colleague who's left the "easier" path behind. They will be honored.

Are You a David among Goliaths?

Are you a "David" among your colleagues? Do you know other teachers who are? How do you/they persist, despite the conventional teaching surrounding you/them? What keeps a "David" from succumbing to the "Goliaths"?

NOTE

1. This metaphor is explored by Malcolm Gladwell, "How David Beats Goliath," *The New Yorker*, May 11, 2009, 40–49.

Part III

WHAT MUST WE CHANGE?

Facing what doesn't work enables educators to find ways that work better.

Part III calls into question four serious impediments to effective teaching and offers practical alternatives.

Education, like other institutions, has embedded practices that obstruct sensible, relevant, and productive teaching. Most of these practices originated inside the paradigm of factory-model schools that were built to meet the demands of the industrial era. Managers (men) led from the top and hired cheap labor (women) to carry out scripted lessons to groups of children often sorted by IQ. Despite the demands of a rapidly changing global world, this hierarchical structure still prevails.

The isolated classroom teacher remains the unfortunate legacy of this paradigm. Despite major efforts across the country to implement standards and strengthen curriculums, most teachers continue to teach as they always have—and more so because they feel they must keep up with the demands of high-stakes tests.

When teachers choose to uproot ineffective embedded traditions, they adopt an emperor-is-not-wearing-any-clothes attitude. They pay attention to the effects of practices cited in part III that interfere with reaching the potential of each and every student, namely, tracking, unions, interruptions, and the persistence of whole-class lessons.

Teachers become more empowered when taking leadership in reforming these practices. They free themselves and their students to become people who live the lives they deserve, gain the freedom they crave, and find the happiness they desire.

Chapter 10

Abolish Tracking

Who's not going to get it? Who will already know it or get it quickly?

The habit of preparing one lesson for the whole class resides deep in teachers' DNA. But, when confronted with these two questions, teachers immediately bring individual students to mind. The door swings open to consider alternative approaches.

These questions have become favorites for Pam Peters, a lifelong teacher and now a popular teacher trainer. She likes them because they force workshop participants to rethink their whole-class approach to lessons. They immediately know the names of students who would struggle with a given lesson and also those who would grasp the material quickly—or already know it.

Pam shows two videos of teachers who adjust their teaching to meet the different levels of understanding among students. In the first video, a science teacher assigns three groups of students alternative ways to investigate a concept. She gives the middle group an at-grade-level lab activity, which used to be her whole-class lesson; she gives the advanced group a simulation designed to stretch their thinking; and she provides struggling learners with a computer to assist them in handling data.[1]

In the second video, a math teacher assigns three groups of sixth graders alternative approaches for solving the same concept: one group she gives manipulatives to work with; the other two groups she gives textbooks, one at grade level and the other more advanced.[2] Pam points out that both of these teachers want to make learning accessible for every student. It's what coaches do in response to players' skill levels. Her workshop participants usually do not question this analogy.

After some conversation, however, the notion arises that the groupings depicted in the videos may represent either a hidden form of tracking or a type of ability grouping. Participants view the "readiness" groups for the lesson as likely to be the same groups for every lesson. Some even state that the teachers in the video should not have allowed students to work at different levels because some of them would be stigmatized while others rewarded.

Pam then puts on a third video in which a fourth-grade teacher demonstrates incorporating student interests while attending to their readiness levels.[3] She first asks them to choose an American Revolution historical figure that they would like to learn more about. After dividing them into three groups based on their choices, she places on each table a basket with multiple levels of books. The video then shows students reading books at their comfort levels.

The next part, however, challenges Pam's participants. The teacher passes out three different-colored cubes—red, green, and blue—to individual students sitting at their respective tables. She then asks all of them to refer to the "compare and contrast" side of each cube. She tells the students to whom she gave red cubes to draw a picture of their historical person, a member of their family, and write a comparison; those with green cubes compare and contrast using a Venn diagram; and those with blue cubes create an open-ended compare-and-contrast diagram.

The teacher has no qualms about assigning different-colored cubes to different students, nor apparently do her students. But Pam's teachers do! "I can't abide having students know that some are 'better' than others." "It's not right to group kids like that." "How do you think the 'red-group kids' feel seeing their 'green and blue' classmates doing higher-level work?" The conversation often becomes heated. Sometimes, Pam is able to reframe the issue from a broader perspective—and sometimes not.

Paradoxically, participants criticize all three video teachers for setting up "readiness" groups as a form of ability grouping. Yet, at the same time, they often defend their own school's decision to make permanent homogeneous groupings for "bright," "average," and "slow" students. By the end of the discussions, the message of the videos often becomes lost as teachers defend their groupings. Pressures to perform well on state and federal assessments, they argue, demand they teach as fast as possible and in the way they know best. Creating flexible "readiness" groups takes too much time; having their fixed "ability" groups is more efficient.

Pam then circles back to a fundamental question and asks, "Why do we insist on teaching using the same assumptions and methods our teachers used? Has it crept into our DNA? Perhaps terms, such as 'bright,' 'average,' and 'slow,' are embedded in the language of the profession."

This is a difficult issue. Pam remembers struggling with it early in her career. Besides, the longer she taught, the more students surprised her when abilities suddenly surfaced. She does not recall when she recognized her perception of "slow" students might be due to their self-identification as "slow"; it was a strategy they used to protect themselves from being thought of as not smart. Nevertheless, she often found herself prejudging students' ability levels when she should have waited.

In those years, she was a caring, energetic, and committed teacher. She did her best to make her classes lively, engaging, and meaningful. Above all, she was fair. But one day she met Jennifer Sinclair in the supermarket several years after Jennifer was in her class. She was struck by Jennifer's comment: "I really enjoyed your class, Mrs. Peters, but one thing bothered me. You decided early which students were smart and which were not—and you never changed your mind." Pam was stunned. From that day, she vowed to try to stay open to the potential of each student—and later to every teacher in her workshops.

When Pam tells about her encounter with Jennifer, she invites participants to consider these questions:

Do we hear what we are actually saying when we discuss students and grouping?
Do we really believe some students are "bright" and others "slow"?
Do we believe we can achieve more with our "bright" pupils than we can with our "slower" pupils?
Do we prefer "bright" (cooperative) kids who play the game of school well and are "easier" to teach?
Do we assume the "lower kids" (uncooperative) are less teachable?
Do we really think we no longer track students as we were tracked?

Pam then shows clips of *Stand and Deliver*,[4] in which Jaime Escalante demonstrates the effectiveness of holding high expectations for all of his calculus students and how his expectations become infectious. Pam wants to crack open the language of tracking she sees etched in most teachers' minds.

However, she does not point the finger of blame. Teachers, after all, deal with large numbers of students. In middle and high school, most have well over one hundred per day. Therefore, having an expedient terminology is useful. Because they have to constantly sort and grade students, having categories facilitates that process. And after all, labeling is endemic in our culture.

The real danger in using this terminology is its threat to student potential. It's a different matter to see a student as struggling or falling behind in his efforts to learn at a given moment. Having this perspective, a teacher can help him progress to the next level. It's another matter to predetermine that he is a "slow" or "level one" student. Once categorized, his fate will have been sealed. Teachers no longer seek his potential—and he no longer will believe in himself.

86   Chapter 10

Teachers can shift their thinking. Some teachers are open to surprise, to "Aha! moments" that signal a student's sudden grasp of a concept, an understanding, or insight. They teach invoking the mantra, "Expect the surprise and it will come."

The habit of sorting resides deep in the profession. It was the foundation of the factory-based public school system developed in the twentieth century. However, once teachers become aware of the harm of sorting they find ways to become open to every student's potential. Having surprise in their mind alerts them to the possible, away from the numbness of prejudgment.

What can teachers do to break out of this predicament? They begin by realizing students do not have a fixed intelligence (see chapter 6, "See the Big Picture"). Once they know that IQ does not determine intelligence and that self-control is more essential, they let go of labeling students as "slow" or "bright." They focus on high expectations and nurture each student's potential.

Pam then shows clips of two other exemplary teachers:

- Marva Collins, whose Chicago elementary student on *60 Minutes* responds to Morley Safer's hard question about his school, "Why do you like it? It's just too hard," with "That's why I like it, because it makes your brain bigger."[5]
- Rafe Esquith, whose Los Angeles ELA fifth graders read, among other books, *Of Mice and Men*, *The Joy Luck Club*, and *To Kill a Mockingbird*—*and* produce a full-length Shakespearean play every year.[6]

Pam encourages participants to see these two teachers not as exceptional but as illustrative of what they too can do for students. She reminds them of the story of Alan Turing whose persistence broke the German secret codes and shortened World War II by two years. His work saved an estimated fourteen million lives. She makes the point that each teacher, each person, affects the lives of others. Not on the scale of Turing perhaps, but true nonetheless. She recommends that they see *The Imitation Game*,[7] the acclaimed movie on Turing's life.

Escalante, Collins, and Esquith show how teachers can

- hold high expectations for all students,
- believe in every student regardless of perceived abilities,
- ask the most from each student every day, every class,
- nurture each student along the way,
- and instill in learners a fascination for learning.

Or, in their own words,

- Jaime Escalante: "You're going to work harder than you ever have before. The only thing I ask from you is 'ganas,' desire. If you don't have 'ganas,' I will give it to you, because I am an expert."[8]
- Marva Collins: "There's no magic here. Mrs. Collins is no miracle worker. I do not walk on water; I do not part the sea. I just love children and work harder than a lot of people—and so will you."[9]
- Rafe Esquith: "There are no shortcuts."[10]

Teachers who still view students as fixed quantities—as "bright" or "slow"—can break away from this mindset. They could recall a teacher who judged them unfairly. Sometimes, such judgments stay in one's psyche for years. But choosing to let go of labeling helps prevent the same legacy for their students. As teachers find their own paths to greatness, they create these paths for students. They heed the wisdom of Marianne Williamson (erroneously attributed to Nelson Mandela who quoted it at his inaugural):

Our deepest fear is not that we are inadequate. Our deepest fear is that we are powerful beyond measure. It is our light, not our darkness, that most frightens us. We ask ourselves, who am I to be brilliant, gorgeous, talented, fabulous? Actually who are you not to be? You are a child of God. Your playing small does not serve the world. There's nothing enlightened about shrinking so that other people won't feel insecure around you. We are all meant to shine as children do. We were born to make manifest the glory of God within us; it's in everyone. And as we let our light shine, we unconsciously give other people permission to do the same. As we're liberated from our own fear, our presence automatically liberates others.[11]

Jaime Escalante, Marva Collins, Rafe Esquith, and the great teachers we've known do not "play small." Why should we?

~ ~ ~

The seminal work of Carol Dweck told in her book *Mindset: The New Psychology of Success* provides insight for understanding how to perceive students. Dweck describes two possible mindsets: a *fixed* mindset and a *growth* mindset. People who have a *fixed* mindset believe their abilities, personality, and moral character are fixed; their responses to circumstances either prove or disprove their worth. People who have a *growth* mindset, on the contrary, believe their initial talents, interests, aptitudes, and temperaments can be changed through effort. Every challenge becomes an opportunity.[12]

Simply recognizing these two mindsets has a profound impact. Teachers stop to think about how much they allow outside factors to tell them about their students, such as test scores, judgments of previous teachers, and class placements. These factors when combined with their initial impressions of students often fix in stone who they are—and will be.

Dweck reminds us, however, had we been Mozart's teacher in his first ten years as a composer, we might have written him off as mediocre. Were we to have been Edison's teacher in his early years, we might not have recognized his entrepreneurial skills. Pam Peters brings Dweck's work to the attention of teachers at her workshops. She urges them to make the following commitment and post it on their refrigerator:

> I will not judge any student's potential by what he has done in the past or what he has done today. I will see him anew today. I will accept whatever he is not good at as a challenge and opportunity for me to make his brain bigger—and mine!

Teachers can choose not to judge students based on IQ or single-placement tests. Less capable students and athletes can—and do—outperform their talented counterparts. Successful coaches know that good teams thrive with players of mixed abilities. Research also shows that mixed-ability classes benefit all learners.[13] And, as Richard Lavoie indicates, regular students always benefit from being in inclusion classes.[14]

Janice Kemp, a participant in one of Pam's workshops, recounted an instance in her graduate class when she forgot to put her name on a paper. As the professor asked two of his best students if the "A" paper belonged to one of them, his jaw dropped when he saw it belonged to Janice. He appeared to assume that she was incapable of such a paper—and worse, he made her feel bad. Upon reflection, Janice realized how often she and her colleagues assume, as did her professor, that some of *their* students are less capable.

Another teacher in Pam's workshop shared what she'd heard at a conference. An elementary special education teacher assigned her students reading books, which they were enjoying. After several weeks, however, the supervising teacher discovered that this teacher had given them "advanced" books by mistake. She immediately replaced them with "more appropriate" materials. This incident reminded Pam of an episode of *The Simpsons* in which Bart was placed in a remedial class and wondered how working slower would help him catch up to the other kids.

Near the close of one of her workshops, Pam overheard Jessica, a ninth-grade history teacher, say, "I don't know if I could teach this concept to my 'lower-level' kids." No one challenged her assumption and instead nodded in agreement. Pam was awestruck by the finality of Jessica's statement and its implications. Jessica's colleagues seemed to believe, as well, that their "top" classes could discuss and debate while their "lower" classes could not. "How sad," Pam reflects. "Are any of my ideas gaining traction?"

Comments such as Jessica's evokes Jerome Bruner's famous dictum, "We begin with the hypothesis that any subject can be taught effectively in some intellectually honest form to any child at any stage of development."[15] Few serious educators disagree with Bruner's sentiment. Yet teachers and schools appear to ignore it. What if, instead, schools took Bruner's words to heart and used them as a mantra? Tom Vreeland, a volunteer tutor who had unwavering optimism about students' potential to learn, stuck with his students who twice had failed to pass the Massachusetts high-stakes test. Eventually, they did.[16]

Pam likes to share Malcolm Gladwell's story of Robert Golomb, a virtuoso car salesman who has an exceptional intelligence in dealing with people. His resolve to take care of every customer who comes through the door prevents him from prejudging. He refuses to preassess customers' looks, that is, factoring in—unconsciously perhaps—their age, race, and gender. Nor does he gauge their inclination to buy or not. He remains open and treats everyone fairly—and doubles the average sales of other salesmen.[17] Pam suggests that teachers act as Golomb and delight in being open to the potential of all of their students and "making sales" well beyond the average.

> Be aware that you choose how you speak about your students. Listen carefully to the words you use. Do you say 'low-level' or 'high-level,' when discussing students? Once you see how detrimental these terms are, you listen for them with your colleagues. Some participants begin to grasp what she is saying.

> You all can recall classmates, friends, and family who have succeeded beyond expectations. You can recall students who surprised you despite your early assessments. When you think about it, you have become smarter through the act of teaching. Everyone has potential—and as you accept this truth you become better. So, when you hear colleagues use these terms, you can reframe the conversation.

When teachers consider the two questions addressed at the beginning of this chapter, "Who's not going to get it?" and "Who will already know it or get it quickly?" they know these questions apply only to a moment in time—and not to the students themselves.

REFLECTION

Teachers who label students give up on them. The "average" students stay average. They make choices that keep them in their place. They rarely distinguish themselves. They fulfill expectations earning C's and D's. The "bright" students maintain their place by memorizing for A's. Few take risks. They can suffer anxiety over grades. And, despite dedicated teachers' efforts to the contrary, special education students feel "special," as in "less than" their peers.

Dan Hilliard struggles not to use such terms as "bright," "slow," and "average." After hearing the two questions posed at the beginning of this chapter, he reframes his thinking about his students' potential. In conversations, however, he occasionally uses these terms, as they are part of the school's common language. Even parents use them freely—but usually only positive terms.

Dan read Carol Dweck's *Mindset*. He's developing a growth mindset both in his life and teaching. It frees him from making judgments of his students—and of himself. He has recommended Dweck's book to his principal for the staff to read.

POINTS TO PURSUE

Break Away from the Tyranny of Language

Like all professions, teachers learn their own lexicon. Some terms seem to be embedded, such as "slow," "bright," "honors," "level one." Unfortunately, such terms constrain teachers (and parents) from seeing potential.

Ask yourself—and ask colleagues—what keeps teachers locked into categorizing students? If you see a student break out, do you see it as an anomaly? What might you do to change your thinking? How might you look for surprises from your students? And how can you look for the unexpected?

Find Ways to Challenge Students at All Levels

Given the numbers of students in classrooms, the task of challenging all of them is difficult. The expansion of special education services has made it more possible for schools to support struggling students. Some schools even have gifted and talented programs for the better-than-average students.

How can you advocate for students in your classroom who perform above and beyond your curricula? How will you provide them with challenges to develop their thinking and creativity? What can you learn from coaches and teachers in the arts?

Learn from the Great Ones

Jaime Escalante, Marva Collins, and Rafe Esquith are examples of exceptional teachers. No doubt, you know of other teachers you would consider to be great.

What can you do to infuse great teaching qualities in yourself? Can you let go of playing small—"I'm just a teacher"—and step toward greatness? Can you acknowledge the greatness you already have?

Seek a Growth Mindset

Carol Dweck has become the poster person for teaching that is growth oriented. Read her seminal book *Mindset*. Invite others to join you for what should be intriguing conversations.

Can you make a commitment to become more growth oriented—not only for your students but with yourself?

See Yourself As a Coach

Taking Bruner's hypothesis seriously brings up the analogy of teacher-as-coach. In *Mr. Holland's Opus*, Glenn Holland denies he's a coach to Lou Russ, an athlete who wants to learn to play a bass drum.[18] Yet, Mr. Holland becomes just that as he teaches Lou to play successfully.

Can you see yourself as a teacher-as-coach? Can you coach when you know you need to cover a lot of material? How can you reconcile these roles?

Make their Brains—and Yours—Bigger

Discuss the following statement with colleagues, adapted from Marva Collins's student's words of wisdom: "I will not judge any student's potential by what he has done in the past or by what he's done today. Instead, I will accept what I am not good at as a challenge and opportunity for making my students' brains bigger—and mine!"

How can this challenge become central in your school's conversations about teaching?

NOTES

1. "Differentiating Instruction: Creating Multiple Paths for Learning I" (ASCD, 1997). "Differentiation of Activities by Readiness."
2. "Differentiating Instruction: Creating Multiple Paths for Learning I" (ASCD, 1997). "Differentiating Content by Readiness."
3. "Differentiating Instruction: Creating Multiple Paths for Learning I" (ASCD, 1997). "Differentiation of Content by Interest" and "Differentiation of Activities by Readiness."
4. *Stand and Deliver* (American Playhouse Theatrical, 1988).

5. Carol Dweck, *Mindset: The New Psychology of Success* (New York: Ballantine, 2006), 194–95.

6. Mel Stuart, *The Hobart Shakespeareans* (Docudrama.com, 2006).

7. *The Imitation Game* (Winston Company, 2014).

8. *Stand and Deliver* (American Playhouse Theatrical, 1988).

9. Zay Smith, Chicago *Sun-Times*, quoting from Marva Collins and Civia Tamarkin, *Marva Collins' Way: Returning to Excellence in Education* (Los Angeles: Jeremy Tarcher, 1982/1990), 47, in Carol Dweck, *Mindset*, 199.

10. Mel Stuart, *Hobart Shakespeareans*.

11. Marianne Williamson, *A Return to Love* (Dunmore, PA: Harper Collins, 1992), Chapter 7, Section 3.

12. Carol S. Dweck, *Mindset*. Thanks to Mary Anton-Oldenberg for bringing this book to my attention.

13. See, for example, John Sutton and Alice Krueger, eds., *EDThoughts: What We Know About Mathematics Teaching and Learning* (Aurora, CO: McREL: Mid-continent Research for Education and Learning, 2002) (220), 4–5.

14. Richard Lavoie, "It's So Much Work Being Your Friend." Lavoie also says inclusion students do not always benefit. See Richard Lavoie, "When the Chips are Down" (Learning Store: http://www.learningstore.org/we1004.html or excerpts on YouTube).

15. Jerome Bruner, *The Process of Education: A Searching Discussion of School Education Opening New Paths to Learning and Teaching* (New York: Vintage, 1960), 33.

16. Tom Vreeland, Mount Everett High School, Sheffield, Massachusetts.

17. Malcolm Gladwell, *Blink: The Power of Thinking Without Thinking* (New York: Little Brown, 2005), 88–96.

18. Stephen Herek, *Mr. Holland's Opus*, 1995.

Chapter 11

Abandon the Crabs in the Cage

There is a type of crab that cannot be caught—it is agile and clever enough to get out of any trap. And yet, these crabs are caught by the thousands every day, thanks to a particularly human trait they possess.

The trap is a wire cage with a hole at the top. Bait is placed in the cage, and the cage is lowered into the water. One crab comes along, enters the cage, and begins munching on the bait. A second crab joins him. A third. Crab Thanksgiving. Yum. Eventually, however, the bait is gone.

The crabs could easily climb up the side of the cage and through the hole, but they do not. They stay in the cage. More crabs come in and join them—long after the bait is gone.

Should one of the crabs realize there is no further reason to stay in the trap and attempt to leave, the other crabs will gang up on him and stop him. They will repeatedly pull him off the side of the cage. If he is persistent, the others will tear off his claws to keep him from climbing. If he still persists, they will kill him.

The crabs—by a force of the majority—stay together in the cage. The cage is hauled up, and it's dinnertime on the pier.

Teachers stick together. Given their long history as blue-collar union laborers in factory-model schools, they unite around one another. They develop strong social bonds and loyalties and seldom commit to act independently. They function inside a strong hierarchical structure and act in deference to their superiors whether they respect them or not. They rarely imagine administrators as colleagues; they are, after all, the bosses. Their deep loyalty to one another protects them from outside threats coming from "authorities."

Ben Klunder, a new teacher, was surprised to hear on his first day veteran colleagues complaining in the faculty room. He had come into teaching from a liberal arts background. He knew the profession was not well respected, but he couldn't wait for his chance to be a teacher. His first weeks with his ninth-grade Language Arts classes were more exciting than he imagined. He was looking forward to becoming friends with his new colleagues.

He was surprised, however, with their demeanor at a faculty meeting. Instead of grappling with issues and focusing on bettering the school, no one paid attention. The more the principal spoke, the less interested they became. After the meeting, Ben asked his department head, Delaney Goodman, why the meeting was like that.

Delaney explained that the school recently underwent a difficult time. "Four years ago, our new principal at that time tried to impose his ideas on all of us. He did not consult anyone beforehand, nor did he enlist any of us to help him. He caused deep resentment. A few of us quit, but most of us retreated into old patterns. Resistance was better than compliance. As you know, we have a new principal. It will take time for our faculty to acclimatize to him. It's a slow process."

Delaney proceeded to explain that the faculty still resents being forced to attend meetings in which they have little or no say. So, they feign attention, correct papers, and carry on side conversations; some even fall asleep. They joke about how they subvert meetings, and often roll their eyes to show their disgust. Some get up and leave at the appointed time in the contract even if the meeting is not over. Actually, the principal does not enjoy most meetings either. He has to lead them, as he's expected to.

Later that evening, Ben thinks how much better faculty meetings would be if he and his colleagues would take initiative to establish a collegial relationship with the administration. He took out his journal and wrote:

> What if we change our attitude? What would happen if we worked with the principal to make the meetings meaningful? Instead of sitting through endless announcements and "administrivia," together we could design workshops to improve instruction. Imagine the effect of four hours per a month—thirty-six hours per year—of real professional learning. If I were to have had such workshops during, say, forty years in the classroom, I would have nearly fifteen hundred hours of collaborative professional learning—and my colleagues and I would become a more collegial and competent faculty.

Veteran colleagues try to find false solace by complaining about matters such as restrictive schedules, single-letter grading systems, extra duties, angry parents, uninformed school boards, state mandates, and unmotivated students. Complaints often become excuses, which allow faculty to place blame as if they have had no part in creating problems. They point fingers instead of recognizing their complicity in scheduling, grading and reporting systems, and rigid contracts.

Ben quickly understands that teachers are instrumental to the culture of his school. It is one matter to complain about what is not working, but it is another to take responsibility for making changes for the better. They often seem to take a crabs-in-the-cage mentality instead of striving to invent new and better ways to teach. "So much wasted effort," he thinks.

Among the complaints that Ben hears in the faculty room are about other colleagues who do not pull their weight. Yet, some of those same teachers do not pull their weight, but he says nothing. Another trait among the faculty that really surprises him is how teachers allow one another to perpetuate old ways. No one seems willing to critique teaching practices.

At faculty meetings, some veterans put down new teachers' initiatives. They voice sharp criticisms like, "We do not do this around here," or "We've tried that before and it doesn't work." Ben feels uncomfortable challenging such comments. He wishes he could. By keeping silent, he realizes he is condoning the "culture of nice"—*but* it might assure him a place in the social structure of the school.[1]

However, such condoning mentality hurts everyone. When veterans slight new teachers during faculty meetings, they shut down their potential to impact effective change. They affirm the status quo. Soon, new teachers either conform, or perhaps as likely quit—and if they still want to teach move to another school.

This situation reflects a crabs-in-a-cage mentality in which everyone sticks close together on the floor of the cage. Any attempt by one to "climb out"—to make an effort to change—frightens others into pulling him back. By sticking together, teachers build an enclave, one that ironically protects them not only from threats of change but also from the influx of new ideas.

Teacher unions can reinforce this mentality. In the early years of factory-designed schools, unions proved important and beneficial. Collective bargaining allowed teachers to advocate for decent wages and working conditions—still a fight for many—and protection from unfair dismissals.

But in recent years, unions have transgressed into the business of education. As a result, they often become a stumbling block for change and innovation. Their role has grown not only in negotiating salaries and benefits, their primary purpose, but also in enforcing seniority for veteran teachers regardless of their competence, determining schedules, workloads, job descriptions, and teaching hours.

The union mindset focuses on security and protection. The practice of harboring less competent members is particularly insidious. Delaney told Ben about how an art teacher, who everyone knew was inadequate, garnered support from the union when the school board held a public hearing to question his competency. "This teacher was cutting corners and not fulfilling his contract. Yet, only one staff member was willing to testify in support of dismissal in front of the board at a public meeting."

Nearly as insidious, especially for students, is the reluctance of unions to support innovations unless specified in the teacher contract. Given that most contracts are negotiated for multiple years, they become roadblocks for change. "If it is not in the contract," the argument states, "we cannot and will not consider it until we renegotiate."

In some districts the union hierarchy exerts a stranglehold on its membership. When a member attempts to act outside the contract, it invokes the crabs-in-the-cage principle. Union officials have chastised members for wanting to paint their own classrooms—even after maintenance refuses—or for arranging to hold parent conferences outside specified contract hours. In some districts, union leadership manages to stay in office for years and is able to enact frequent grievance procedures to block any and all proposals for changing instructional practice. In some districts, past presidents even maintain control years beyond their time in office.[2]

Tenure has become another obstacle that prevents creativity and independence. In most districts, teachers spend their first few years on probation, proving their worth—mainly by staying out of trouble. They, then, secure a professional contract or tenure. Ironically, assessments during these first years often focus on behavior and not on the quality of instruction. Unlike college and university professors who must prove their academic credentials to earn tenure, teachers need only do a satisfactory job—or appear to.

When visiting her doctor, a patient is confident that her doctor is up-to-date in his practices, as he is required to take periodic recertification exams. If he were able earn a certificate to practice for life without rigorous recertification, she would not continue as his patient. Yet, the teaching profession presses to equate tenure with job security. In many districts, the profession requires little more than attending workshops and courses to collect professional development credits. They rarely conduct—or allow—serious assessments of teaching practice.

At a brain-research workshop led by a nationally respected presenter, Benklunder noticed that two-thirds of the participants left after lunch to shop rather than complete the workshop; since they had already signed in, they received their credit hours for the day. Needless to say, Ben was embarrassed, not only for the presenter but also for the profession. The presenter told him afterward that such behavior is not unusual.

Once receiving tenure, teachers are virtually guaranteed a lifetime contract. For example, two teachers in the same department teaching the same subject in the same school can perform at very different levels. Yet they expect to have their contracts renewed annually. An egregious example happened in the case of one science teacher who taught twenty-eight times as much as another teacher down the hall in the same school.[3]

Teachers know who are the most effective teachers in their school and who are not. Yet, they rarely consider themselves as one of the weaker teachers. A principal and good friend from a neighboring school told Ben that after interviewing all of her teachers, she learned that they only perceived other teachers as weaker—never themselves. Parents, too, know which teachers they want for their children, but often have to count on the luck of the draw.

Ben surmises about his colleagues' crabs-in-the-cage mentality. He again takes out his journal and asks:

> How can we break out of our persistence in support of mediocrity?
>
> Why don't we pay closer attention to the evidence that confirms our central role in student achievement?
>
> How can we become open to data analysis of performance levels to complement our personal judgments?
>
> Why do so many of my colleagues support simplistic satisfactory/unsatisfactory performance rating systems of their teaching that assure that over 95% of them are guaranteed a satisfactory rating?

Michael Jones, in the *Boston Globe*, sums up the absurdity of this rating system in one sentence: "At 72 of [Boston's] 135 schools, not a single teacher was given an unsatisfactory evaluation. Fifteen of these are on the state's list of chronically underperforming schools."[4] When teachers remain hunkered down with the crabs-in-the-cage mentality, they not only perpetuate mediocrity and failed practices, but they also deny the opportunity to identify and verify factors that define greatness.

Dr. William Sanders, a senior research fellow at the University of North Carolina, designed the seminal Tennessee Value Added Assessment System (TVASS). His system provides convincing evidence at that time that teacher effectiveness is the leading factor in student achievement. In fact, according to Sanders it is ten to twenty times as significant as the effects of other factors, such as socioeconomic status, race, urban versus rural, and heterogeneous versus homogeneous groupings.[5]

Whether or not teachers agree with Sanders's research model and conclusions, they know some are better teachers than others. It behooves each teacher to know the difference and then strive to teach as the best among them do.

Other researchers, notably William Damon, lament the passivity and apathy of students and the discouragement of teachers.[6] At the same time, Damon recognizes teaching as "the very heart of schooling. Because a child's learning requires a framework of guiding relationships . . . the teacher is the single most important resource of any school."[7]

However, recent evidence indicates a shift. Edutopia, funded by the George Lucas Foundation, reports that "the most significant variable is socioeconomic status, followed by the neighborhood, the psychological quality of the home environment, and the support of physical health provided."[8] Given the fifteen years between Sanders's study and this one, Edutopia's conclusions reflect changes in culture. Still, in any school, teachers have more contact with students than their parents do. Even at 30 percent—probably much more in many instances—teachers are crucial. Education is a human activity, not a series of test results.

By insisting on securing and protecting tenure rather than being open to performance reviews, teachers implicitly support a play-it-safe mentality. If students fail to learn, teachers often make the argument they do not try hard enough. "If our good students do well," they contend, "we must be doing something right." Such behavior admits to not taking responsibility to design teaching to meet every type of learner.

Teachers can take initiatives to improve instruction, seek and receive feedback, and support one another. A faculty would be wise to establish a Golden Toilet Award for any colleague who takes a risk to try something new and then fails.[9] When teachers fail, they know they've tried. If they never try, they never find out whether their ideas might work.

At the same time, schools should honor teachers who succeed. They need not pretend all teachers "are fine" and thus ignore colleagues who design and implement exceptional practices. Teacher of the Year, even Teacher of the Month, misses the point. This form of recognition is often more political than instructional. Instead, make it common practice to acknowledge exceptional work whenever it appears. Teachers then learn about the good work of their colleagues—and become better themselves. Teacher of the Week, Teacher of the Day, Teacher of the Moment. It's a no-brainer, really.

And, why not encourage teachers to share Golden Moments, to celebrate the wonderful times that make teaching worthwhile. Such as breakthroughs with parents and students, or new collaborations that open doors among colleagues, or moments when a student finally "gets it." Such celebrations bring diversity and exploration into a school culture and move faculty away from feeling pressure to stay under the radar. Nobody wins when everyone stays at the bottom of the cage.

Ultimately, the crabs-in-a-cage syndrome supports a subculture in which the main purpose is to guarantee jobs. Although teachers work in isolated classrooms, they make a tacit agreement to teach in much the same way. Conforming to the accepted behavior of their culture means no one will bother them.

When teachers give good grades, especially to "honors" students (particularly in high-powered districts), they please everyone and avoid complaints. When they limit the number of students they send to the office, administration views them as effective teachers. On the other hand, in cases where teachers face difficult groups (often from the luck of the draw) administrators become annoyed when increasing numbers of students are sent to them. They assume the teacher is doing a poor job—and may often prejudge without any in-class observation or offers of help.

~ ~ ~

One day after a department meeting, Ben Klunder says to Delaney Goodman, "Sometimes, when I reflect on the crabs-in-a-cage phenomenon, I understand why we teachers stay there. We face constant public scrutiny and criticism. Everyone has opinions about education."

"You're onto something here," Delaney replies. "It's been my experience that when the economy tanks, we are often blamed; when it thrives we remain invisible. When budgets tighten, we suffer. When state test scores drop, we hear criticism. When parents see future, they talk as if they know how to fix us; since they attended school for years, they know all they often act as if about education.

"And, I've seen this happen when an administrator does not like a teacher. He can make her life miserable to the point where she wants to quit—and sometimes does. We find it frustrating when others do not appreciate the complexities of what we do every day. Sticking together helps to assure survival. You can see where the crabs-in-the-cage analogy might fit in."

Ben begins to sense the big picture. "Yes, but I think this mentality fails to serve us—and ultimately our students. If the accepted culture in our school advocates that teachers lecture and give quizzes, tests, and papers as the primary assessments, I may need to think twice before teaching differently. I've heard some veterans express their displeasure with alternative methods calling them 'progressive' or 'risky.'"

"Good students, too," Delaney chimes in, "may resist new approaches, because they do not want to change how they do school. They master earning A's by memorizing for tests and writing thoughtless formulaic essays. I was like that. Today, this mediocrity explains why colleges have to have set up remedial reading and writing centers. And, it confirms why many students become bored and drop out."

Delaney and Ben see it like it is. The crabs-in-the-cage mentality often starts at the top. Principals who taught as sages on the stage prefer quiet, orderly classrooms with teachers standing at the front. They prefer to not rock the boat. Some actively support personal *congeniality* rather than challenge the staff to develop professional *collegiality*—a far more difficult task. They stay away from spending time in classrooms, except for the required scheduled observations and evaluations. These are dog-and-pony shows. By these actions, principals unwittingly support the crabs-in-the-cage mentality.

Some principals, however, challenge restrictive school cultures and union contracts. They advocate, for example, walkthroughs, learning walks, or mini-observations—somewhat analogous to hospital grand rounds—where principals and teachers make quick visits to classrooms and provide descriptive, nonevaluative feedback. These approaches break through the closed culture of isolated classrooms. In schools using walkthroughs, teachers appreciate the feedback once they trust its intentions. And principals appreciate it, as well, as they learn what actually happens in classrooms.

Teachers can take responsibility to teach at their best. They know how important they are for improving instruction. The crabs-in-the-cage mentality, however, puts a stranglehold on improving teaching. When a teacher stays on the floor of the cage and agrees to conform to outmoded practices, he is committing malpractice.

As author Steven Pressfield writes, "The highest treason that a crab can commit is to make a leap for the rim of the bucket."[10] Great teachers make this leap every day.

REFLECTION

Dan Hilliard has conflicting concerns about his union. When he first became a teacher, he joined and participated in union activities and even became treasurer for a year. But recently, his union leadership has expressed concerns about his radical ideas. One of the officers questioned him about his practice of meeting parents after school hours, as it is in violation of the contract. Dan has not confronted the union's concerns, but he worries about possible difficulties.

He is also concerned that some teachers seem to hang on until they retire. Tenure has given them security. Because they know they will not be challenged, they often hunker down and do only what they've always done. They resist new initiatives, knowing that it will mean more work.

Meanwhile, Dan continues to push the envelope. Teaching, after all, is first about what is good for his students and their families, not about the contract. It's not about clinging onto the cage floor.

POINTS TO PURSUE

Assess the Role of the Union in Your School

Ben Klunder was surprised to learn that some of his colleagues did not perceive his school as he did. After a few faculty meetings, he saw that he was not on the same page as his most vociferous veteran colleagues. It was as if they were like crabs at the bottom of the cage, wanting to stay there.

To learn about the likelihood of a crabs-in-the-cage mentality in your school, begin by assessing the role of the union. You can determine if it serves your contract well—and how well it serves innovative teaching. Having conversations with colleagues about the union can be enlightening. Are there other crabs-in-the-cage issues in your school?

Redressing a Negative Faculty Room

Many new teachers are surprised at the negativity of the faculty room. In some schools, the same people hang out and grouse about the administration, colleagues, students, and the community. Not all schools.

What can you do if your faculty room is filled with complainers? How can you reorient attitudes of your colleagues, particularly veterans? How might you redirect conversations toward what works in your school—or what could work? Or, you could also do what many choose—not go into the faculty room.

How Might You Expand Your Teaching Role?

If you are a new teacher like Ben Klunder, you, too, may feel unforeseen constraints on your teaching. You feel slowly being shut out from the embedded culture controlled by the school's veterans.

How might you take initiative as a faculty member in your school, knowing that you might be confronting the union contract? Perhaps at a meeting you could introduce the Golden Toilet Award or the Golden Moments concept? It might get people thinking off the floor of the cage.

Initiate Cooperation with Your Administration

Faculty meetings need not be the sole jurisdiction of the principal. Ben comes to the realization that he and others can take a role in improving these meetings.

Seek out like-minded colleagues and together approach the principal to find ways to improve professional learning for everyone, particularly at faculty meetings. If your union takes a "strict-contract" attitude, try to work around it as much as possible.

Making the Leap!

How can you take initiative to raise expectations for all teachers in your school—and for yourself? How could you encourage them to emulate Steven Pressfield and "make a leap for the rim of the bucket"? Bringing up such a proposition takes courage, even when you know that you are thinking first of your students.

NOTES

1. Elisa MacDonald, "When Nice Won't Suffice: Honest Discourse is Key to Shifting School Culture," *Journal of Staff Development*, June, 2011.

2. It would be unfair not to acknowledge instances of union leadership that exert a positive influence on improving education. Brian Gearty of Blue Hills Regional Vocational School in Canton, Massachusetts, and Robert Becker of Wachusett Regional School District in Holden, Massachusetts, are examples of two innovative union leaders I have met. Unfortunately, such people are too rare.

3. Michael Schmoker, *Results Now*, 37, cites David Berliner's reports of the chaos in curriculum.

4. Michael Jones, "Grade the Teachers: A Way to Improve Schools One Instructor at a Time," *Boston Globe*, November 1, 2009.

5. Marilyn Marks, "The Teacher Factor," *The New York Times*, Education Life Supplement, January 9, 2000.

6. William Damon, *Greater Expectations: Overcoming the Culture of Indulgence in Our Homes and Schools* (New York: Free Press, 1996), 32.

7. Ibid., 200.

8. Education Trends, "8 Myths that Undermine Educational Effectiveness," at http://www.edutopia.org/blog/myths-that-undermine-educational-effectiveness-mark-phillips?utm_source=facebook&utm_medium=cpc&utm_campaign=blog-myths-undermine-ed-effectiveness-countdown-link, June 10, 2014.

9. Robert Evans, "National Seminar for the Experienced Pro," Mallery Seminars, Philadelphia, Pennsylvania, 2001.

10. Steven Pressfield, *The War of Art* (New York: Warner Books, 2002), 20–21.

Chapter 12

Stop the Interruptions

It has to do with power. Every time anyone shamelessly interrupted my class, the message was clear: "My time is more valuable than yours. Whatever you're doing cannot possibly be as vital as whatever I'm doing."

Why do teachers have to struggle to find uninterrupted time? What in the school psyche allows office personnel—principals, guidance, and secretaries—to interrupt over the public address system (PA)? What allows janitors during classes to operate floor-cleaning machines in the hallways or lawn mowers outside windows? People claim that teachers are an essential piece in a child's education, yet such actions in schools undermine their efforts.

Coleen Armstrong is right. Whatever she is doing in her classroom is not as valuable as what others do. It is a power struggle.[1] But an unnecessary power struggle, an unjustified power struggle. Successful businesses put customers first, so schools should put teachers and students first. When the principal interrupts over the PA, the lesson disappears! Depending on the length of the announcement and its content, returning to the lesson—if possible—can take several minutes. "Will the following students please come to the office?" has an even more emotional impact.

Patti Grenier, former superintendent of schools in Barnstable, Massachusetts, and now a consultant at Teachers21, shared at a workshop that an average of seven minutes are lost with each PA announcement. Think about that. If five interruptions occur during the day, thirty-five minutes of teaching is lost. For a week, that means three hours! For thirty-six weeks, forty-eight hours!

Armstrong's insight is the-emperor-is-not-wearing-any-clothes expose' of this travesty. In dire contrast, in Japan, the classroom is considered sacred. Learning takes priority. No interruptions are tolerated.[2] In contrast, in

American schools, where interruptions are the order of the day, Japanese visitors flinch when the PA (Big Brother?) issues a command—or when teachers barge in on one another.

This last comment deserves scrutiny. If you are a teacher, how often do you drop in on other teachers in the middle of the period to borrow something or simply to say hello? How often do you interrupt your own students during a lesson instead of letting them have extended time? Have you thought about suggesting to your colleagues to consider the impact of the traditional assembly-line schedule of forty-to-forty-five–minute periods? How might you make it a point to advocate for more uninterrupted learning time?

Lorraine Hong offers a different perspective from Armstrong, one that is more subtle and perhaps more insidious.[3] Hong describes how increasing intrusions caused her to lose her passion for teaching. In her school as part of an hour-long writing period, the principal told her and her fifth-grade colleagues to include ten minutes of keyboarding. While her principal considered this a simple request, by the time the computers were set up and students settled, the lesson took fifteen to twenty minutes to implement.

Later, a new math curriculum was put in place that required teaching sixty minutes per day. Hong found it impossible to schedule it on Mondays and Fridays, because students were required to leave for "gifted" programs and for special-education pullouts. She summed up her frustrations in an apt analogy:

> When the days are fragmented and move at the pace of fast-food eateries rather than four-star restaurants, teachers have no time in which to build the provocative experiences that nourish layered learning—experiences that provide teachers with the continuing intellectual and creative challenges that allow them to be professional educators rather than short order cooks.[4]

Four-star restaurants—what a way to visualize classrooms! So contrary to the repetitious hamster-wheel–driven lessons after lessons, spinning endlessly. Lessons without comprehension, because of pressures from federal and state assessments and overcrowded curriculums. Hong and Armstrong articulate what most teachers appear to accept as part of school culture. However, teachers can combat these interferences—and in Armstrong's words, "take back their classrooms."

Teachers would be wise to assess the effect of this interruptive culture. Instead of consenting to every addition to the curriculum, they can express their apprehensions. The continuous growth of patchwork curricula—adding more content without taking any away—decreases the quality of what's being taught. A mile-wide, inch-deep curriculum reduces learning. In contrast, in-depth investigations based on big ideas, active literacy, critical thinking, and thoughtful assessments engage students—and teachers.

Every time a teacher interrupts her students with "It's time to put away your materials" or "You have to leave now," she sends a wrong message. Students see that working fast and getting the right answers in short segments make for success. Analytical thinking, reflective conversation, and interactive processing, on the other hand, take time to develop—and for long-term learning need time to take root.

Another form of interruption comes from digital devices. In classes where students are allowed to have cell phones with the notification feature switched on are provoked to respond immediately. Such interruptions delay returning to the task at hand by as much as fifteen minutes. Attending to electronic communications to fill in "dead time" precludes daydreaming from which eureka ideas can arise.[5] And it disrupts coding short-term memory into long-term memory. In a class where students are constantly referring to text messages, any chance of developing thinking and creative ideas becomes nearly impossible.

When interruptions rule, learning retreats to the back burner. The schedule dominates. When the intercom makes an announcement in the middle of a class, the priorities are clear. When a secretary calls over the intercom to ask for student health forms, learning grinds to a halt. When guidance calls for a student, everyone listens. When a student turns to the messages on his cell phone, he's no longer in class. Whatever ideas were waiting to be discovered disappear.

Sean Mullens, a first-year music teacher, recalls his comment in a conversation he had with colleagues at a beginning teachers' workshop. "I really feel bad that I interrupt your classes when I pull out students for music class." Mary Thompson, a special education teacher, concurred. "I, too, feel badly when I interrupt a lesson to pull out a student to work with me."

As the conversation progressed, it became clear that conflicts with "specials" are a central concern for both classroom teachers and specials' teachers—but for different reasons. Having to work with fragmented schedules ultimately hurts everyone, especially students.

Instead of acknowledging the inevitable, Amir Sharma, a new fifth-grade teacher, suggested taking another tack. "Why not bring this issue up at a faculty meeting? Why not demonstrate that students—and we—are being shortchanged by this system. I have heard veteran teachers in my school saying the same thing. I bet if everyone puts their heads together, we might come up with ways to minimize interruptions. We will define and claim our space and declare that quality instruction is our most important goal."

Pam Peters, who was leading the workshop, liked what Amir suggested. "I agree with the sentiment in this room. Let's see if we can think in the spirit of Coleen Armstrong's power struggle and a 'take-back-the-classroom' mentality. Let's see what you can come up with." She then asked them to break up into smaller groups and come up with ways to resolve the problem.

After twenty minutes of heated discussion, each group was asked to share its ideas. Sean Mullens spoke for his group. "We could begin by asking to eliminate the more obvious interruptions: lawn mowers, vacuums, snowblowers, the PA, and cell phones—ours included. And, no unannounced visitors are permitted including colleagues. No exceptions. We have a plan to make this happen.

"We will gather 'interruption' data for a month. When we are interrupted we will note what happens to our lessons. Once we collect evidence we can compile the data and bring it to the administration. We then will move the conversation away from complaining to improving conditions for instruction."

"I cannot imagine the PA operating during class time if everyone declared it off limits," Mary Thompson chimed in. "I've heard of schools that already function without it, including large high schools.[6] And, I cannot imagine if we develop a culture of no interruptions that office staff, guidance counselor, or administrators would not abide—and fellow teachers would not enter a classroom uninvited during a lesson either. I would be most grateful, and so would my American History students."

Portia Lavine, a Language Arts teacher from a more progressive school, spoke up. "One exception is walkthroughs, or learning walks, which work because they are integral to the system of instruction in our school. Everyone is aware they are coming, even students. My colleagues and I like them, as they provide us with valuable feedback. We become better teachers for it. And our administrators are becoming more sensitive to all that we do. Since we all know they're coming, they are not considered interruptions. They're part of our instructional matrix."

A possible side benefit of a no-interruptions policy is that it allows administrative staff to become more involved in classroom teaching. Instead of calling individual students out of classes throughout the day, college guidance counselors could schedule classes for college application preparation. A principal might find time to teach a class in his subject area. Any time the administration participates in the teaching process, it reinforces the message of the classroom as the focus of the school—and reduces class size for everyone.

"In my school," Ignatius Perkins, a fourth-grade teacher, pipes up, "we schedule electives one day a week for each grade. On Monday, the first grade has art, music, computer, and extended physical education, on Tuesday the second grade, and so on. Not only do we have uninterrupted days on the other four, but we also had the opportunity to collaborate for one whole day per week! I've also heard of other schools who schedule specials for a grade on two half-days, which makes for two half-days a week for collaborative planning."

"Wow!" Pam Peters interjects. "With this approach you achieve two essential changes in the culture of the school: fewer interruptions *and* less isolation of teachers!"

~ ~ ~

Classrooms ultimately belong to students. They should be considered sanctuaries. Once teachers recognize this principle—and recognize the precious little time they have to create opportunities for effective learning—they will not tolerate interference. They already contend with far too many outside dictates that cut into their teaching—including excessive interruptions to prepare and administer standardized tests. As long as teachers are complicit with an interruptive school culture, they perpetuate short-segment teaching that results in short-term learning. By reducing interruptions, they make possible the primary imperative of the classroom.

Perhaps Principal Tim Healey said it best after observing a secretary making an all-school PA announcement on a trivial matter: "Mediocre schools make decisions that are based on what is convenient for secretaries and administrators. Great schools make decisions that maximize and guard instructional time."[7]

REFLECTION

Dan Hilliard discovered early on the deleterious effect of his school's PA system. At least three times per day, the office would make announcements to request forms, indicate team bus schedules, call for individual students, notify about after-school events, and occasionally broadcast a message from the principal. Dan noticed how difficult it was to bring his students back into his lessons, especially after they had been deeply engaged.

When Dan brought his concern to veteran teachers, some shrugged, "It's the way it is." But he would not let it go. He conferred with his team and together they agreed to count how many interruptions came from the office—and from maintenance—and to use stopwatches to time just how long. If possible, they would also try to assess how much time before students to regained focus, admittedly a difficult task.

After several weeks, they brought their data to Principal Margaret Fellows. They were not surprised that she recognized the severity of the problem. However, she was usually open to different ideas coming from faculty and students. She promised she would do her part to end interruptions from the office. She agreed to use the PA only at specified times at the beginning and the end of the day.

She surprised them when she asked if they and any others would like to study the interruption issue further, specifically, to look into those from maintenance, for sending students to "specials," and the impact of extracurricular areas. "In particular," Margaret emphasized, "we should determine the effect of curricular add-ons. I am noticing increased frustration among staff. Assessing this area will be a challenge. I hope you will help." Dan and his colleagues quickly agreed, as they also find dealing with add-ons difficult.

"What a difference it would make," Dan said to his colleague Allegra Bernardi, "if we could count on teaching without any interruptions; not only would we be able to teach more effectively, but our students would have more opportunity to be stay involved!"

POINTS TO PURSUE

Collect Data on Interruptions

Coleen Armstrong points out the obvious. Every teacher knows school has an interruptive culture. Have you ever wondered why this is necessary?

Taking Armstrong's lead, do what Dan and his team did and document your school's interruptions. Once you collect your data, approach your principal. Have a backup plan if she resists.

Take Lorraine Hong's Insights to Heart

Less obvious and perhaps more insidious are the interruptions described through Lorraine Hong's eyes. Having some students leave in the middle of lessons is common. Piling on curriculum has become the norm in many districts.

Identify curricular allocations that interfere with your teaching. Note, too, the number of students who leave during lessons. Can you advocate changes to reduce the conflicts? Have discussions with colleagues to see what you can do to make learning smoother—to make your classrooms into "four-star restaurants."

Create Classrooms to be Sanctuaries for Learning

James W. Stigler and James Hiebert make clear the distinction between U.S. classrooms as interruptive and Japanese classrooms as sanctuaries. Given the plethora of distractions in your classroom and school, what can you do to make your classroom a sanctuary for learning? How can you create the self-respect necessary to make this possible?

Sanctuary classrooms come from being honored from the inside as well as from the outside. How can you reduce the number of interruptions you create? How can you teach students, as well, to understand that not responding to digital devices during class will improve the atmosphere?

Making "Specials" Less Interruptive to the Classroom

Given the randomness of students leaving for "specials," can you think of a less interruptive approach? As suggested in this chapter, propose that each grade have either the morning or the afternoon scheduled for "specials" two days per week. When you make uninterrupted teaching your priority, you begin to think about different possibilities and configurations—even inside your classroom.

Make Your Classroom a "Four-Star Restaurant"

Take Lorraine Hong's image to heart and visualize yourself as a teacher in a four-star classroom. What is already there? What else do you need? What interferes that makes you feel like a short-order cook? What do you want to discard? Instead of eliminating digital devices, how might you use them to "feed" a four-star classroom?

NOTES

1. Coleen Armstrong, "Do Not Disturb!" *Teacher Magazine*, May/June 1995.

2. James W. Stigler and James Hiebert, *The Teaching Gap: Best Ideas from the World's Teachers for Improving Education in the Classroom* (New York: Free Press, 1999), 55–56.

3. Lorraine K. Hong, "Too Many Intrusions on Instructional Time," *Phi Delta Kappan*, May 2001, 712–14.

4. Ibid., 714.

5. "Will the BlackBerry Sink the Presidency?" by Sharon Begley in *Newsweek*, February 16, 2009, 37, excerpted in the *Marshall Memo* 274, February 23, 2009.

6. For example, Peabody High School and Wachusett Regional High School in Massachusetts, each with nearly 2000 students, do not allow the PA to be used during the day.

7. Tim Healey, "Creating Greatness," *Principal Leadership*, February 2009, 31, in *Marshall Memo* 272, February 9, 2009, 1.

Chapter 13

End One-Size-Fits-All Teaching

I think I used to be more like Mr. Appleton, because I gave a lot of lectures. But now, I am more like Mrs. Baker, as I do many fun activities as well as some lecturing. I'm afraid I do not use many of Ms. Cassell's ideas.

I agree, I'd like to be more like Ms. Cassell, but I think I would have to be careful if I wanted to have a life outside of the classroom!

Teachers like to talk about themselves. Pam Peters and her consultant colleagues often comment about this phenomenon. Early in their Differentiated Instruction (DI) course, they assign Carol Ann Tomlinson's now-classic essay among educators, "Mapping a Route Towards Instruction."[1] Tomlinson develops her essay around three teachers who teach about ancient Rome. Pam asks participants to write a reflection about themselves in comparison to the three teachers:

Mr. Appleton represents the classic stand-up, one-size-fits-all teacher who uses a textbook. He has students read the text in class and take notes. He lectures frequently, expecting students to take notes, as well. He gives out study sheets the day before a test.

Mrs. Baker introduces graphic organizers to help students read the textbook. She brings in pictures, invites students to wear togas, and brings food for a Roman banquet. Also, she shows video clips on gladiators and reads Roman myths to her students. She goes over the chapter before the test rather than having them review it on their own at home.

Ms. Cassell plans her year using long-range thinking. She concentrates on a few key concepts and generalizations, sets clearly defined facts and skills, provides multiple pathways to learn material, and develops essential questions to drive her students' thinking. Her classroom is unified, intricate, and more complex than the other two.

The teachers see themselves in various combinations. In an attempt to make their classrooms more appealing, many state that they used to teach like Mr. Appleton but have moved over to Mrs. Baker's approach. Few say they emulate Ms. Cassell. Many see the value of her approach but, at the same time, they think she should "get a life" because of how much she is willing to attempt and accomplish.

Usually conversations center around the issue of coverage. Participants point out pressure from administration to cover as much as possible to prepare for state assessments. To teach like Ms. Cassell would take too much time. "It would be nice to be similar to Ms. Cassell much like it was before state assessments when we could spend time teaching what we enjoyed."

The irony of this reasoning ignores that teaching as talking alienates students—and it ignores the conclusions of research. The National Research Council's definitive compilation on brain research states, "Teachers must teach some subject matter in depth, providing many examples in which the same concept is at work and providing a firm foundation of factual knowledge."[2]

Teaching for "coverage" does not guarantee retention. When teachers explain, they often are the major beneficiaries. No matter how well they explain, there's no guarantee students will learn. However, if teachers provide opportunities for students to explain what they know, they will have a better idea of what they have learned.

Yet, teachers feel caught: "If I don't cover what *might* be on the test, my students will not have an opportunity to learn it," declared one of Pam's participants. "When I cover everything in a mile-wide inch-deep approach, I recognize that not many will retain it. At least I can defend that I am doing my job and covering what needs to be covered." But, as a colleague insightfully shared at the same workshop, "When we teach something and students do not learn, then nothing has happened!"[3]

At the conclusion of the conversations about Mr. Appleton, Mrs. Baker, and Ms. Cassell, Pam often senses her groups reach an impasse. Still, the elephant in the room has been exposed. Pam points out, "I think you should do everything you can to make it possible for every student to learn. How can you do any less? Exciting classrooms are essential!"

When a teacher perpetuates Mr. Appleton's standup pedagogy, her digitally wired students will likely be destined for boredom and disinterest. Only a few will learn from taking notes. When a teacher emulates Mrs. Baker's activity-centered teaching, her lessons will be more interesting but will lack coherence and direction. Students may enjoy the learning, but may not connect the dots when bouncing from one activity to the next.

When a teacher takes Ms. Cassell's approach, she is in for more work—and for more satisfaction. Each lesson, each unit, and the whole year will fit into a coherent sequence and include carefully selected knowledge and skills, principles of learning, and essential questions.[4]

However, both of the approaches are deeply embedded: Mr. Appleton's in the upper grades and Mrs. Baker's at the elementary level. Pam does her best to encourage participants to consider working toward Ms. Cassell's paradigm. She acknowledges that such a commitment may require a major overhaul in practice—more for some and less for others. "In our DI course, I will do my best to help you make your classrooms exciting, engaging, and effective."

~ ~ ~

The path to Ms. Cassell is complex. Pam then asks the participants to do an exercise that she learned for her colleague, Jerry Goldberg[5]:

"Fold your arms, please, in your natural way."
"Those whose left arm is on top of their right arm, raise your hand." Then, after a pause she says, "You are visual learners."
"Those who have the right arm on top, please raise your hand. You are auditory learners."
"Anyone who disagrees with this 'research,' raise your hand. You are kinesthetic learners."
Then, she asks everyone to fold their arms the opposite of their natural way.

Most participants find this last step uncomfortable. Pam brings home the obvious point: "I don't put much stock in this 'research.' Yet, we do have students who fold their arms opposite to us; that is, their ways of learning differ from ours. Aren't we obligated to reach out to these differences? Shouldn't we respond in ways that enhance each student's learning? I think we have no choice."

Pam hopes that as a result of exercises like the one above—and from ideas in the course—that participants will shift their mindset away from one-size-fits-all lessons toward trying alternative pedagogies. For example, she introduces 10-2 Thinking as a move away from Mr. Appleton's lecture delivery and toward engagement (see chapter 1, "Implement 10-2 Thinking").

She also shares a colleague's story of how he shifted his teaching away from standing and talking at the front. He opened his teaching to include more "purposeful engagement," which enables intelligence to grow in his students—and in him.[6] Throughout the DI course, Pam offers multiple ways for teachers to meet the needs of all their students.

Pam also frames DI techniques inside a backward design mindset to help teachers move closer to emulating Ms. Cassell. "Whenever you teach, you must have purposeful intention; align the learning sequences; set clear objectives; aim for understandings, not regurgitation; and closely connect home practice to your objectives. When students see everything fitting together, they will find learning exciting and more useful."

Pam also encourages participants to move away from textbooks as the center of their teaching. "Covering the text and filling out worksheets, turning the page and filling in one worksheet after another, becomes monotonous. Taking responsibility for framing and implementing what to teach, on the other hand, gives you control of what students will know, understand, and be able to do. They align their curriculum so students will learn better."

Pam offers an example. "Take two history students. One, let's call her Pauline, sits in a classroom at her desk and takes lecture notes every day for two weeks. Her teacher gives a couple of quizzes and finishes with a test (usually on a Friday) the day after he reviews the material (much like Mr. Appleton). Pauline's been in this routine for weeks.

"The other student, Brian, engages in directed discussions analyzing and assessing material. This week he focuses on the complexities of cause and effect of wars and the resulting moral issues. Sometimes, Brian and his classmates engage in whole class activities; other times they work in small groups, in a pair, or in a triad. The teacher uses Give One/Get One for review. (See Textbox 5.1, Give One/Get One as Review, in chapter 5 "Make Meaning.") She sees herself as a coach who assesses her 'team' during the review and then determines how to arrange the 'material' for the upcoming 'test.'"

Pam then summarizes, "Pauline receives information from her teacher and must take responsibility for learning it *outside* of class. Brian engages with his teacher *inside* the class, then reviews and reinforces it at home. While both students may earn A's, Brian will retain more—and will have more tools for responding to future classes. He will be developing lifelong learning skills."

On the closing day of the DI course, Pam passes out copies of the "Teaching Manifesto" (see Appendix). This manifesto encourages teachers to expand the horizon of their teaching. It invites them to take steps that lead them to deliver less and engage more. It asks them to become open to the myriad of good research and ideas to improve their practice. The manifesto addresses what a teacher can do on her own and with her colleagues. "I hope that you will sign the Manifesto as a commitment to improve your practice and to make your classrooms exciting for your students—and for you."

~ ~ ~

Ultimately, teachers choose whether they teach like Mr. Appleton, Mrs. Baker, or Ms. Cassell. They can carry on as their predecessors and teach one-size-fits-all lessons. They can diversify their teaching to meet the needs of each student. They can choose the TAPS Template for Teacher Planning as a guide for making this commitment. They can sign the Teaching Manifesto. And in line with Carol Ann Tomlinson, they can create their own map toward instruction and seek all the help they can muster to make it happen. Teachers are, after all, deciders of their destiny.

REFLECTION

The one-size-fits-all lesson has been the teachers' staple for generations. Dan Hilliard's move into the center of his room began a journey toward diversifying his teaching. Throughout his schooling, he sat through whole-class lessons. Dan understands that one-size-fits-all thinking has become oxymoronic in today's global world. He has become open to the plethora of methods available for engaging his students so that they learn and love to learn. He wants to revamp his teaching to meet his students' needs—and to make his teaching more satisfying.

When Dan read Carol Ann Tomlinson's "Mapping a Route Towards Instruction" in his DI class, he discovered that he was more like Mrs. Baker than he realized. He has been working hard to make his lessons more differentiated, but he needs to integrate them with his units, as Ms. Cassell has. He hoped that the course would provide him with many good ideas.

POINTS TO PURSUE

Which Teacher Are You on Tomlinson's Spectrum?

As you read the discussions around Mr. Appleton, Mrs. Baker, and Ms. Cassell, where do you see yourself on the spectrum? How did you get to where you are? Are you happy with where you are? Have you changed? If you want to change, how will you begin?

How Much Do You Do One-Size-Fits-All Teaching?

One-size-fits-all teaching has a deep history. As efficient as this approach has been for teachers, clearly it has not worked for all students. Carol Ann Tomlinson's advocacy for DI has opened the door to alternatives.

To what extent do you practice one-size-fits-all teaching which focuses on coverage? Have you thought of ways to break away without compromising your perceived obligations to teach all that's required? What small steps can you take?

Consider using the TAPS Template for Teacher Planning as a guide for deepening your teaching (see Figure 5.2. TAPS Template for Teacher Planning, chapter 5, "Make Meaning"). Share your progress with a colleague.

Being a Ms. Cassell

Pam Peters tries hard to steer her participants to move toward thinking like Ms. Cassell. She knows that it's hard work but necessary.

If you are a "Ms. Cassell" in your school, how will you help your colleagues let go of one-size-fits-all practices? How will you convince them that while being "Ms. Cassell" is more challenging, it is more satisfying. Can you prove to them that their students will benefit—and so will they?

How Do Others View Your Teaching?

If you want to begin thinking more openly about your teaching, invite a colleague to observe you. Ask him to describe how students perform in your classroom. Are they passive or active? Some of the time, most of the time, or all of the time? Take time to converse after his observation. You may be surprised.

Sign the "Teaching Manifesto"

A Teaching Manifesto? Take time to read the Teaching Manifesto (see Appendix) and think about how it relates to your teaching. Then, check off the items you want to aspire to. Sign it, date it, and commit to fulfilling it.

Post it on your refrigerator—or better yet in your classroom. Using the manifesto as a guide may lead you to new teaching practices for which your students—and you—will be grateful.

NOTES

1. Carol Ann Tomlinson, "Mapping a Route Towards Instruction," *Educational Leadership*, vol. 57, no. 1, 1999, 12–16.

2. J. D. Bransford, A. L. Brown, and R. R. Cocking, eds., *How People Learn: Brain, Mind, Experience, and School*, exp. ed. (Committee on Developments in the Science of Learning, National Research Council, National Academy Press, 2000), 20.

3. With thanks for Debra Spinelli who shared this anonymous quotation.

4. See Figure 5.2. The TAPS Template for Teacher Planning, in chapter 5, "Make Meaning," for a graphic representation of Ms. Cassell's approach.

5. Jerry is a former superintendent and a consultant with Teachers21 in Wellesley, Massachusetts.

6. Robert Sternberg, in Carol Dweck, *Mindset*, 5.

Part IV

WHAT CAN WE LEARN FROM BEYOND THE CULTURE OF SCHOOLS?

By taking a longer view, teachers gain strength from seeking wisdom both old and new—and discover how to resolve difficult questions.

Part IV invites teachers to examine out-of-the-box points of view to freshen their teaching.

Educators who want to discover their full potential look beyond the culture of the school and the classroom. The world is integrating disparate elements at mind-bending speed. Educators who hunker down inside the confines of embedded school thinking will become anachronistic and irrelevant.

Strong educators find ways to open their minds to ideas from beyond the norm, from beyond the enclave of school culture. They imagine new roles that serve the greater community. They reframe their perceptions and discover tipping points to enable them to accomplish more than they thought possible. They're relentless in pursuing their ideals.

Taking a long view enables them—especially younger teachers—to sustain their efforts. They imagine their ideal classroom. And, they find solace in invoking the metaphor of being a spiral galaxy that infuses life into their students.

Expanding thinking beyond the classroom, beyond the schoolhouse, makes for a better understanding of place and purpose. Teachers connect imaginatively with administrators, students, and families—and with each other.

Chapter 14

Become a Gadfly

Imagine the effect of receiving consistent feedback from one of your colleagues—a teacher as a gadfly.

As this book has made clear, from the first day a teacher steps into her classroom she works alone and without feedback, except when her supervisor evaluates. Rarely does she have time to discuss teaching practices with colleagues. And rarely, if ever, does she observe a colleague or invite one to observe her. It's simply not part of the culture. Teaching is a private affair subsidized by government—and has been for generations.

Perhaps the myth of teaching as an intimate affair stems from the dialogical encounters of Socrates on the Acropolis. Or from Mark Hopkins, then president of Williams College, sitting on one end of a log, with a student on the other. Then came one-room schoolhouses with but one teacher. Finally, factory-model schools, buildings with long corridors and a woman teacher, assured a unified curriculum, each tecaher delivering it alone. No wonder teachers remain isolated.

Why not, then, introduce the idea of a gadfly—a teacher, without his own classroom, to serve all the classrooms in the school? George Wesson, a lifelong teacher and now a consultant, came up with this idea one evening as he was preparing to spend a day in a school doing walkthroughs. He wrote the following memo in his usual flamboyant style:

Memo to colleagues from George Wesson

The Gadfly concept as I see it:

As the gadfly, I arrive at my small office in the morning and check my computer to see if any teachers have made requests for help. "Aha, Mrs. Wilson needs the material I promised to teach this morning; Mr. Keogh wants help planning a third-grade trip to our local science museum . . ."

I first go to Mrs. Wilson's fourth grade with the requested material and prepared to teach a lesson to her children. She stays to observe and discuss with me her impressions of the lesson. I proceed to Mr. Keogh's third grade to meet with his team to plan the museum trip. . . .

Throughout the day I rove as an observer, questioner, commentator, teacher, co-teacher, seminar leader, and idea person. I float from room to room by invitation. I advocate for meaningful, exciting, rigorous, engaging, humorous, stimulating, and worthwhile learning—for students and teachers. I imagine helping teachers to purge methods that fail, implement best practices, and create new ones. I set up feedback loops. I am not a judge. I am a pied piper among my peers.

As a gadfly, I break down the generational isolation of the classroom. I find ways for colleagues to release their skills and gifts to one another. I see them interacting on many levels: talking about teaching, creating new ideas, and designing aligned curriculums. When a teacher requests that I take over a class, she either stays, or spends time with a colleague, or prepares on her own. Whenever I can, I create opportunities for ad hoc conversations to develop collegiality.

For my homework, I reflect on my day and in response to staff requests look for web resources, materials, books, articles, and resource people. I respond to emails or text on my phone if necessary and prepare what to bring the next day.

I think the main task of the gadfly is to break down classroom isolation, which has been unwittingly self-imposed and endemic in the system.

What do you think of my idea of the gadfly?

Sincerely,
George

As George aptly describes, the gadfly supports and nurtures creative possibilities for exciting classrooms. He provides feedback that gives colleagues the confidence and tools to improve teaching. He also takes part in staff meetings to help keep conversation focused on teaching.

The gadfly should come from within a faculty, perhaps as a rotating one-to-three-year appointment or as someone who will be on an in-school sabbatical. Having a gadfly changes the school's culture. The gadfly breaks down the embedded isolation. He encourages teacher initiative. He supports collegial relationships that can evolve into professional learning communities or self-management teams—teachers working together with administrators. Collaboration throughout the school allows the whole to become greater than the sum of its parts.

Become a Gadfly 123

What can the gadfly do? At a faculty meeting, George gives the following examples:

- Introduce activators to excite and engage students
- Use summarizers to build retention
- Create options for struggling students
- Provide alternative materials for advanced students
- Demonstrate how to form readiness groups
- Teach self-assessment practices
- Demonstrate responses to different learning styles
- Introduce brain research techniques
- Design flipped lessons where students learn first at home
- Arrange and rearrange desks to facilitate lessons
- Introduce assessment products in place of tests
- Frame essential questions for lessons, units, and courses
- Initiate access to Web 2.0 tools

While some of these ideas are practiced in some classrooms, many teachers are not familiar with them. As they share, other innovative methods will emerge. George imagines that once teachers taste better practices they will want more.

~ ~ ~

After hearing favorable responses from his consultant colleagues, George drafts another memo, further clarifying his idea:

> Follow-up memo on the gadfly from George Wesson:
>
> Imagine the effect of receiving consistent feedback from one of your colleagues, a teacher as gadfly. His purpose is to make every classroom better. Imagine the effect on the gadfly himself. He who finally has an opportunity to share his pent-up ideas! Because he needs help with his pedagogy, he knows that everyone does.
>
> Teachers should not have to teach alone any more. Great teaching demands that every time a teacher steps into her classroom, she will do everything she can to engage students. The gadfly is there to help make it possible.
>
> Alone, teachers struggle to let go of treating students as targets needing improvement, as regurgitating robots who pass tests. But with the help of a gadfly, they can make lifelong learning central to their teaching. An ever-present gadfly helps teachers to break the teach-to-the-test paradigm and discover best practices.

The gadfly as a member of staff without a classroom becomes a member of everyone's classroom. He is an insider who helps to improve teaching.

His presence validates not only the *need* to improve practice, but also the *ability* to succeed. The gadfly affirms the desire of colleagues to teach in exciting classrooms—and provides the will and resources to do it.

REFLECTION

Schools are hierarchical. Administrators sit at the top, led by a superintendent and his central office staff. Below them is the principal and his staff, next are the teachers, and below them paraprofessionals. The term "superintendent" reflects the factory-based origins of the public school.

When Dan Hilliard was hired, he naturally expected his principal to be in charge of his teaching. Surprisingly, during his initial five years, his principal never appeared. He told Dan that he hired him because he came from a well-respected college and had his master's degree. He was confident that Dan would do fine. Fortunately, his department chair visited him often and took time to share his observations. Now, his present principal, Margaret Fellows, is required to evaluate new teachers twice a year for the first three years and veteran teachers once a year. The feedback she gives is very supportive—and offers valuable ideas and strategies.

However, Dan has a new department head who does not visit often. He misses the consistent feedback, as he finds it difficult to weigh all the implications of his teaching. When he hears of the idea of teacher-as-gadfly, he becomes intrigued. After all, he is somewhat of an idealist. Yet, how would such a position be funded? Who would determine who would be a gadfly? Could he do it? Dan will try to convince Margaret to advocate for a gadfly for the school.

POINTS TO PURSUE

Consider the Gadfly for Your School

The idea of having a gadfly in your school may seem foreign at first. Suspend your disbelief—if you have it—and explore with colleagues the potential of appointing a gadfly. What might you do to introduce the concept? How might you inspire a serious conversation about the potential of a gadfly functioning in your school?

Once people begin to accept the possibility of a gadfly, who might be willing and capable of doing it? Should the school hire an outsider? What are the budget implications? Who would you advocate for this position?

Create a Gadfly in Your Department or Grade Level

Think about a gadfly in other contexts. What if, for example, you and like-minded colleagues agreed to become gadflies for one another? If you are a department head, how might you restructure your position to act as a gadfly? Perhaps you could do it for selected time periods, for example, for a week each month. Perhaps, you could be a "gadfly" for colleagues during planning periods?

Propose the Gadfly Idea in Your School

Even if you are skeptical, simply bringing up the notion of a gadfly might inspire teachers to become more willing to open their doors to one another. At least, it might be a start. Anything to break down the embedded isolation of teachers.

Chapter 15

Leverage Tipping Points

Imagine a school full of teachers who have a "vitality, a life force, a quickening," and view themselves as tipping-point contributors.

Malcolm Gladwell keeps close touch with key ideas in our culture. In *The Tipping Point* he writes that social change can happen quickly with only little input, in the same way viruses cause epidemics—what he calls tipping points. Radical change occurs under the right circumstances. He makes an analogy with a measles epidemic in kindergarten. One child introduces the virus, which immediately spreads, reaches a critical mass, then quickly runs its course. A situation may be placid one moment and explosive the next.[1]

Annie Thomas became a teacher because she wanted to subvert the sterile patterns she'd seen throughout her schooling. She chose to teach middle school Social Studies. She liked commiserating with the volatility of early teens—their excitement one day, their hesitancy the next. She intended to bring in materials with which they could engage, learn from, and want more.

Teaching has been harder than she imagined. After five years, however, she's begun to find her groove. "Now, I really like the challenge of meeting these kids who are so different from me when I was their age. I am getting closer to making their education relevant and useful. At least, they are responding better."

However, Annie is often baffled by her colleagues' reluctance to seek better ways to teach. Most of them cling to past practices. However, her colleague Javier Gonzalez implemented an effective social contract with his students to guide their behavior. Except for Annie, his colleagues have not given his approach a try; many continue to have problems with the behavior of their students. Paul Durant, another colleague, developed ways to escape the tyranny of the required textbook, but no one else except Annie and Javier has asked him how he does it.

Annie has noticed the same trend with other issues. Constructivism, which has roots in Dewey, Piaget, and Vygotsky, remains largely unknown. In her reading, she discovered that the progressive Open Education movement faltered before it could find a foothold in schools; administrators and traditional teachers dug in to preserve the status quo. Montessori's rich successes remain largely outside the reach of public classrooms.

As part of her professional development, Annie has taken seriously Carol Ann Tomlinson's DI methods.[2] As a result, she has changed her teaching. She also has adopted ideas and strategies from Understanding by Design (UbD) workshops and thus has changed her approach to planning.[3] Because both of these pedagogies are proving effective with her students, she imagines that they may eventually reach a tipping point in schools. Not soon perhaps, but eventually.

One evening, after a particularly tense faculty meeting, Annie took out her journal. She had proposed that her faculty consider introducing DI and UbD into the curriculum. She was surprised at the resistance from many of her colleagues and the principal. She asked herself the following questions:

- Why have innovative efforts in schools often failed—more likely actively resisted?
- Why don't good new ideas—even good old ideas—spread as viruses?
- What inhibits my colleagues from responding to off-the-wall ideas, trying them out, and being willing to adopt what works?
- What good comes from professional development (PD) that introduces new strategies year after year if teachers do not take advantage of them?
- Is it possible for me to create a tipping point in my school?
- What keeps most of us where we are, year after year, generation after generation? Are we stuck in the crabs-in-the-cage mentality?[4]

Annie appreciates PD when the presenters are well-prepared, offer new ideas, and provide excellent follow-up materials. Sometimes her colleagues appear to accept the new ideas. Weeks later, however, she sees that few teachers actually use them. She walks by their classrooms and sees them standing at the front and doing what they have always done. Not everyone for sure. But many of them.

~ ~ ~

Annie looks beyond her classroom for ideas to invigorate her teaching. One evening at a friend's home she learned about Pike's Place Fish Market in

Seattle. After reading the book *Fish! A Remarkable Way to Boost Morale and Improve Results* and visiting the Market's website, she becomes convinced that she should explore its fresh and zany attitude. Of course, she would not throw fish—big ones!—at her students as the Market does to its customers; she can, however, inculcate its philosophy—its four principles:

Choose your attitude
Play
Be present
Make someone's day[5]

She always tries to be upbeat. She is an inveterate punster who inflicts groans on her students, yet they always want to hear more. Still, she thinks that she may be taking school more seriously at times than she needs to. Reflecting on the Pike's Place Market principles, she wrote in her journal:

- I can be upbeat about my students and circumstances regardless of how I am feeling on any given day.
- In addition to puns I can put more playfulness into my lessons and encourage students to express their humor.
- I can be more present with student responses and less present to what I think I want to say.
- I can certainly bring a smile to a student that, in turn, uplifts everyone.

Annie is convinced that intention in teaching—in life as well—is important. Yet, intention does not always lead to what she wants. She discovers from Paul Hawken, "We have no control of the outcome ... the only thing we can control is our intent."[6] She persists with her intentions as a way, perhaps, to implement tipping points to spur further changes until only remnants of poor past practices remain. The intention itself is not a tipping point, but enacting the intention may set it in motion.

Another series of insights about improving teaching came from Chip and Dan Heath's *Made to Stick: Why Some Ideas Survive and Others Die*.[7] Annie likes their emphasis on stickiness—Gladwell writes about this—ideas that are easily understood, remembered, and effect change. If she could make stickiness central to her teaching, her students would become more engaged. In her journal, she copies the six principles that the Heaths develop in their book using the acronym SUCCESs:

Simplicity: determine and prioritize your core message and communicate it using an analogy or high-concept pitch; keep it simple, don't dumb down.

Unexpected: gain and hold attention creating curiosity gaps to make students want your message; use exciting lead-ins, dynamic questions, and mystery queries.

Concrete: use sensory language (for example, Aesop's fables), paint a mental picture, employ the Velcro theory of memory as having multiple hooks; specificity connects.

Credible: ideas gain legitimacy from outside authorities (or antiauthorities) or from within using human-scale statistics (for example, one child for Save the Children or the Smile Train); let students test it out before they buy.

Emotional: people care about people, not numbers; be aware as identity appeals can often trump self-interest.

Stories: drive action through simulation (what to do), inspiration (the motivation to do it), and springboard stories (helping others see how an existing problem might change).[8]

The Heaths are onto something—and they have developed materials with teachers in mind. Teachers who read their book, make use of their website, and take their message to heart will rethink their pedagogy. Students enter classrooms full of their own sticky ideas, most of which have little use. If Annie creates stickiness in their brains, she will break the cycles of monotony—and no longer see them sitting passively at their desks.

In department and faculty meetings, Annie hears murmurings from colleagues who want their lessons to stick better. She speculates, "Can the teachers in her school reach a tipping point and let go of acting as conduits of an imposed curriculum? Can they take ownership in what they teach?" Annie is convinced that when they do, teachers will transform the minds and hearts of students—and themselves. They will invoke an epidemic of learning.

Annie posted a quotation from Martha Graham in the faculty room to encourage colleagues to rethink their role:

> There is a vitality, a life force, an energy, a quickening that is translated through you into action, and because there is only one of you in all time, this expression is unique. And if you block it, it will never exist through any other medium and it will be lost. The world will not have it. It is not your business to determine how good it is nor how valuable nor how it compares with other expressions. It is your business to keep it yours clearly and directly, to keep the channel open.[9]

"Imagine a school full of teachers who have a 'vitality, a life force, a quickening,' and view themselves as tipping-point contributors," Annie wrote in her journal. "How would they interrelate? What would be happening in their classrooms? How would their students feel? What would they be learning? Perhaps the intention to become a tipping-point provider is enough!"

REFLECTION

Dan Hilliard feels fortunate that he has taken time to learn about new strategies for his classroom. He really likes DI despite its challenges, especially in planning. He also is a devotee of UbD, as it brings coherence and relevance to his courses, units, and lessons.

He is intrigued with Malcolm Gladwell's *Tipping Point*, but has not figured out how to connect his idea to his lessons. When he discovers Chip and Dan Heath's *Made to Stick*, however, his mind jumps. He already includes stories in his teaching to perk his students' curiosity. He includes concrete examples as well, but he often slips into the abstract, which appeals only to some students. The key revelations of *Made to Stick* help Dan to choose his priorities and keep it simple. He has recommended the book to his principal, Margaret Fellows, for the faculty to read but hasn't heard back.

POINTS TO PURSUE

The Out-of-the-Box Teacher

Think of someone in your school who teaches out-of-the-box. Annie Thomas's colleagues Javier Gonzalez and Paul Durant each acted out of the box but did not gain much traction with the staff. Perhaps you know colleagues who are like them—maybe you are one.

What is the role of these people—or your role—in your school? Whether or not out-of-the-box teachers are viewed positively, how can they become catalysts and spread new ideas into neighboring classrooms, down the hall, and throughout the building?

Try New Ideas and Strategies Often

Old habits are difficult to break. Some are deep traditions that have been embedded in schools for generations. The lecture is one obvious example (see chapter 1, "Implement 10-2 Thinking").

One way to break out is to commit to trying a new idea or unfamiliar strategy as often as you can. Process how well each works with your students. Invite them to comment on your effort—perhaps it will encourage them to up their effort.

Enact the Four Principles of Pike's Place Fish Market

One of the pillars of this book advocates that teachers benefit from looking beyond school culture when seeking better ways to teach. The practice of this

Seattle-based enterprise provides a wonderful metaphor for creating a lively, productive classroom.

Explore the implications of implementing the four principles of Pike's Place Fish Market in your classroom, perhaps even in your school. Plan carefully how you'd launch them with your students (check their website http://www.pikeplacefish.com, or buy one of their books, *Fish!* or *When Fish Fly*) and carefully observe the effects.

How might you introduce these principles to colleagues?

Make Intentions a Priority

"Everything rests on the tip of intention," said the Dalai Lama. Setting new intentions can be challenging. If you choose this path, be willing to persist! As Paul Hawken wrote, "We have no control of the outcome. . . . The only thing we can control is our intent." If you are confident in your intent, don't let failure derail your effort.

Implement Chip and Dan Heath's Principles

Chip and Dan Heath's stickiness speaks directly to teachers. The authors provide a valuable perspective of the teaching process. Make a plan to study *Made to Stick* (the book and the website http://www.madetostick.com). Invite colleagues to study with you. Dig in and try out its six SUCCESs ideas. Let students know what you are doing. Ask them for feedback throughout.

Persist in Innovating Your Teaching

Martha Graham reminds us that we have a unique expression that only we can put into the world. As Annie Thomas wrote in her journal, "Imagine a school full of teachers who have a 'vitality, a life force, a quickening,' and view themselves as tipping-point contributors."

Have you ever thought of a new way to teach but dismissed it as too radical? Take Martha Graham at her word and resurrect that idea. Perhaps it will have an impact and become a tipping point, perhaps not. If not, give yourself the Golden Toilet award for taking a risk and failing.

NOTES

1. Malcolm Gladwell, *The Tipping Point: How Little Things Can Make a Big Difference* (New York: Little, Brown and Company, 2002).

2. See chapter 13: "End One-Size-Fits-All Teaching" for an elaboration of Carol Ann Tomlinson's Differentiated Instruction.

3. See chapter 23: "Become Stakeholders" for an extensive conversation on Grant Wiggins and Jay McTighe's Understanding by Design.

4. See chapter 11, "Abandon the Crabs in the Cage," for a detailed discussion of this concept.

5. Stephen C. Lundin, Harry Paul, and John Christianson, *Fish! A Remarkable Way to Boost Morale and Improve Results* (New York: Hyperion, 2000).

6. Paul Hawken, on *The Paula Gordon Show*, January 15, 2010, at http://www.paulagordon.com/content/suicide-interventions.

7. Chip Heath and Dan Heath, *Made to Stick: Why Some Ideas Survive and Others Die* (New York: Random House, 2007, 2008). An essential for teachers!

8. Ibid. This summary was adapted from material on the authors' website, which offers free materials specifically for teachers. http://www.madetostick.com.

9. Martha Graham to Agnes de Mille, *Dance to the Piper* (New York: De Capo Press, 1980), 335–36, in Paul Hawken, *Blessed Unrest: How the Largest Movement in the World Came into Being and Why No One Saw It Coming* (New York: Penguin Group, 2007), 9.

Chapter 16

Teach As If

We should act as if the universe were listening to us and responding. We should act as if we were going to win.

Once there was a man who never could remember how to swipe his card on the bus on the way to work. Each day, the driver or the other passengers helped him. It turned out he later won a Nobel Prize. Teachers can ask: "Who am I teaching? Do I have a future Nobel Prize winner before me? Perhaps she's a student who appears not to have a clue?"

Mehmed Abaid takes his teaching seriously—and always has. His parents came from Iran to Michigan, where he was born. He loved school, always looked at the bright side, and did well in college. Now, he loves teaching his high school Language Arts classes, especially ones with eager students. He constantly reflects on his role and is open to new possibilities. Each year, he discovers different ways to teach. He understands that good ideas feed teaching—often manifesting from beyond the classroom.

One of his favorite discoveries came from a *New Yorker* interview with Philip Pullman. Pullman argues for pursuing what matters in the face of people who wish to control others. He calls them "theocracies . . . the tendency of human beings to gather power to themselves in the name of something that may not be questioned."[1]

Theocracies. Unquestioned leadership. Mehmed has not thought much about this although at times he has sensed it. He occasionally struggles with his administrators but never lets them interfere with his teaching. And here is Philip Pullman taking on authorities. Pullman admits in his argument that theocracies eventually win out, but:

that doesn't mean we should give up and surrender.... I think we should act *as if*. I think we should read books, and tell children's stories, and take them to the theatre, and learn poems, and play music, as if it would make a difference.... We should act as if the universe were listening to us and responding. We should act as if we were going to win.[2]

As Mehmed thinks about it, he senses that most teachers survive because they appease theocracies, a habit harking back to the factory-designed schools of the early twentieth century. They resist reform by acting *as if* they've reformed. Yet, teachers still reside at the bottom of a hierarchical ladder. Despite working alone in private, isolated classrooms, they defer to people at the top, people who often perpetuate us-versus-them relationships.

"What if instead we believe that we are the key deciders in our classrooms?" Mehmed ponders. "What if we act *as if* we were in charge, as the decision-makers? Why not act *as if* we have an active role in governing our schools, as our university colleagues do? What might happen?"

Taking Pullman's counsel, he and his colleagues could create a sense of empowerment both for themselves and for their students. Teachers could ask provocative questions and take time to ponder outcomes to model active learning. Teaching *as if* would encourage everyone to engage in exciting classrooms irrespective of bogus requirements and oppressive theocracies.

Mehmed wonders why he and only a few of his colleagues risk invoking *as if* possibilities. "Why don't we enact offbeat methodologies rather than fulfill the mandates of others? Why don't we do it our way rather than follow what we're 'expected' to do? Sometimes we convince others of our intentions, but mostly we stay by ourselves. In fact, we like being different. Choosing the *as if* path creates meaning for our teaching."

Shortly after reading the Pullman piece, Mehmed discovered Eliot Eisner's "deep stuff that schools should teach"—five ideas to push the boundaries of orthodoxy in schools:

- Judgment—students deal in problems having more than one answer
- Critical thinking—exploring big ideas "with legs"
- Meaningful literacy—reading, writing, numeracy—*and* music, visual arts, and dancing
- Collaboration—moving beyond solo performance to meaningful collaborative work during school
- Service—students learning to reach out beyond individual achievement to the community at large[3]

Eisner's five ideas encourage Mehmed to step out from under theocratic thinking. Eisner's framework supports Mehmed's desire to invite students to explore rather than to regurgitate, to investigate rather than to repeat, and to learn in community rather than to compete for grades. "What if all of us took his five ideas to heart? What would be different about our school?

"Imagine the excitement when solving complex problems instead of giving notes to copy. Imagine inviting students to write reflections in class in response to unresolved issues, instead of only writing at home. Imagine connecting with the greater world rather than pursuing textbook chapters that lack any narrative. Imagine teaching for learning rather than for test taking."

Yet, implementing frameworks like Eisner's would take time away from covering required material. Mehmed and his colleagues already feel pressure to teach fast. Still, Eisner's five ideas offer a strong invitation to let go of coverage and to trust uncoverage and exploration. Taking such a position, however, puts one outside of the prevalent theocracy. Given the pressures of federal and state assessments, making such a decision is difficult.

Eisner is one of a growing number of educators calling for teachers to concentrate on learning. Robert Marzano, whose exemplary research calls for significant reform, has articulated ten questions to direct teachers away from the tyranny of the theocracy of coverage.[4] His questions address critical areas for teachers to consider as they aim to create exciting classrooms. Questions about communicating goals, accessing new knowledge, engaging students, and establishing rules and positive relationships.

For example, Question #1 is: "What will I do to establish and communicate learning goals, track student progress, and celebrate success?" Question #5 is: "What will I do to engage students?" And Question #9 is: "What will I do to communicate high expectations for all students?"

Imagine using Marzano's questions as guides for collaborative discussions. Imagine how these questions would help tap into understandings of the teaching process. Imagine becoming open to change as a result of these conversations. And, imagine what would happen to theocracies.

~ ~ ~

When we act *as if*, we heed again Pullman's words and "act as if the universe were listening to us and responding. We should act as if we were going to win." Students listen as we listen and respond as we respond. We are free to teach our hearts out. We find confidence in our purpose, in our invitations to learn, in our celebrations, in our integrity, and in living our truths to make a difference.

When teachers decide to implement these ideas, they show belief in themselves as decision-makers—at least act *as if* they are. They nurture their students to become lifelong learners—curious, persistent, insightful, self-reliant, caring, cooperative, and community-minded. To become citizens the world needs.

So much happens when teachers choose to live in their teaching. What appears beyond their domain suddenly has relevance. They see connections, insights, and serendipity. When powerful ideas appear, such as Philip Pullman's *as if* and Eliot Eisner's five principles, they open up to new possibilities. They don't assume to know the future. They allow imagining *as if* one of their students could become a Nobel Prize winner. Ultimately, it keeps them from succumbing to theocracies—and from creating their own.

REFLECTION

When Dan Hilliard read Philip Pullman's *as if* in *The New Yorker*, he imagined himself teaching whatever he wanted. He could put aside the expectations of his theocracy. He hesitated, however, when he remembered that making such a decision should only be in the context of an aligned, purposeful curriculum. Simply teaching what he wanted to teach would be wrong; he might even be creating his own theocracy. Still, he liked Pullman's call to listen to the universe and bring his own values to the table. He vowed to bring his best every day.

Dan also values good ideas and strategies from others. He liked reading about Eliot Eisner's "deep stuff that schools should teach," as it inspired Angela Bernardi and him to have probing conversations. Dan has recommended that he and his colleagues take time to assess how Marzano's Ten Design Questions can improve their curriculum and teaching.

POINTS TO PURSUE

What Has Moved You to Rethink Your Teaching Practice?

Have you had epiphanies about your teaching, as Mehmed Abaid had with Philip Pullman's "as if?" Anything to move your teaching away from embedded habits? Has an outside idea moved you to rethink your teaching? What happened? Do you know of some ideas that you've held back, hesitated to try? Why not share them with colleagues and listen to their reaction.

How Have You Responded to Theocracies?

Had you ever thought about theocracies and their power in schools? Have you felt pressure from them? If you have succumbed, are you aware of the possible consequences on your students—and you? What steps could you take to free yourself? Should you? If you think you should, how would you seek help from others?

Incorporate Eisner's Five Principles

Eliot Eisner's "deep stuff" is not unique. Plenty of writers and critics of education have proposed alternative paradigms; John Holt, Herbert Kohl, and Jonathan Kozol are among the best known. John Dewey tried early in the twentieth century to reorient classroom practice.

For starters, take Eisner's five principles one at a time and explore with colleagues their meaning. See if his principles awaken you to better ways to think about your teaching. As you come to understand them, implement them into your teaching and observe their effect. Invite your students to give you feedback.

Assess Robert Marzano's Ten Questions

Robert Marzano has persisted in having teachers become more effective. His writings have been praised for their clarity and thorough research.

Google "A Teacher's Guide through Marzano's Ten Design Questions." Better yet, read his book *The Art and Science of Teaching: A Comprehensive Framework for Effective Instruction.* Take time with colleagues to consider each of Marzano's Ten Design Questions and Marzano's proposed Action Steps. Reading and discussing them will take time. It will more take time and harder work to implement them. It will be worth it.

Take Seriously Philip Pullman's "As If"

"Fake it till you make it," often attributed to Alcoholic Anonymous' Twelve-Step program, opens the door to using positive thinking to achieve an end. Mehmed Abaid's beguilement with Philip Pullman's *as if* led him to think of changing his internal conversations—those self-communiqués that define who he is as a teacher—and as a person perhaps.

Adopting *as-if* thinking, you can become open to what transpires and to what touches your heart. You may become a different teacher.

NOTES

1. Laura Miller, "Far From Narnia: Philip Pullman's Secular Fantasy for Children," *The New Yorker*, December 26, 2005 and January 1, 2006, 3.
2. Ibid.
3. "Elliot Eisner on the Deep Stuff That Schools Should Teach," in *Marshall Memo* 17, December 15, 2003, 3–4. http://marshallmemo.com.
4. Robert Marzano, *The Art and Science of Teaching: A Comprehensive Framework for Effective Instruction* (Alexandria, VA: Association for Supervision and Curriculum, 2007).

Chapter 17

Take the Long View

Invoke the kaleidoscope metaphor.

As a consultant, Pam Peters loves tapping into the minds and hearts of her beginning teachers. Meeting with the teachers either after school or on Saturday mornings, she discusses the trials, tribulations, and trappings of being a new teacher in what is becoming a more challenging profession. Her letter to Marie Lambourne, a Biology teacher in a suburban school, symbolizes the kind of thinking Pam values.

November 2014

Dear Marie,

I admired your courage and honesty today at our new teachers' class. You shared the woes of your first months and opened the door for others to share theirs. While you may not feel much better, at least you learned that you are not alone.

When you crossed over to the other side of the teacher's desk, Marie, you quickly discovered more than met your eye as a student. You watched your teachers glide through lessons year after year. However, now that you are taking your turn, you feel you are stumbling. You imagined that your students would gravitate to your love of learning, but you've seen them chatter, roll their eyes, and doze off. You entered your ninth-grade science classroom having magic in your heart only to see it quickly fizzle. No wonder you are hurting.

I can't blame you. You've said that you want to bond with students as you bonded with some of your teachers. Yet, whatever you try turns out differently. Many of your students ignore your enthusiasm, hardly pay attention, slouch at their desks, and rarely do homework. Only a few appear to appreciate what you do.

You told us that your department head has observed you only once in the past three months. He has offered a few suggestions, none of which have worked. Your mentor listens to you in the lunch room and suggests alternatives. However, she has no time to be in your classroom. You feel alone, deserted with thirty armchair desks full of uninterested students.

What can you do? I wish that I had some easy answers. But, alas, I do not. I do, however, have one suggestion. You might begin by stepping back and take the long view of your life as a teacher. You have already told me you wanted to become a teacher when as tenth grader you took science from Mr. Rowe. You admired his unique manner, his gift of storytelling, and his understanding of the deeper purposes of biology. You wanted to teach biology just like him.

Now you are in your own science room, but your teaching does not come close to Mr. Rowe's. I'm sure you are disappointed. But, if you take the long view and visualize the time needed to put it all together, you will see that you will not become Mr. Rowe—nor should you. Becoming a teacher, a good teacher, takes years—at least five—in which you give 110 percent every day. You become you, Marie teacher. It is an iterative process that demands commitment, energy, and persistence. I know you will accept the challenge.

In our Saturday morning classes, you have heard from colleagues who claim to have few difficulties. Their students like them, as I imagine your students down deep like you. I remember a couple of years ago in another beginning-teacher workshop, a third-grade teacher shared week after week that she had no behavioral issues. She had a rare opportunity to teach without conflict. Her colleagues were in awe, as they were all facing disciplinary issues and other challenges. However, the next year her third grade proved more difficult.

In our class, we have been discussing ideas and approaches about classroom management, lesson design, and assessment. Only some of these ideas may appear workable for you at this point. Your style and the context of your classroom limit what you can try. What works for one teacher may not for another. Unfortunately, I know of no recipes for success, because teaching combines the science of practice with our personal artistry.

Whenever my teaching appeared topsy-turvy and out of sorts, I turned to the kaleidoscope metaphor. The colorful glass pieces swirling about represented my students, parents, colleagues, administrators, ideas, and concerns. The more disconnected, disoriented, and disappointed I was feeling, the faster the stones tumbled. Some days they would spin so fast that everything blurred.

But when I took time to step back, I found more control—at least a better perspective. The pieces slowed and patterns began to emerge. When they slowed to a stop, I discovered insights, clarity, joy, successes, connections, and epiphanies. Meaning, direction, and purpose showed up. I felt I was where I belonged. I remembered that I was doing what I had been called to do. Such instances may not occur often, especially early in your teaching. Remember, Marie, teaching ultimately is not about what happens *to* you; it's about what you *do*—and *can do* for your students.

Experiment with the kaleidoscope metaphor. When you sense it spinning fast, see it as a message to take time for yourself. Take deep breaths, enjoy a quiet meal, a movie, or a conversation with a friend. Step back and remember you are a young teacher who will become better and better—and will.

As the tumbling slows, be alert. Look for possibilities as to how to shift gears, to make changes, to discover new paths. Recognize the kaleidoscope as a reflection of your mind and heart as it sorts and clarifies. Sometimes it feels like a mentor. The more open you are the more the metaphor will speak to you.

When the pieces become still, pay close attention to their arrangement. Take advantage of what you are seeing and take time to reflect. Write in your journal; write a letter to yourself or to a colleague; talk into a voice recorder; call a friend or relative. Whatever works for you, take that time. You will solidify your newfound insights and make them part of your practice. You will become what you practice.

Remember, you bring your best teacher self to school every day. Now that you are on the other side of the teacher's desk, remember to take the long view and pay attention to what you see in your kaleidoscope.

After school when you get into your car, Marie, take a deep breath and tell yourself, "I'm here! I made it through the day!" Reflect upon the good moments; for example, when you told me the first time that Debbie passed in her homework; the day Mary smiled when she walked in your room; the time Rebecca, your mentor, told you Joe Roberts—one of your most challenging kids—loves your class; and the other day when Paul, your principal, complimented you about how you handled a parent conference.

Only after such celebrating should you think about what did not go so well. Keep everything in perspective! Keep the long view!

Namaste,
Pam

P.S. By the way, remember to buy tickets for a concert, so you'll be sure to take the time to do something for yourself!

REFLECTION

New teachers face challenges that threaten their commitment nearly every day. Given that half of them leave the profession within five years, a new teacher should be cognizant of her need for support, care, and love. Dan Hilliard in contrast to Marie, felt blessed in his early years. He became close to Mel Goodwin, his department chair. "Mr. Goodwin" and he co-taught a senior section during his first three years. As a result, Mel took a deep interest in Dan's teaching, often observing him and providing feedback. Years after Mel retired, Dan learned that Mel regarded Dan as the best young teacher in the department. Mel had taught him well.

For years, Dan has used the kaleidoscope metaphor. He particularly likes it as a metaphor for visualizing the different aspects of teaching. It has been particularly useful when challenged. He enjoys sharing it with newer colleagues on his staff. He has found that it provides a much-needed perspective.

POINTS TO PURSUE

As a New Teacher, Do You Know What Support Is Available?

One of the first emotions a new teacher faces in her classroom is how alone she is. Thirty students face you behind your closed door. No one is there to help. And, you've never done this before!

As a new teacher, do you know what support you have? Do you know what support you would you like? The sooner you admit that you cannot do everything alone (even though you may feel that others expect you to), the sooner you will seek help. If you don't have a mentor, find a colleague (new or veteran) with whom you can engage about teaching. That conversation may open many doors. If not, seek someone else.

As a New Teacher, Develop Collegial Relations As Soon As You Can

As a new teacher, make it a point to form close relationships. Plan not only to arrange social engagements with colleagues, but also schedule regular times to meet to discuss teaching and classroom issues. Don't be surprised if you find that your new colleagues are better at being congenial rather than collegial.

While congeniality is valuable, forming collegial relationships is more important in the long run. Make every effort to have serious conversations about your teaching. Begin with short ones in the hallway or faculty room.

People will see you as serious about wanting to learn how to teach well. You will be able to offer them good ideas as well.

As a Veteran, What Do You Do to Help New Teachers?

Veteran teachers tend to stick with what they know. Some think they should not impose their thinking on others. Nothing could be further from the truth. As a veteran, you should see yourself as doing all you can to strengthen the teaching community.

Have you paid attention to the newer members of your staff? If you are a mentor, have you made time to support your mentee, to be in his classroom at any time and in any way necessary? If you are not a mentor, have you offered to forge a professional relationship with a new teacher? It's an experience you'll not want to miss.

Invoke the Kaleidoscope Metaphor

Sometimes, we become stuck in the linearity of the teaching life. Metaphors can serve as doorways to other sides, to other ways to see and understand. Pam Peters hopes that her reference to the kaleidoscope metaphor will help Marie sort out her troubles and see her way to succeed.

Try this metaphor to see if it helps you maintain focus, purpose, and patience. Share your thoughts with colleagues about this idea.

Chapter 18

Imagine the Ideal

What is an ideal doorman?

At his eighth-grade team meeting Steve Sinclair shared an idea he learned more than twenty-five years before. "At a conference of Social Studies teachers, Fred Jervis, Founder and President of the Center for Constructive Change, asked us: 'What is an ideal doorman?' People at the table offered a litany of qualities: 'appears well dressed,' 'holds the door,' 'gives smiles,' 'acts efficiently,' 'carries bags,' 'hails a cab quickly,' and 'knows the neighboring restaurants and their menus.' Fred then concluded, 'Once you know the characteristics of an ideal doorman and you want to become one, you can plan backwards to get yourself there.'"[1]

Steve went on to say, "This is a simple but profound concept, one I have used in my teaching ever since. Once you ask the question, you'll be surprised how easy it is to generate answers. For example, remember last year when I taught my unit on Egypt? I asked my eighth graders to interview second graders who had been studying Egypt for several weeks as their central subject. They already learned far more than my students ever would.

"Before I began the unit, I explained the final outcome: 'In three weeks, you will have completed a mini-book for your paired second grader.' I showed samples. Jan Cerrucci, our librarian, located top internet sites for research and placed books on Egypt on reserve. From there, my students and I planned backwards—and it worked well."

His colleagues appeared intrigued. They knew Steve as an innovative teacher who consistently tried new methods. Sometimes, they felt that he needed to slow down. But, he had been like that since his first year in the classroom.

They agreed to try Fred Jervis's thinking and visualize their ideal classrooms. That night, Steve was inspired to write in his journal. "What would *my* ideal classroom look like? Sound like?" As he began thinking, he felt that unlike Plato's ideal form, his classroom would be distinct. As long as schools have classrooms, each one needs to become personal and unique. He wrote:

In *my* ideal classroom, my co-teachers and I create a space with its own aura. We have a few desks and chairs but also couches, upholstered chairs, area rugs, plants, curtains, and perhaps a teacher's desk set off to the side. Students' fine art and stimulating ideas grace the walls. Music plays at in-between times. There is no litter.

Students arrive expecting the unexpected but certain they will learn. Everyone greets each other by name and with a smile. Learning begins the moment they enter and carries on as they leave. No bells. No public address announcements.

Students are free to move about the room when not in groups having lessons. They are free to stand, sit on windowsills and counters as long as they do not obstruct others. Stand-up learning for some is the best option.

My colleagues and I evoke deep respect for our students and treat them as honored guests. We accept them as they are and welcome them into a safe learning place. We help them bring focus in their work. We teach them to take breaths to center themselves. We enjoy what we are doing with them and with each other. We teach without stress.

We ask more questions and give less answers. We create conversations using reason, evidence, and temperance. We invoke empathy, encourage different viewpoints, and expect rigor. Each student can and will learn. We do all we can to make it happen.

We concentrate on what they do well. We nurture their weaknesses through their strengths to help them gain confidence and thrive. We value thinking and allow time for students' brains to ponder, explore, and consider. We value the struggle necessary to develop worthwhile insights.

We work. Productive, useful, thoughtful, attentive, honest, and persistent work. Purpose is evident. Rigor means to strive without fear of judgment. We provide frequent and consistent feedback. We transform failures into successes. Teaching and learning become everyone's business. Students learn to teach themselves.

We strive to answer the question, "What's worth knowing?" even though we do not know what jobs await our students, or what technologies, or what problems they will face. We take responsibility to teach tools for lifelong learning.

We build a culture of creativity, a culture of innovation. We resist making academics the sole concentration. Instead, we build learning around all facets of the mind and heart. We provide equal access to the arts, humanities, and sciences and understand that they have equal value in the learning lexicon.

We allow their work to become evidence for learning. The quality of work reflects the quality of our teaching. We strive to provide authentic performance assessments. We do not grade students against each other, but instead we give honest, summative assessments of their progress in relationship to clear goals and standards.

We use technology, including the Internet, smart boards, overheads, DVDs, computers, cellphones, iPods, and iPads. We include online learning in a framework of sensible thinking, reading, writing, discussion, and creative media and arts. We remain open to emerging technologies and their potential to enhance learning.

We value face-to-face encounters. We do not allow technological interactions to supersede them. We use new technologies when they serve everyone's purposes. Yet, we spend long periods of time without electronic distractions to build habits of concentration and deep thinking. And we treasure humanity's uniqueness, its gift to itself, by learning together through love, laughter, sharing, cajoling, reading, writing, discussing, engaging, playing, eating, walking, and so on.

We provide equal opportunities for learning. We move on to new learning only when everyone demonstrates that they're ready. Teaching means to invite. Invitation is the best motivator.

We build relationships to create a culture of appreciation. Our ideal classroom invites its own sacredness, its reason for being. It acts as a tribe, so to speak, sharing rituals, mythology, and culture. Our classroom lives beyond the school day—everyone feels free to connect, ask for help, and share learning in person, by phone, or online.

We are present to everyone and everything. We listen. My colleagues and I always seek the next-best way to making learning exciting for our students—and for us.

Steve enjoys visualizing the ideal as it helps him align priorities and awaken possibilities. Few teachers take the time, however, as they feel overwhelmed with daily tasks. Yet, when Steve walks through the hallways of his school, he sees countless rooms with desks in rows and columns with the teacher up front. "Why do so many of us continue to work inside this old paradigm," Steve asks himself. "Why do they persist to teach in this way?" Later, he again writes in his journal:

I keep coming back to these now familiar, persistent questions:
What keeps so many of my colleagues boxed in?
What keeps them insisting on replicating the ways of their predecessors?
What prevents them from letting go of convention and seeking the ideal?
How are teachers able to ignore the presence of the future and not feel its energy tugging at them to reform their practice?

~ ~ ~

The questions that Steve asks himself are less about blame and more about curiosity. If only more of his colleagues were to ponder the ideal classroom, they might begin to step away from the old paradigm. They would discover the precious delight inherent in teaching. Steve remembers back in the 1970s when open education inspired alternative approaches. His classroom at that time included areas for reading, cooking, drama, music, painting, illustrating, science, math, writing, calligraphy—and a bicycle-repair shop. Colorful fabrics divided spaces—in days before fire departments banned them—and student artwork and calligraphy hung on the walls.

He and his two colleagues co-taught all subjects side by side. Students used planbooks to organize and self-assess their learning. Steve taught in his alternative classroom for six years until the powers-at-be absorbed it into a traditional team in his middle school.

"Perhaps a time will come," Steve thinks, "when we will break out of the mold of the regular classroom. When we will discover new patterns and new ways to interact and relate. When each classroom will be free to establish its own identity."

Building ideal classrooms from the bottom—a curious idea! Teachers can do it if they believe it is possible. One ideal at a time.

REFLECTION

Once teachers move away from standing before students, new possibilities emerge. The more Dan Hilliard uses active strategies, the more he sees his classroom as unique. He speculates sometimes what his ideal classroom might look like. He thinks about removing some desks, adding a couch and soft chairs, bringing in plants, and taking extra care when displaying work. He incorporates more essential questions in his lessons, ones that have no obvious answers.

He continues to refrain from making comments after each student speaks, something he discovered on that day when he sat in Sam's seat in the middle row. He brings in ideas and strategies from other disciplines when relevant, especially from the arts. If he is to evoke the ideal, he needs to be realistic. He does not want to be gimmicky for gimmick's sake. Seeking the ideal means having intention, direction, unity, and sequence at a minimum—and rigor.

Dan asks his principal, Margaret Fellows, to devote a faculty meeting on visualizing the ideal classroom. Yet he wonders, how will his colleagues react? After some thought, he sees the ideal applying not only to a classroom but also to a subject area, a department, and grade level. Margaret agrees to the meeting, but she wants Dan to include teachers to help plan it. She does not want to impose it as her agenda but wants buy in from everyone. Dan agrees to work with her to involve faculty.

POINTS TO PURSUE

How Can Visualizing Your Ideal Classroom Affect Your Teaching?

When you choose to imagine the ideal, you become open to possibility. You start to see in a new light. You begin to think of exciting alternatives. You might decide to approach a new unit in an unusual way. Instead of giving one writing assignment, you might ask students what they would like to write about. You might even circle desks around the edge of the room before they arrive.

Whatever you do, you need to know your intent. As for moving the desks, what would be the purpose of such a rearrangement? Where would you sit? What would happen in the middle? What might evolve next? What other arrangements might you consider?

What If You Decide Not to Use the Textbook?

Textbooks are difficult. They are expensive. They become out of date. And, they are difficult to read.

Imagine deciding to toss out your textbook, particularly when it is outdated? At least decide to take it away from its central role in your curriculum. How do you think your students would react? How would you then get students to the material they need to learn? What might they do differently for home-practice? Would you need a bigger budget?

Rethink the Classroom

What if you were to simply ask your colleagues the straightforward question: "What can we do to create classrooms to stimulate more excitement and less passivity?" Do you think they would take you seriously? Can you imagine what ideas might emerge?

What if you asked your students the same question? Would you be willing to listen to their suggestions—and even try some?

Assess the Role of Grading

Grades have been present for time immemorial. No doubt, you went through school being graded. It's hard to imagine teaching without them.

Still, have you thought about the impact that grades have on learning? Do you really think the way you grade is effective? Can you imagine alternatives to grading and still motivate your students? What do you think will happen if you remove grading from the equation of teaching?

Seek Out Known "Great" Teachers

Everyone knows about great teachers. Especially the famous ones in films: Mr. Chips, Mr. Holland, Jaime Escalante, Rafe Esquith, Marva Collins, John Keating, among others. Watching their teaching lives can give goosebumps. They inspire.

Yet, great teachers exist everywhere. You could be one of them. Find teachers who students and parents love. Visit them to learn their secrets. You might discover elements for your ideal classroom. You might find a new colleague.

NOTE

1. Fred Jervis, founder and president of the Center for Constructive Change, Durham, New Hampshire, speaking in Hanover, New Hampshire, August 1982. Despite his blindness, he gave a memorable presentation.

Chapter 19

Invoke the Cosmos

It's turtles all the way down.

Some days we find ourselves swirling amid epiphanies, momentary insights, or revealed truths. We see a resistant student suddenly proclaiming her grasp of a concept that had eluded both her and her classmates. We catch a parent recognizing his child's newfound successes. We discover our principal anticipating our plan to improve our team. These moments happen in unlikely places, at unlikely moments, in the middle of the night, in the shower, on a walk, when reading—or simply by sitting still.

Steve Sinclair often waxes philosophically with his colleagues and in his journal. A History major in college, he wanted to teach high school Social Studies. He liked to mingle with adolescents, hear their ideas, and help them find their place in the world. He migrated to junior high school and later to middle school where he found his calling. Eighth graders became his thing. Being with them feels most natural to him.

Steve also takes opportunities to explore new thinking. He attended seminars with David Mallery; the highlight was a week at Westtown. He took an innovative course in Social Studies at Carnegie Mellon and an early computer course at Wesleyan. He also treasured his summers at the Institute of Religion and Science (IRAS) at Star Island.

One bright summer morning at chapel on Star Island, he had one of those moments of insight. Brian Swimme, cosmologist and chaplain at the conference, shared a remarkable discovery by astronomers. They had observed a spiral galaxy—a galaxy with one center alive with active stars—coming into contact with an elliptical galaxy—a galaxy with two foci stuck inside itself with no active stars. What did the astronomers see? The spiral galaxy appeared to be bringing the elliptical galaxy to life![1] Steve did not remember the rest of Brian's talk, because he was immersed in seeing teachers as spiral galaxies bringing life to children.

Steve took Swimme's metaphor as an invitation for him and his fellow teachers to live an engaged and curious life and bring that understanding to students. "As adults and teachers," Steve thinks, "we have to take time to know who we are. We become conscious of our mission. We accept the realities before us. We seek possibilities for transforming them into the greater good. We are 'icons of the future possibility of living and empowering life.'[2] We become spiral galaxies and breathe life into our students!"

Steve entered teaching eager to touch lives. Every day he imagines making a difference to his students, parents, and school. Rarely does he have passive days. He stays alive to what he teaches and seeks the new and different, even when he teaches the same subject or grade level year after year. His students love his compassion and commitment. He's never burned out. He's a spiral galaxy teacher, full of life, eager to share and generate creative lives in others.

Yet, today's parents have to contend with a persistently invasive culture. In response, they rear their children inside cocoons of endless directed activities. Children appear suspended, lifeless between two foci: one of face-to-face relationships with family and friends and the other of a faceless relationship with electronic "friends."

Children have less time to make choices, less time to play as they spend more time alone. They shuffle from one activity to another, both after school and on weekends. In between, they sit before televisions and computers, and attend to cellphones, smartphones, tablets, video games, and the Internet. They come to school less able to initiate, choose, and inquire. They wait for direction. They are uncomfortable in face-to-face encounters and appear adrift without electronic devices under their thumbs.

Despite the glitz of ever-newer technologies, ironically, children appear to live inside stagnant elliptical galaxies with little or no self-generated energy. Steve recalls Susanne Rubenstein's insight of more than fifteen years ago. She wrote about her high school English students who claimed that they could not have dinner table discussions because they did not have dinner with their parents.[3]

Our latchkey culture has left children and adolescents at home alone; the myriad of electronic technologies only adds to the isolation. Schools lament the listlessness of increasing numbers of obese children who have little desire to participate, to try, to engage. Teachers notice greater and greater apathy. Art teachers—in schools and in museums—express frustration with their lack of imagination. Children act as texts without context. The image of them as two foci living inside an elliptical galaxy is compelling.

When teachers act as spiral-galaxy teachers, they activate energy. When they see students as elliptical dual-foci beings, they can uncover their spiral-galaxy potential. When Steve acts as an activator, he resonates at the heart of the universe. Human consciousness is unique among all creatures—at least on this planet—as humans reflect on our place in the universe. Quantum mechanics teaches that the act of looking affects what we see—the observer affects the observed.

If, however, we were to see people and objects as alien life forms, we would be denying our interconnection with them. "But," as Steve wrote in his journal, "we have all been born of the same source. We exchange atoms with everyone and everything around us. We recognize our students as integral to our lives, as part of the extended human family, as part of the same universe.

"Suppose a spiral galaxy and an elliptical galaxy touched and the reverse happened—the spiral galaxy were to die? Would not the universe be conveying a different message? Instead of affirming life as essential to the universe knowing itself, it would be declaring the opposite. Thank goodness we humans are a unique part of a creative universe, and as a part we reveal the universe. What happens at the macrocosm echoes in the microcosm." As Ken Wilber puts it:

> There's an old joke about a King who goes to a Wiseperson and asks how is it that the Earth doesn't fall down. The Wiseperson replies, "The Earth is resting on a lion." "On what then is the lion resting?" "The lion is resting on an elephant." "On what is the elephant resting?" "The elephant is resting on a turtle." "On what is the . . ." "You can stop right there, Your Majesty, It's turtles all the way down."[4]

~ ~ ~

The universe favors life. It insists on its emergence. By no means could the universe generate itself as it has in the past 13.8 billion years in random fashion. The universe exudes intelligence. Just how this occurs, humans can only surmise, but it appears obvious in the results it has produced. At the same time, humans will not survive as a species any more than the Earth will survive when the sun dies in four billion years. We live in precious times.

Already, 99 percent of all species that ever existed on Earth have become extinct. Yet, clearly, life has been an outcome of this particular universe. Certainly, it does not take up residence exclusively on planet Earth. Life will live beyond our time.

We begin to understand ourselves by acknowledging each of us as a fragment of a greater whole, a single stitch in a garment. As a fragment we participate in life around us, making our contributions and accepting the contributions of others. Each of us emerges unique. A teacher entering her classroom for the first time does not replace the previous teacher in the way a new light bulb replaces a worn light bulb. Instead, she arrives as a unique fragment—or filament perhaps—that has never been nor ever will be again.

We are, in Ken Wilber's terminology, holons, simultaneously whole and part.[5] "Each grain of sand or snowflake is a holon in and of itself. But only in aggregation as a part of the whole does one contribute to the beach or the blizzard."[6] As wholes, we act as agents, as active holons in the world embodying the change we want. Or, in the words of Gandhi, "Be the change you wish to see in the world."

At the same time, we act in communion. If we do not, we will not survive. We find meaning in community. Solitary fragments are shards, brittle and disconnected, like one broken off from the whole in a huge ceramic mosaic. Not only will we be isolated, but we will also be missed.

Steve Sinclair's perception of Swimme's metaphor seems grandiose at first when he compares it to him in his classroom. Yet, the metaphor reminds him of his universe home. He sees himself and his colleagues as part of the continuum of the Universe Story and in particular, as conduits and creators of human history.

As Wilber wrote, "It's turtles all the way down."

REFLECTION

When Dan Hilliard first heard Carl Sagan lecture on the Cosmos, he saw himself in its unfolding story. His friends chide him about this perspective, but he won't let it go. Years later, he read Brian Swimme and Thomas Berry's *The Universe Story*, and Ken Wilber's *A Brief History of Everything*, which only solidified his convictions. He sees himself as a teacher born of star stuff, taking his turn in human history to fulfill his—and its—purpose. His purpose resides in his teaching, and he gives himself to it every day.

At the same time, within the grand macrocosm he pays attention to what's in front of him. Each student, each colleague, and each grain of sand—each fragment, if you will—counts. Life's fullness requires his fullness.

Dan tries to intrigue colleagues to read and discuss these ideas, but only a few take any interest. He shares his thoughts in class whenever it seems to fit and finds many of his students curious to know more. One year, he spent six weeks teaching the origin of the universe as an elective. His students were enthralled.

POINTS TO PURSUE

How Do You Relate to the Spiral/Elliptical Galaxy Metaphor?

Steve Sinclair has been a budding philosopher since college. His friends saw him as their philosopher in residence. When he heard Brian Swimme's galaxies metaphor, he immediately connected it to his teaching. He pondered the meaning of the expansion of consciousness in the universe. That humans are the universe knowing itself. That the universe really is "turtles all the way down."

Are you willing to take Steve's perspective and teach inside questions you can at best only surmise? Are you willing to activate your students' brains—and yours—in pursuit of understanding yourself and your purpose in the greater scheme of things?

Seek to Understand Your Place in the Universe

If you've never considered the universe perspective, read Carl Sagan. Better yet, view him on YouTube, or watch *Cosmos*, the television series. Sagan opened minds and hearts to the wondrous universe in which we live. Since his teachings, astronomers and physicists have seen deeper into our 13.8 billion-year universe.

For a more recent perspective, read Brian Swimme and Thomas Berry's *The Universe Story* and Ken Wilber's *A Brief History of Everything*. Also, view Neal deGrasse Tyson's sequel to Sagan, *Cosmos: A SpaceTime Odyssey*.[7] Find some colleagues to join you. Invite everyone to be open to incorporating the universe perspective into their teaching.

Reflect on Holon and Holons

Take time to ponder the implications of Stacey Ake's wonderful description of Koestler's concept of holons: "Each grain of sand or snowflake is a holon in and of itself. But only in aggregation as a part of the whole does one contribute to the beach or the blizzard."

What does this mean to you? What does it mean to your teaching?

NOTES

1. Brian Swimme, at the Institute of Religion in the Age of Science Conference, Star Island, Portsmouth, New Hampshire, August 2005. His seminal work with Thomas Berry, *The Universe Story: From the Primordial Flaring Forth to the Ecozoic Era—A Celebration of the Unfolding of the Cosmos* (New York: Harper

Collins, 1992), has brought forth the new creation story based on recent cosmological research.

2. This phrasing comes from the thoughtfulness of Stacey Ake, associate teaching professor of philosophy in the English and Philosophy Department at Drexel University, in a personal communication.

3. Susanne Rubenstein, Wachusett High School, *Teacher Magazine*, August/September, 1999, excerpted in the journal *ClassWise*, October, 1999.

4. Ken Wilber, *A Brief History of Everything* (Boston, MA: Shambhala, 1996), 20.

5. Ibid., 20ff. Wilber shares Arthur Koestler's ideas of holons.

6. Stacey Ake in a personal communication.

7. Neal deGrasse Tyson, *Cosmos: A SpaceTime Odyssey*, a 13 part series on PBS, 2014.

Part V

HOW DO WE FIND OUR CALLING?

Seeking to know our inner teacher, we discover teaching as a personal and collective calling.

Part V invites teachers to embark on a never-ending search for meaning and a willingness to transform—essential qualities for becoming a complete teacher.

Successful teaching—a successful life—requires understanding who we are and what we want. We discover the deep richness that teaching can bring us—and to the lives of our students, their families, and our colleagues. We seek our inner teacher. "Know thyself," proclaimed Socrates, "an unexamined life is not worth living."

We recognize the nature of our calling. We take our own path. We pay attention to the practices we implement, determine their effectiveness, and keep only those that work. We reexamine our philosophy and the nature of our journey as we become the chief stakeholders in our teaching. We articulate for ourselves and for our students the knowledge, understandings, and skills we intend to teach.

Finally, we recognize the crucial role we have in the successes—and failures—of our students. We sense the differences we make every day. We acknowledge the honor that teaching bestows. We work toward realizing our potential to serve our students, their families, and the community.

Chapter 20

Grow Our Seeds

What matters was her desire to do school—a hint of a calling perhaps—that revealed more than the act itself.

He could hardly hold back. In the middle of a department meeting, Harold Dennison blurts out, "Hardly a day passes when I am not reminded that I am called to teach! My classroom has always been a joy. Every day something unexplainable happens. In my relationships with students, their families—and with you! I see infinite possibilities. I am blessed every day to learn as much and often more than my students."

His colleagues are not surprised. They know Harold as an enthusiast from his first day twenty years ago. He came from a liberal arts college determined to reform teaching. His classroom reflects his personality. He hardly keeps the same arrangement of desks including his own. He has a couple of couches along the back wall and three soft chairs. His walls are decorated with student writings and drawings framed in colored paper. One of his windows appears as stained glass—made from colored tracing paper. He has put curtains on his windows. He has lots of plants. Harold has made his classroom a world of its own.

Shortly after he declared his deep love of teaching to his colleagues, he discovered James Hillman. He particularly likes Hillman's "acorn theory" where "each person bears a uniqueness that asks to be lived and that is already present before it can be lived."[1] Hillman has expressed how Harold feels about teaching. "I know teaching resides deep within me," he says to himself, "I feel it every day."

According to Hillman, as each acorn emerges into its own oak, so each human emerges into its own being. Identical twins are no exception. Harold connects with Hillman's acorn concept because he has seen the uniqueness of each child. While he hesitates to subscribe to Hillman's concept of daimon—a guardian angel that guides and directs us, Harold agrees that he does have a calling. And he agrees that events align to make it happen.

How can a teacher determine whether or not he's been called? He may feel it when he wakes up with yet another idea and rushes to write it down. He may know it when he sees a student suddenly grasp the concept of surface tension while watching a wiper blade move across a windshield.[2] Ursula Boyle knew it when she spent twice the required hours for a course, writing, reflecting, and responding. Jenn Drew and Leighann Wright sensed it when they took a course *not* for credit or professional development, but because they wanted to learn and share their learning with colleagues.

Harold feels it on days when the bell rings, and wonders just where the time went after ninety minutes of conversation with his eighth graders. He feels it in countless other ways when lightbulbs go off in his head, when epiphanies suddenly arrive, when students gleam with joy, when Clevie saw the light for the first time, when Joey apologized before being asked, when Shanaya found her first friend . . . so many ways.

Harold has a persistent passion, a sense of the sacred in everything. He asks questions with a child's curiosity. He makes a cup of coffee for the pleasure of making a cup of coffee. He pounds a nail with joy knowing what he is building. He serves others with delight as if he were his own customer. He teaches as if he were his student. Each act has meaning. Each act belongs.

He is surprised sometimes how he got to where he is. "Why am I so blessed to have found what I love to do every day? Why was I willing to become a teacher when so many of my classmates were getting more lucrative positions? Why did my parents accept my desire to teach when they knew that I could have gone into business with their friends?" Harold has never doubted his commitment. Sometimes he wonders if James Hillman is right: "Do I have a daimon guiding me?"

From his earliest years, he loved teaching about Marxism and Communism. The more he explored the Russians, the Chinese, and the Cubans with his students, the more he tried to reconcile the public face of Communism to what he thought might be lurking behind their borders. He was thrilled when President Obama initiated talks with Raul Castro at the Summit of the Americas in Panama in April 2015. He yearned to travel to Cuba. Through a remarkable combination of circumstances, he secured a two-week leave of absence from his classroom the following April to take a trip with fellow educators to Cuba.

When Harold thinks back to his childhood, he remembers what attracted him, what pulled him in, what invited his curiosity. Throughout his life, he would meet people who slipped into his web as if they had always been there, while others did not find a home with him. His likes and dislikes come and go often with no apparent reason. He cares passionately about some issues and ignores others, while his friends do the opposite. He became obsessed with baseball, soccer, reading, and photography but ignored other offerings. Why he made these choices, he's not sure.

Sometimes, Harold has had nondescript moments that linger. He remembers that once, when he was about ten years old, he was standing on a sidewalk on Maple Street when he saw his uncle, who was a druggist, across the street talking with Mary Donaldson. Harold was taken aback because his friends—and everyone else it seemed—said that Mary was different, and for lack of a better term, slow. She often dressed in tattered clothes and had a speech defect. Sometimes, Harold and his friends would mock Mary behind her back.

Later that evening, Harold asked his uncle why he took time to stop and talk with Mary. His uncle said that everyone is worth talking to. This moment stuck with Harold. He learned then—he did not know it at the time—not only to pay attention to professors, teachers, shop owners, lawyers, druggists, and city officials, but also to postal clerks, garage attendants, janitors, cooks, and the homeless. Whenever he can, Harold makes it a point to know their names and their stories.

~ ~ ~

Do the memories we keep, such as Harold's memory of his uncle and Mary Donaldson, instruct us toward our own calling? Are they fertilizer for our seeds? Do we see them because they have been placed before us?

Harold has a Cuban story that speaks to this. It was an afternoon on his April trip when he went to a school in central Havana. He saw a small group of children in a classroom by themselves. One of them was acting as the teacher. Her manner was stern, assertive, and exhibiting a no-nonsense attitude. Harold stood alone, unnoticed, outside the door. He was fascinated.

As the young girl stood in front of her "children," she revealed a curious intensity. No smile. Very serious. She never saw Harold. He wonders to this day if this child ever became a teacher. She appeared to internalize the demeanor of an authoritarian school master. She was, after all, a child of the Communist system. Maybe she saw herself at the moment as a surrogate parent for the state and needed to assert full responsibility for the character of her students.

In the end, it's not the way this Cuban child, or any child, plays school that matters much. What matters was her *desire* to do school—a hint of a calling perhaps—that revealed more than the act itself. This young Cuban, a product of what Harold perceived was a conformist culture, appeared to be nurturing her own seed by choosing what she wanted to do without pretense. At least, that's the way Harold saw it.

REFLECTION

Dan Hilliard recalls his junior year in college when he was hired to take care of thirty children of bankers attending a summer conference. It was then he found his desire to become a teacher. For the first time in his life he had been given responsibility without having to do someone else's bidding. His task was to keep the children safe and happy—how he did it was up to him.

By the time he stepped into his first classroom, he was where he belonged. He has never doubted it. He knows colleagues who also have a strong sense of their calling. They seem confident and flexible—and willing to explore their teaching to make their classrooms engaging and exciting. He wishes all teachers felt this way.

POINTS TO PURSUE

Do You Subscribe to James Hillman's Acorn Theory?

Harold Dennison knew he wanted to teach. He likes to say that he did not choose it, but that it chose him. When he came across James Hillman's acorn metaphor "that each person bears a uniqueness that asks to be lived and that is already present before it can be lived," he understood.

As a teacher or principal, have you sensed your uniqueness? Are you aware that you are unlike any educator who came before you or who will come after you? Do you know what is unique about you? About each of your colleagues?

Take time to reflect on your special attributes and celebrate who you are.

Are You Willing to See Yourself As Special, Unique?

Harold later read these words from John Updike: "There's a kind of confessional impulse that not every literate, intelligent person has. . . . A crazy belief that you have some exciting news about being alive . . . what separates those who do it from those who think they'd like to do it. That your witness to the universe can't be duplicated, that only you can provide it, and that it's worth providing."[3]

Are you willing to explore that notion "that your witness to the universe can't be duplicated"? Are you willing to see yourself as unique, special, a one-of-a-kind educator?

What Events Have Defined You?

Harold Dennison's memory of his uncle speaking with Mary Donaldson remained deep in his psyche. Later, his trip to Cuba convinced him even more of his place as a teacher. These and other such experiences have stuck with him and help define who he is.

What events have become seminal in your life? How have they helped to define you? How do they define you as a teacher? Do you have a sense there's more to come?

Are You Willing to Invoke Play in Your Classroom?

Seeing the Cuban child hold forth with her peers, Harold wondered how play could become more a part of his classroom. He wondered if he could provide more time for his students to play. Perhaps, play should become a larger part of his school.

Would he learn more about who his students are, as he imagined for young girl in the Cuban school? Would students learn more about who they are, what they value, and what they want in life? Would teachers learn more about them?

What can you do to justify play when you feel pressured to apply more time on task to cover curriculum and prepare for federal and state tests?

NOTES

1. James Hillman, *The Soul's Code: In Search of Character and Calling* (New York: Warner Books, 1997), 6.
2. Example from Matthew Adiletta, Intel fellow and director of Communication Infrastructure and Architecture in the Intel Architecture Group, speaking at Clark University, March 26, 2001.
3. John Updike, from his 1990 *Boston Globe* interview, January 28, 2009.

Chapter 21

Rethink Our Philosophy

Showing up

"Your assignment for the next class will be to write a two-page philosophy of education," said Professor Ronald Anderson, six weeks into Harold Dennison's graduate philosophy of education class. How ironic to be asked to write his philosophy before he taught his first lesson! And on two pages! Harold leaned on the wisdom of Plato, Whitehead, Black, and Dewey. For thirty-five years, Harold never considered writing another.

Then, in his final year in the classroom, he did. Perhaps it was because it was his last year and he wanted to clarify his own understandings of teaching. Perhaps it was his effort to make better sense of his values and concerns. Perhaps he was simply curious about what he would write. Whatever the reasons, he found the exercise intriguing, insightful, and self-revealing.

As he was writing, Harold understood that the core of his values came from his life and work, rather than from the wisdom of philosophers. He was surprised at his focus on practice. He understood himself better as a teacher—and what he wanted to bring to his students. Had he taken time to write a philosophy periodically throughout his career, he might have had a clearer focus on the qualities—and deficits—of his teaching. He certainly would have developed a stronger self-awareness.

Now that Harold is a consultant, he wonders if it's a good idea to ask his teachers to write their philosophies when they are so busy. Papers pile up, grades become due, supplies need replenishing, deadlines have to be met, and meetings and conferences add to the workload, let alone the demands of their personal lives. How will they find time and space to commit to write and share their philosophies of education? What if they do not consider themselves writers? Why should they bother, anyway?

Harold decides to propose the idea of writing one's educational philosophy in his workshops. In the packet he gives them, he puts it this way:

> Do you want to know yourself better as a teacher? Do you know what your personal core values are? Do you wonder what your students would say about your beliefs and values? Your parents? Your administrators?

Try this idea:

- Agree to write your educational philosophy in only two pages or less;
- Focus first on what you do, then on what you believe and value;
- Include as many concrete details as you can;
- Then, set up a meeting time to share your philosophy with trusted colleagues;
- Encourage each of them to write his own philosophy;
- Agree to meet again to share everyone's philosophy.

The first couple of times he introduces this idea Harold does not convince many participants to write their philosophies. So, he decides to assign them to write one as part of their portfolios. He rewrites his instructions and adds the following:

> Setting down your core beliefs can be intimidating, particularly if you've never done it. Be open to what transpires. Making the commitment is the first step (I've done that by giving you this assignment). Doing it is the next. Once you do you will be surprised, as you will tap into your real teacher self. When you come to share it with colleagues, you will come even closer. The following prompts may help you find points of entry:

- When I first taught, I believed . . . but now . . .
- Students used to . . . but now they seem . . .
- I used to teach only whole-class lessons, but now . . .
- From the first day, I believe I . . . and now I still do believe that . . .
- While I average grades, I place more value work done later in the term because . . .
- I am struggling with the idea of including cellphones and iPads in my teaching . . .
- I found being alone in my classroom hard at first, but now I like it because . . .
- I used to like being alone in my classroom, but now . . .
- Compared to my first years, I now learn more and share more with colleagues about . . .
- Assigning homework has become a greater challenge because . . .

- I feel pressure to meet state tests, so I cannot teach the way I want to . . .
- I read . . . and it has changed my teaching . . .
- Sometimes, I wonder if I have a life outside teaching . . .
- It's not as much about what I teach, but rather I am a teacher who . . .

Happy writing!

After giving the assignment, Harold tells participants that if they want to read his rewritten philosophy from his last year in the classroom it he will email it. He suggests that they write their own before reading his. He wants them to stay fresh in their thinking.

Statement of Philosophy, February 1998

Paying attention. After years of contemplating, reading, and discussing, my philosophy of life and teaching is about paying attention. Paying attention allows me to be in the present. When I listen without distraction, without preoccupation, without thinking of the next appointment, I become a part of those around me. When a student asks a question and I listen, I answer with a chance to find meaning for both of us. Otherwise, our words pass by, each of us soon without a memory of the conversation.

Philosophy at its best is practical. What one does becomes one's philosophy. I remember the challenge in graduate school of writing a two-page statement of my philosophy of education. I wish I could find it and see what I said. I remember it was full of platitudes reflecting my love of Plato, Dewey, Black, and Whitehead. I find no separation between my practice at work, at home, and on the street. It's the challenge of living a good life, a caring life—and it meets me everywhere.

Showing up. Sometimes that's all it takes. Being there. To be fully present. It is not simply putting in an appearance, but being a presence. The best days are those where I am in the midst of it all, an integral part of the swirl. Whether leading a discussion, sharing a pun, observing a colleague, listening to a parent, complimenting the kitchen help, thanking a friend . . . whenever I am attentive wherever I am makes a difference.

It's in the details. Setting up my chairs for the incoming class. Copying and collating a test or a handout. Cleaning the table after having lunch with my advisees. Saying thank you and finding opportunities to say it. Writing comments to parents about their children. I like the business of life. Doing it well makes it possible to do it well again. It's habit.

Reading. Aldous Huxley, Jon Kabat-Zinn, Lao-Tzu, Thich Nhat Hanh, The Dalai Lama, Ken Wilber, Brian Swimme, Annie Dillard, and others. I like entering others' minds and trying to understand their perspective. Wilber's *A Brief History of Everything* does it in a big way.

I like to invite my students to be writers, particularly on provocative, challenging subjects. I read their insights, which frequently touch me deeply.

Seek meaning. I attend services and a weekly spirituality discussion group at my Congregational Church. I like our minister's collective search process, which includes many paths. I also attend a weekly Hindu meditation group and attempt some meditation on my own with varying success. Seeking in silence is often rich, particularly for one who likes to talk. Entering these doorways opens me to possibilities.

Doorways lead to bridges. Bridges provide a context for connecting. I thrive on bridges where I find understandings and resolutions. A bridge is a safe place to see into one another's world, to explore ideas, to encourage empathy, to resolve conflicts. That's why I taught in England, Canada, and the former Soviet Union during glasnost. Meeting others halfway opens creative possibilities and invites reconciliation. I have a richer understanding of others—and of myself.

Being on the edge. I think I have always been this way. Recently, when asked to teach Ancient History in the eighth grade, I began with the Big Bang. After all, why begin at Mesopotamia when civilization was already in place, such a recent event in cosmic time? Ancient History is not supposed to begin with the Big Bang.

Being a messenger. Several years ago, I created what I call wisdom beads, colored pony beads into which I inserted rolled sayings. I began by taking quotations from the Dalai Lama and Lao-Tzu. On the day before winter break, I invite my students each to take a bead from a bowl with the understanding to pay attention to its particular message. We then share them. I also have a set I share with the faculty and staff.

In the end it's all about commitment. A commitment to be of service to others—to do whatever it takes for children, for parents, for colleagues, for the school, for the community. My commitment combines competence, excellence, rigorous attention to relationships, and a sense of the awesome responsibility of teaching.

Harold's assignment to write philosophies proved rewarding. Most participants found that the process invited them to understand themselves. They enjoyed both sharing their philosophies and listening to others. Some became convinced that they should adapt this assignment for students as a means for them to know themselves better.

~ ~ ~

After sharing his philosophy with teachers, Harold revises his own. Recently, he has begun one to share with his workshop teachers:

My Philosophy Reconsidered, February 2015

It's been more than fifteen years since I last sat with my eighth graders. On that last day, the last class, we were sitting in a circle as usual, discussing what,

I can't remember, when suddenly we were late for the final middle school assembly.

Arriving late, no one seemed to mind. Neither did Chris Barnhill, our principal. "What a way to leave the classroom for the last time," I said to myself. "So embroiled in conversation that we lost track of time. For a few moments we beat Time, that insidious enemy of teaching. We never had enough. My students and I took it anyway. I wished I remembered what we were discussing."

Since then, my classroom has been with you, my fellow teachers. I have enjoyed making this shift, despite having been warned teachers can be difficult. "They tend to chat among themselves," my new colleagues told me. At first, I saw some of this but since calling it to your attention, it has ameliorated.

But, calling attention to behaviors has a short shelf life. The real operative in my teaching is its quality. No amount of interactive, innovative pedagogies can make a difference without quality. But to define quality can be illusive. . .

So Harold begins another statement of philosophy. He will come back to it another day. Meanwhile, he focuses on his teachers and writing. He thinks he might write a book to help them find their path toward engaging and exciting classrooms. However, he visualizes his book ultimately for students who he hopes will be the beneficiaries of his ideas. Who knows?

REFLECTION

When Dan Hilliard wrote his first philosophy of education in graduate school, he did not think it would have much meaning for his teaching. He had only observed some classrooms during his senior year in college. He liked John Dewey, so he based his essay on Dewey's progressive ideas. He liked the practicality of his philosophy.

Toward the end of his career, his colleague, Pat Blackman, had to write a philosophy of his teaching for his master's degree. He invited Dan to write one as well. At first Dan hesitated, but when he started to write, he discovered that he shifted considerably from that first effort.

When Pat and he shared their philosophies, they discovered more similarities than differences. It was surprising because they often disagreed with one another at faculty meetings. Now they understand each other better and, more importantly, know themselves better. They both agree that writing their philosophies is a valuable exercise.

Pat and Dan decide to establish a bimonthly conversation group to reflect on and discuss the deeper principles and values of their work with students— and with each other. They hope that colleagues who join will write their philosophies to further stimulate discussion.

POINTS TO PURSUE

Reread Your First Philosophy of Education

Harold arrived at graduate school fully committed to teaching. He was not surprised when Professor Anderson asked him to write his philosophy of education. But, having to write it showed him how little he knew.

Do you still have your first philosophy of education paper? Do you remember your reaction to having to write it? If you can find it, reread it. Then, write a new one, up to two pages. Invite colleagues to write one as well. If they need help, show them the prompts in this chapter.

What Do You Do to Reexamine Your Teaching?

Harold thought that writing periodic philosophies might have kept him more aware of his teaching. Still, he had been reflective throughout his career.

Do you have an approach for periodically reexamining your teaching, such as a diary, a blog, or sending emails to teachers in other schools? Which ones have been the most valuable? Share your thoughts with colleagues. You may discover other ways.

Take Writing Seriously—Yours and Your Students'

Writing is never easy. You should not be embarrassed to explore your thoughts in writing, especially since you expect students to write well. By looking closely at your practice, you make it easier to ask the same from your students.

Just as reading makes you better able to entice students to read meaningfully, your writing enables you to better guide students when they write.

Chapter 22

Achieve Our Dreams

We teach who we are.

Randy Pausch's fifteen minutes of fame sticks in Harold Dennison's mind. Pausch's gave his "Last Lecture" when he had inoperable cancer, with only six months to live. His theme "Lessons learned: how *you* can achieve your dreams and enable the dreams of others" riveted listeners in the audience and now more than seventeen million listeners and counting on YouTube.[1] His wisdom touches everyone—and Harold in particular.

Pausch spoke as though he had ascended a mountaintop, discovered wisdom, and came back to share it. As Harold listened, he wondered how many of us have such wisdom ready to be tapped. "Does the threat of impending death, of an approaching end, awaken us? Or, does it awaken us at least to be open to such wisdom from people like Randy before they leave us?"

In the spirit of Pausch, Harold writes in his journal:

What if we imagine we had only six months left to teach?
What if we see these six months as *the* opportunity
to teach as we have always wanted to?
Would we discover our own wisdom and feel compelled
to share it with our colleagues and students?
Would we become free to teach as our real selves rather than
feeling we must fulfill the expectations of others?
Could we actually evoke this sense of urgency?

Harold figures it would be a challenge to pretend he had "only six months left" to teach. After all, he will have the next year, and the next, and the next until he retires. Yet, in the second semester of any year he has less than six months to teach his current students. "Maybe I should think in terms of Pausch's 'only six months left.' Certainly not as urgent but nonetheless true."

Constraints provide pressure—and perhaps allow a sense of freedom. Deadlines help keep us focused. They provide borders and keep us attentive to what needs to be done. Without them, we can lose our place. When teachers create constraints, students gain a clearer sense of what they need to know, understand, and be able to do.

Harold remembers a shift in the quality of work with self-hardening clay in his open classroom years ago. Because students were misusing and wasting clay, his colleague, Chris Thomson, established straightforward and clear procedures: First, students could only use enough clay to fit in one hand. Second, they could not make a recognizable object, such as a cup and saucer or an animal. And lastly, within their abstract shape they had to put at least one hole.

The result was a series of remarkable sculptures, which led to the discovery of a faux glaze when students rubbed the sculptures with polished rocks. They did this while sitting quietly or listening to stories. Unwittingly, Harold and Chris had found a way to build meditation practice into their home groups.

In his last year in the classroom, Harold felt the meaning of Pausch's "only six months left." He became more conscious of his presence. Soon he would no longer have a classroom in which he would hold deep conversations in a circle with his eighth graders. He would no longer assign them to innovative projects or unusual writing assignments like his Ivan Denisovich journal across Russia.

Sometimes, Harold caught himself saying words and phrases for the last time like "Your assignment for tonight . . .," "Today, we will read . . ."; "Thank you for being here." As if to cement his departure from teaching, a year later his school tore down the building in which he last taught.

Had Harold taken to heart Pausch's "only six months left" throughout his career, would he have been a different teacher? Because he saw how important Pausch's insight was, he wrote in his journal:

> I certainly would have had heightened awareness about who I am, why I teach, and what I bring to the classroom. I would have paid more attention to my students' responses as I spoke—and as I listened. I could have been more reflective and fully present every day. By seeking to discover my inner knowing—available to all of us—I would have brought it to the surface earlier than I did.
>
> Though I did take advantage of my freedom to create units of study and made them imaginative and interesting, I wish I had paid more attention to how each and every student responded. I had a tendency to become carried away with the novelty of my ideas without always attending to their impact on each student. As long as most of them appeared to be on board, I was happy.
>
> I would have paid more attention to how each student learned. In my early years, I delivered academic knowledge and skills in as an entertaining way as

possible. And, as with my colleagues, I based my assessments on quizzes, tests and papers; the best grades seemed to belong to the "bright" students and lower grades to those at a "lower level." I did not pay close enough attention to what each student learned and to my part in it. I wish I had learned sooner about learning styles so I could have diversified my teaching.

I wish I had been more sensitive to my colleagues before judging them. I tended not to engage with them, particularly when I saw them teaching in ways I did not respect. Perhaps had we had better dialogues, we all could have become better teachers.

Impossible as it was, I wish I could have had access to recent research on brain-based learning and other innovative methods and approaches now available to teachers. Had I known more about collaborative planning and teaching as exemplified in professional learning community initiatives, my colleagues and I would have been better teachers. I experienced glimpses of these ideas, but, alas, they were not in place in my time.

I wish I had the courage to have graded papers without names.

"Perhaps this might turn into a book," he said to himself.

Whether or not teachers think of teaching as if it were for their last six months, the invitation to shift from teaching as talking to teaching for learning remains on the table. Teachers change when they decide to change. Parker Palmer frames it best: "We teach who we are."[2] We first bring our self-knowing into our classrooms, and from there choose our practices. What we do, after all, starts with our intention.

The Dalai Lama said, "Everything rests on the tip of intention." Teaching is, after all, an intentional activity. If a teacher intends to push as much material across during her lessons, she will do that. If a teacher intends, on the other hand, to spend more time alongside her students rather than stand and talk, she will find ways to do so.

If any teacher still doubts the need to create a sense of urgency to change her teaching, perhaps this anecdote will convince:

> Harold was sitting in the reception room at the doctor's office waiting for a ride home when he happened to watch a local-access television program featuring a school superintendent and three high school students.
>
> For nearly a half-hour, the superintendent and students exchanged laudatory comments about the qualities of their high school. The students made comments, as the superintendent nodded, including, "Our campus is better than some colleges"; "We have the most professional TV studio of any school"; "Our school is better equipped than many universities." Harold thought the program may have been scripted.
>
> Then, without warning a girl said, "Given that we have ninety-minute class blocks, I wish we did not have to take notes for the entire time."
>
> The superintendent did not blink.

The DNA of teaching-as-talking, which requires students to take notes, still resides deep in schools. This is the way it is—what Michael Schmoker calls "the brutal facts."[3] Harold wonders if this practice will ever change. He became a school consultant primarily to encourage teachers to let go of this practice. However, he knows he cannot *make* them change. Throughout his career, forcing teachers to change—himself included—did not work. Instead, he intends to invite teachers to want to change, to want to explore new ways to teach, new ways to engage students, new ways to be alive in the classroom—to achieve their dreams.

As the Taoists profess, a journey of a thousand miles begins with the first step. Taking that step requires courage, commitment—and support.

REFLECTION

Dan Hilliard is embarrassed that his profession has been lax in enforcing standards. However, he is tired of the rhetoric that compares the medical profession to teaching. He wishes that the current tenure system—three years, and you gain a contract for life—was a thing of the past. He prefers stricter recertification standards, not simply taking random courses for credit or putting in recertification hours. Students deserve more than that.

He has decided to pursue National Board Certification from the National Board for Professional Teaching Standards (NBPTS).[4] The work will be hard, but will provide him with knowledge and understanding of the latest and best practices. He wants to be challenged.

Dan is concerned that some of his colleagues settle for less. He feels for students who get stuck with teachers who use old lecture notes, who work strictly by contract and by the clock, and who take little interest in the personal lives of students. Until higher standards for all teachers become mandatory—as they are for other professions—such teachers continue to receive renewed contracts. Dan is particularly upset with those who are on the verge of retirement and count the days—and act that way.

POINTS TO PURSUE

View Randy Pausch's "Last Lecture"

Take time to watch Randy Pausch's YouTube video, "The Last Lecture," (and read his book, *The Last Lecture*). His freshness, vigor, and sense of humor offer wisdom that reminds teachers how they can be with students and their families. His message is provocative, encouraging, and uplifting.

Once you've seen the video, try out the "only-six-months-left-to-teach" approach, as Harold Dennison did in this chapter. See what happens.

Pay Attention to Your Intentions

Harold Dennison is a reflective teacher. He knows that he sets the tone of his students' learning. He knows, too, that he is flawed. He has had to pick up the pieces often in his teaching years. He understands that his intentions are his guide for what he wants to achieve, what he wants his students to achieve.

Have you considered the power of intentions as expressed by the Dalai Lama? Are you aware of your intentions, every day, and in every lesson? Choose one area of your teaching you'd like to change the most: set your intention; then reflect on your transition. Invite a colleague to observe and support you. Pay close attention to your students' reactions.

How Can You Discover the Elephant in the Room?

While waiting in the reception room at his doctor's office watching a local TV program proselytizing the glories of a suburban school, Harold had an epiphany. He wondered how much his own school shielded its eyes to the realities lurking below its public face. "What are our elephants in the room?" he asked himself.

Are you aware of the disconnections between professed practices and what really happens in your school? Do you sometimes say one thing to your students when you know it isn't quite right? Do you know of the elephants in the room in your school that need to be exposed?

Challenge Yourself to Become a Better Teacher

Dan Hilliard recognizes his need to become a better teacher. Despite his successes, he is certain that he should know more. His decision to seek National Board Certification may not make any difference to his Board, but it will for him.

You can become a more professional teacher by following Dan Hilliard's footsteps and applying for National Board Certification. Once in the program, you can be assured that you will become more well-rounded and knowledgeable about the teaching profession—and about you as a teacher. You may be surprised at how much more there is to learn.

NOTES

1. Randy Pausch, "Last Lecture: Achieving Your Childhood Dreams," http://www.youtube.com/watch?v=ji5_MqicxSo—A worthwhile one hour and a half! See also Randy Pausch and Jeffrey Zaslow, *The Last Lecture* (New York: Hyperion, 2008).
2. Parker Palmer, *The Courage to Teach: Exploring the Inner Landscape of a Teacher's Life* (San Francisco: Jossey-Bass, 1998), Introduction, 1. Still the most profound book on reflecting on the meaning of teaching.

3. Michael Schmoker, *Results Now* (Alexandria: Association for Supervision and Curriculum Development, 2006), "Introduction: The Brutal Facts About Instruction and Supervision," 1–10.

4. See National Board for Professional Teaching Standards, http://www.nbpts.org.

Chapter 23

Become Stakeholders

The first boy said, "I bring you gold." And the second boy said, "I bring you myrrh." And the third boy said, "Frank sent this."

Teaching to the test has bothered Harold Dennison since the early days of No Child Left Behind. Those tests do not focus on students as students but on students as receptacles. Because so many of his former colleagues spend weeks on "drill and kill," as he likes to refer to it, they lose valuable teaching time. However, in schools that do not emphasize test prep, students can do well.[1]

His favorite critique of present educational practices is the now famous TED Talk, Ken Robinson: "How schools kill creativity."[2] Robinson reveals the fundamental flaw in teaching in today's pressurized, overextended, and misdirected classrooms. Teaching to the test means to fly through facts without regard to meaning. Children absorb fragmented knowledge that prevents them from finding significance in the world, let alone in themselves. Robinson's anecdote sums it up: "The first boy said, 'I bring you gold.' And the second boy said, 'I bring you myrrh.' And the third boy said, 'Frank sent this.'"

Harold also likes a more recent Ken Robinson TED talk, "How to escape from education's death valley."[3] In his inimitable style, Robinson takes the emperor-is-wearing-no-clothes approach to the current state of education. He makes clear that its narrowness focuses on tests that measure clerical-level thinking. Schools as they are structured are antithetical to human beings. Teachers are put in an untenable position of having to cater to narrow-focus tests that measure anything but what it is to be human.

Robinson's conclusion matches Harold's belief that devolving the responsibility for schools on teachers and principals is essential. Enough of the hierarchy.[4] Robinson cites the metaphor of Death Valley—where nothing grows—when the Valley received seven inches of rain in 2007. The next spring, flowers appeared.

Schools are like that, seeds of possibility waiting to be nurtured. Take power away from federal and state authorities and give it to teachers and principals. Finland does it. Its schools have a broad curriculum, no standardized tests, and—Robinson emphasizes—no dropouts. Harold invites his workshop participants to see both of Robinson's TED talks.

Given the state of schools, Harold is surprised that many students still do schoolwork, let alone homework. The ubiquitous presence of text messaging, tweeting, Instagram, video games, iPods, cell phones, television, and the Internet hold far greater appeal. On-screen interactions with peers—often when home alone—prevail over face-to-face time and keep students away from homework. Sometimes Harold imagines them using their devices as pebbles skipping over water. They move quickly but not deeply. They make innumerable contacts but do not linger. They connect but do not embrace. They travel fast but do not saunter—and do not know how.

Harold sees more and more people spending inordinate amounts of time with them. As a result, they spend less time dwelling inside their minds. How much time would a person who averages thirty-five thousand text messages per month—outside her job—have for reflection?[5] Will the relentless attraction of social media lure people to become conduits of information rather than initiators of thinking?

Children arrive in kindergarten as mobile kids with exploring thumbs, natives to the electronic devices they gleefully touch. They step through the classroom door eager to explore, but their teachers say, "No, not yet." Waiting curbs their curiosity. By third grade, they're less curious, less interested, less connected. They ask fewer questions. Teachers postpone exploration in the name of coverage, of impending state and federal assessments, of preparing for the next year. They are teaching very different children who process the world in new ways, appear impatient and inattentive, and seem more urbane, yet less mature.

At a summer faculty workshop, Drew Gibson, a history teacher in Massachusetts,[6] shared his wish to have students become shareholders in his classroom. His argument focused on the importance of teachers in encouraging students to take ownership in their learning. "We don't want them to act as 'cognitive slaves,' who only do the minimum to reach their goals." Citing his understanding of the slave South, Gibson related his unmotivated students to slaves, who act passively in part because they have no stake in the work they are forced to do.

As the discussion progressed, others agreed that students who only do the minimum care less about their future. They also agreed that they have a responsibility to motivate and create ways to evoke effort. Students who become stakeholders take ownership in what they do and focus their attention. Teachers who become stakeholders take ownership in what they teach. They make their classrooms exciting.

Increasingly, Harold hears teachers' concerns about the influence of Google. Many feel it is fast replacing students' memories. They hear students say, "Why should I remember information when I can Google whatever I need to know?" Nicholas Carr wonders if Google will become our collective human brain.[7]

Harold hints at this conundrum. He innocently asks participants, "What is the capital of Iowa?" He pauses and then says, "Google!" His point is that students know they don't need to memorize states and capitals. "Why have such information in my head when I can find it instantly?" But, Harold cautions his teachers to be sure they convince students always to determine the validity of information on the Internet and evaluate its applicability—an essential tool for all Internet users.

Still, a larger question remains: What do people need to learn, to memorize in the twenty-first century? The multiplication tables? Regions of the world? Literary terms? The causes of the Civil War? Now that we live in a culture in which Google surrounds us in ever-expanding ways, teachers need to address what students *do* need to know. They need to ask the following:

What do students need to know, understand, and be able to do?
What competencies must they have so they can face a changing future?
What values should we nurture for them, for our communities, and for the global world?
How can students—and we as teachers—become stakeholders in our learning?

Focusing on standardized tests misses the point. Harold likes Susan Engel's practical thinking. She writes, "Why not test the things we value, and test them in a way that provides us with an accurate picture of what children really do, not what they can do under the most constrained circumstances after the most constrained test preparation?"

Harold appreciates Engel's variable approach for testing children's seven abilities and dispositions: Reading, Inquiry, Flexible Thinking and the Use of Evidence, Conversation, Collaborations, Engagement, and Well-being. "One key feature of the system, I am suggesting," Engel writes, "is that it depends, like good research, on representative samples rather than on testing every child every year." Harold particularly likes her caveat, "We'd use less data, to better effect, and free up the hours, days, and weeks now spent on standardized test prep and the tests themselves, time that could be spent on real teaching and learning."[8]

Staying focused on what matters to children's actual learning makes more sense than testing to determine how well they can do on tests. Harold plans to share Engel's comments with his consultant colleagues—and with his former principal. He wants to open the conversation about outside assessments. Previously, he has been opposed to any testing. Engel's ideas are far from passing out No. 2 pencils and filling in bubbles. He now agrees with her that the right testing can "measure the things we most value, and find good ways to do that."[9]

Harold has been a fierce critic of No Child Left behind, and he does not support Obama's Race to the Top either. However, he has recently reconsidered his thinking about the Common Core State Standards (CCSS) Initiative. He now thinks that the Common Core supports teacher efforts to teach more rigorously. But, teachers must be trusted to be major decision-makers in implementing the Common Core. Every student deserves to be challenged. Every student deserves to have skills that prepare him to teach himself. And every student deserves to have knowledge he can apply to gain further knowledge. Teachers can facilitate these objectives.

The world is fast knitting together, its peoples all needing excellent education. The Common Core may be the United States' best hope. However, as with all reforms, the results will be what actually happens in classrooms. Its standards are reasonable and make sense. Good teachers are already teaching to them. The Core sharpens instructional targets to enable teachers to develop proficiency scales with explicit sets of goals. They also help align assessments and curriculum to support knowledge development and higher-order thinking.

As to its testing programs—Smarter Balance Assessment Consortium and The Partnership of Readiness for College and Careers (PARCC)—the jury is out as to whether they will be more revealing. Students will take them on computers and receive results immediately. They will have to answer more sophisticated questions including having to synthesize information, reason mathematically, integrate multiple sources, write coherent explanations, and make reasoned arguments. Harold hopes that multiple-choice questions will not play a major role. Yet, he is suspicious of Pearson Education's increasing control of the testing process from curriculum to the tests themselves.[10]

Test prep by itself has little or no impact on test scores. In his workshops, Harold sites Judith Langer's important work that contrast, "Beat the Odds" (BTO) schools with "Typically Performing" (TP) schools.[11] In TP schools, students typically work alone or in groups or with the teacher. They focus on particular tasks without substantive discussion from multiple perspectives. No dialogue. No opportunities to challenge one another.

In BTO schools, the learning environment is radically different. The distinguishing features of instruction in BTO schools are the following:

1. skills and knowledge are taught in multiple types of lessons;
2. tests are deconstructed to inform curriculum and instruction;
3. within curriculum and instruction, connections are made across content and structure to ensure coherence;
4. strategies for thinking and doing are emphasized;
5. generative learning is encouraged; and
6. classrooms are organized to foster collaboration and shared cognition.[12]

BTO teachers have a vision, in Langer's words, of "what counts as knowing," and they recognize the importance that all students can learn—*and* teachers can make a difference.[13] To enact all six features, teachers have to reassess their pedagogies. Simply using "sit and get" will not suffice. If a teacher wants to "beat the odds," she needs to find multiple ways to engage and excite her students' thinking and learning.

Harold includes Langer's story of a BTO teacher who asks her students to "fight to teach me." This teacher wants them to disagree with her (and each other) and extend her (and their) thinking. They practice this every day in discussions. "Is there a better way to open dialogue in the classroom?" Harold asks his participants. And the clincher for BTO teaching, he underscores, "the true test of teaching the Common Core comes when the test arrives unannounced, students take it, and they do fine. No prep. No warning."

Although the Common Core focuses on Math and Language Arts, Harold agrees with Stephen Wineburg of Stanford that the Social Studies curriculum is an important component in teaching nonfiction. Teaching from "that 1,000-page behemoth known as a history textbook . . . prepares students to meet the challenges of the world that no longer exists."[14]

Wineburg argues that historical nonfiction offers a rich variety of documents including letters, diaries, secret communiqués, public speeches, among others. Nonfiction also offers opportunities for close reading. "History demands that we think about the meaning of words not to us 150 years later, but to the people who actually uttered them."[15] In response to the Internet's fluidity with truth, Wineburg states, "Today, when information bombards young people from all sides, the question is not where to find it, but once found, whether it should be believed."[16]

However, as with all reforms, what counts is what transpires in classrooms. When Common Core teacher trainers mimic the old "sit and get" professional development, teachers will do what they've always done. When, on the other hand, trainers demonstrate interactive strategies that model the 65 percent student-led/35 percent teacher-led classroom, teachers see the value of this approach and have opportunities to practice. "You become what you practice," Harold reiterates.

~ ~ ~

Teachers have a responsibility to preserve eternal human values that have developed over the past ten thousand years. They need to instill the unique human treasure of face-to-face contact. Otherwise, technological wizardry will supplant it and people will, ironically, become separated from one another. Students who walk home from school with classmates while on cell phones or texting are already living alone. When they arrive home, they find the key, unlock the door, and lock the door behind them. They sit alone with their media devices to befriend. Friends without breath, without touch, without a wet glint in their eyes.

However, Harold advocates that teachers make an effort to incorporate the changing world of technology. Given the power of smartphones and tablets, he visualizes teachers using them at sophisticated levels. By inviting students to pursue meaningful questions and discussing their thoughts with one another, teachers will slow their tendency to behave as skipping stones acting only as conduits on these devices.

At the same time that teachers acknowledge the capital of Iowa is Google, they also establish the crucial importance of learning the arguments in the Federalist Papers, analyzing Orwell's metaphors in *Animal Farm*, interpreting the implications of Catherine the Great's Potemkin Villages, considering the impact of sunspots on climate change, and learning processes that aid thinking, such as the multiplication tables.

And, perhaps more important, teach the joys of rigor, ambiguity, and wondering.

REFLECTION

Dan Hilliard sees his students absorbed by the glitz of electronic devices. Some even attempt to text during his classes. He has been hesitant to take away cell phones, as he does not want to be known as a dinosaur; he does, however, ask them to turn them off. After all, he has an iPhone—and has used it occasionally in class to call a friend for an opinion during a discussion, or to access Google to clarify a fact. Once, he asked his students to take out their cell phones to contact friends for their opinion on a controversial issue. They loved it—and it activated discussion. He plans to do more with phones.

Yet, Dan continues to stress literacy: reading with pen in hand, writing and rewriting, and encouraging rigorous discussions. He takes seriously providing skills instruction in his well-organized classroom. He and Angela Bernardi integrate curriculum with the tests in mind but spend only a few lessons on the structure of the tests themselves. They believe that extensive test prep is a misnomer.

Dan keeps in touch with digital potentials. When he learned about Teacher-Tube videos, "Did You Know? 2.0" and later "Did You Know? 3.0 updated" (aka "Shift Happens"), he asks his principal, Margaret Fellows, if he could introduce these videos at a faculty meeting.[17]

Dan is convinced that everyone should be aware of the information presented in these videos, as they open faculty to resources including YouTube, TeacherTube, iTunes U, TED.com, and Bigthink.com. Dan's own distaste for textbooks has led him to these sources as a means for keeping his materials up-to-date and being appealing to his students.

Dan is convinced if all teachers watch one TED Talk every week or two, they will discover ways to enhance their teaching. He suggests they begin with his favorites, "Ken Robinson Says Schools Kill Creativity" and "How to Escape from Education's Death Valley." If Margaret agrees, he could also show them at a faculty meeting.

POINTS TO PURSUE

How Do You Respond to Children Who Constantly Skip Like Pebbles on Their Phones?

What do you notice that is different about your students from, say, five years ago? Ten years ago? Do you see today's children "as pebbles skipping over water"? Are they less involved—or appear to be less involved in your classroom?

Can you find alternative ways to engage students? Are you able to convince them to dig deeper into what you teach? Do they resist? Do you understand how your students learn best?

What Can You Do to Enhance Student Curiosity and Commitment to Learning?

"Why is it the longer kids are in school, the less curious they seem?" A school administrator asked this question in Tony Wagner's *The Global Achievement Gap*.[18] What might you be doing to contribute to decreasing curiosity in school? What can you do to recapture it, nurture it, and celebrate it? What are the consequences if you don't?

Harold Dennison has been a critic of standardized testing since No Child Left Behind. He continues to wrestle with this issue. Is it possible that the emphasis on testing has narrowed the potential for education to be exciting? Is it possible that testing has disassembled the notion of teaching to the individual student, as these tests look for the same attributes in everyone? Interesting questions.

How Do You Respond to the Concept of Stakeholders?

Harold was fascinated with Drew Gibson's metaphor of seeing children (and teachers) as stakeholders in their learning. He saw it as an effective way to determine whether or not students are engaged. He found the counterimage of cognitive slaves—who only do the minimum to get by—an equally compelling image.

How does Gibson's metaphor apply to your classroom? Do your students see themselves as stakeholders in what happens? Or are they closer to cognitive slaves who do your bidding? Do you feel you are a stakeholder in what transpires in your classroom? As a principal, do you see yourself as a stakeholder in your school?

How Do You Respond to the Impact of Google?

Google has become central in Harold's life, first as a teacher in his later years and now as a consultant. Sometimes, he wonders what life would be without it. At the same time, he's suspicious of its encroachment. He wonders how to approach this problem.

How has Google evolved in your teaching? In your life? Have you reconciled the impact of Google? Do you know what your children need to know, understand, and be able to do—beyond Google?

How Will You Take Advantage of the Common Core?

The work of Judith Langer cited in this chapter opens the door to richer pedagogies. She makes clear the central importance of the teacher. Her distinction between BTO versus TP teachers deserves close scrutiny.

Can you commit to implement the depth of teaching required to raise the level of your students' knowledge and thinking? How can you use Common Core principles to make that happen? How will you engage with colleagues to make your teaching better for your students—and for all students in your school?

How Can You Connect with Today's "Digital Natives" or "Mobile Kids"?

The influx of digital technologies has caused new thinking about today's culture. Do you see adults as "digital immigrants" and not as "digital natives," as Marc Prensky writes?[19] Or do you prefer depicting adults as "refugees" and not like "mobile kids," as Neil Swidey writes?[20]

Whether you choose one or the other (or neither), how can you reconcile students' fluency and ease with these technologies with what you intend to teach? This is a fundamental question.

NOTES

1. Students at the University Park Campus School in Worcester, Massachusetts, scored well on state tests from the beginning without test-prep sessions. Instead, its teachers emphasized strong academic classes with plenty of time for writing and rewriting. A classic example of this on film is *Marva Collins' Way* (1981) where all her students scored well above the norm.

2. Ken Robinson: "How schools kill creativity," TED2006, February 2006, http://www.ted.com/talks/ken_robinson_says_schools_kill_creativity.html. At the time of writing this book, more than thirty-three million people have viewed this remarkable talk.

3. Sir Ken Robinson, "How To Escape From Education's Death Valley" at http://www.ted.com/talks/ken_robinson_how_to_escape_education_s_death_valley?language=en.

4. For an extensive argument for devolving responsibility for schools to teachers and principals, see part V, "Build Trust and Respect," in Frank Thoms, *Teaching That Matters: Engaging Minds, Improving Schools* (Lanham, MD: Rowman & Littlefield, 2015).

5. Justine Ezarik, a Web designer and video blogger in Pittsburgh, interview: "iPhone: A Compact Device With a Very Bulky Bill," *All Things Considered*, NPR, August 16, 2007.

6. Drew taught history at Berkshire Arts and Technology Public Charter School and is currently at Mt. Greylock Regional High School.

7. Nicholas Carr, "Is Google Making Us Stupid?" *The Atlantic*, July/August, 2008.

8. Susan Engel, *End of the Rainbow: How Educating for Happiness (not Money) Would Transform Our Schools* (New York: The New Press, 2015).

9. Ibid.

10. Google "Last Week Tonight with John Oliver: Standardized Testing" (HBO, May 3, 2015) for a scathing report. It's ironic that a comedy show articulates this issue as well—or better—than anyone.

11. J. A. Langer, "Beating the odds: Teaching middle and high school students to read and write well," *American Educational Research Journal*, vol. 38, no. 4, 2001, 837–80. (Source used here from http://www.albany.edu/cela/reports/langer/langer-beating12014.pdf).

12. Ibid., 45.

13. Ibid.

14. Commentary: "Using History to Invigorate Common-Core Lessons" by Sam Wineburg, *Education Week*, Online, December 10, 2013. See also "Steering Clear of

the Textbook" by Sam Wineburg in *Education Week*, December 11, 2013 (Vol. 33, #14, pp. 30, 36), www.edweek.org excerpted in *Marshal Memo* 515, December 16, 2013, 1/3.

15. Ibid.

16. Ibid.

17. See the videos, "Did You Know? 2.0," http://www.teachertube.com/viewVideo.php?video_id=3051&title=Did_You_Know__2_0; and "Did You Know? 3.0," http://www.teachertube.com/viewVideo.php?video_id=115106&title=Did_you_know_version_3_0.

18. Tony Wagner, *The Global Achievement Gap*, 41.

19. Marc Prensky, "Digital Natives, Digital Immigrants."

20. Neil Swidey, "Why an iPhone could actually be good for your 3-year old," *Boston Globe*, November 1, 2009, http://www.boston.com/bostonglobe/magazine/articles/2009/11/01/why_an_iphone_could_actually_be_good_for_your_3_year_old/.

Chapter 24

Begin at the End

Pathways. It is all about pathways.

On the first day of school, teachers feel the pull of the last day whether they attend to it or not.[1] Every year they begin in August/September and end in June. They compose their teaching inside beginnings and endings. Plans sometimes work out as expected but other times not.

Schools exist inside blocks of time and have their own rhythms. Teachers "have kids" for a year. Schools schedule holidays and vacations; semesters, terms, marking periods; lessons, units of study, courses; concerts, musicals, plays; and sports seasons. Teachers—and students—welcome the New Year as a chance to begin anew; beginning teachers find solace in this second chance, as do their students.

Teachers think in weeks, as well. Many choose Thursdays as review days for Friday tests. Wednesday for some is "hump day." Mondays and Fridays, too, have their own karma, their own energy. Fridays come too slowly and Mondays come too quickly for some. Others look forward to Mondays and squeeze as much as possible out of the last hour on Friday.

The first day of school: a clean slate, a fresh start, a new beginning—and a level playing field. Only for that day. Nothing quite like it!

Inside these beginnings and endings, teachers keep pace even as glitches and surprises upset their rhythm. New teachers wonder why no one prepared them for unexpected hits. It didn't seem as confusing when they were in school. Student teaching, they quickly discover, only touches the surface of real school. It's impossible to replicate being alone in a classroom.

How can teachers better prepare to meet the perplexities of daily school life? How can they set priorities and not lose sight of what matters, what they want students to know and care about? Some teachers weather storms well, keep their composure no matter the stress. Others struggle. There are no magic bullets to manage the chaos, no formulas to make classrooms calm and productive. Each teacher must find her own means, her own anchors to stabilize her ship.

A teacher drops anchor when she builds her teaching toward known outcomes. She defines the roads intended, yet she discovers new and better roads along the way. In the words of Robert Frost, she might even claim at some later date that she "took the one less traveled by" and believe it "has made all the difference." But, she won't know until she commits. Many roads lead to Rome; each teacher finds her own.

~ ~ ~

"Pathways. It is all about pathways." So began Harold Dennison's letter to his students and their parents on the first day in his last year of teaching. He often designed pathways for the year ahead, particularly for his open-education classroom. This letter, however, was his best effort in a long time. It not only provided students and parents with his intentions for the year but also gave him a clear sense.

The success of "Pathways" led him to develop a portfolio assignment for a course he teaches as a consultant on backward design. He wants his participants to write an end-of-the-year reflection of what they want their students to learn, understand, and be able to do. To set the proper tone, he invites them to imagine standing at the door of their classroom on the last day of school:

> It's the last day of school. You are standing at your door. Your children are leaving. They will no longer be yours.
>
> You ask yourself: Who are they now? What have they become? What have they learned? What do they understand about themselves? What is important to them? What do they care about? What do they value? How will they relate to the world? What differences have I made? . . .
>
> Take some time to reflect on these questions and others you might ask. Most likely you, too, will look for personal, emotional, and intellectual qualities in your students; hardly anyone mentions tests or grades.

Harold pauses to give them time to ponder his proposal and ask any questions. After some conversation, he proceeds:

> You teach because you believe you can make a difference. You know what you want for your students. Regardless of the demands for testing and accountability, you understand in your heart of hearts your deeper obligations and responsibilities.

You articulate what you want your students to learn, understand, and be able to do—every class, every day throughout the year. You design instruction that reaches out to all learners. You provide means to assess what they learn. You do not always succeed, but you try.

In writing this end-of-the-year reflection, you give yourself a benchmark. Your lessons and units will be framed as part of a whole. They will aim for overarching understandings, significant knowledge and skills, and essential questions that drive your students' thinking. Every day, you will give them opportunities to connect and make sense of what you are asking.

A teacher who gives his students the final exam on the first day of school understands this.

After sharing his standing-at-the-door-at-the-end-of-the-year idea, Harold repeats, "A teacher who gives students the final exam on the first day of school understands this." He invites participants to examine Dan Bisaccio's "Biology Final," which is in their packet (Figure 24.1).[2]

Harold knows that most participants will not choose to emulate Bisaccio, but he hopes Bisaccio's idea will provoke discussion. During the conversation, Harold emphasizes Bisaccio's clear vision of what he wants his students to know, understand, and be able to do. He has an excellent idea of what his students will have accomplished by the time they walk out the door on the last day of school—as they will have as well.

Yet, participants hesitate to consider passing out their final exam on the first day of school, because it defies conventional wisdom. Teachers and professors have used exams for generations to determine grades—and some think, to indicate students' level of intelligence. Not to have exams defies tradition.

Harold's participants recognize, however, that the Biology Final indeed becomes a vehicle for students to become "biologists"—not for getting A's on the exam. In September, when Bisaccio has them define biology in their own words, they write a paragraph or two. In May, they compose thoughtful essays. His "biologists" improve in class, as athletes improve at practices. Bisaccio visualizes his students leaving his lab on the last day as "biologists," not for what they remembered or could recall on tests.

Harold hopes the discussion will provoke teachers to rethink their approach to tests and exams—perhaps reassess their rationale for teaching.

Harold takes time in his workshop to stress the importance of UbD planning, which is based on the work of Grant Wiggins and Jay McTighe.[3] Usually some participants already know about this approach. Others recognize that they instinctively use some backward-design principles. UbD's principles and practices are comprehensive and accessible, albeit sometimes complex. UbD hits a "sweet spot" in teaching. Teachers see not only the whole but also

Biology Final Exam – Dan Bisaccio

More often than not, you will find the definition of "biology" given in a somewhat clinical manner such as "Biology is the study of life and how organisms relate to their physical environs." However, biologists are in the business of seeking answers to questions, and their search encompasses a much more exciting and broader spectrum than this usual definition implies.

This year you will be the biologist and, in seeking the answers to the questions posed below (and others that will certainly arise), you will have the opportunity to discover and understand a much more comprehensive definition of biology than the one previously stated.

From time to time you will be given the following questions to answer ... and, in fact, this is your final exam as well. Each time you answer them, your grade will be based on your development as a biologist. In other words, as the year unfolds, it is expected that you will become more and more the "sophisticated biologist," and your answers should reflect this.

1. Define "biology" in your own words.

2. What characterizes life? In other words: what is the difference between "living" and "nonliving," between "living" and "never-living"?

3. There are 5 Kingdoms of Life: what are they? what is common to all? what distinguishes each as a separate kingdom?

4. From a scientific standpoint: how did life begin on this planet? what characteristics of this planet enabled life to evolve? what were some problems early organisms needed to overcome and how did they do it?

5. Within the 5 Kingdoms, biologists recognize millions of species. What is a "species"? Why are there so many different species? In terms of question 4, how did so many forms of life come to be?

6. Perhaps the most essential biochemical reactions are listed below. In terms of entropy (2nd Law of Thermodynamics), discuss the importance of these reactions as they pertain to life:

$6CO_2 + 6 H_2O + SUNLIGHT \Rightarrow C_6H_{12}O_6 + 6O_2$

$C_6H_{12}O_6 + 6O_2 \Rightarrow 6CO_2 + 6H_2O + ENERGY$

7. In an ecological sense, interpret the essay "Thinking Like a Mountain" written by Aldo Leopold, from his book *A Sand County Almanac*.

Figure 24.1 Biology Final. (From Dan Bisaccio's "Biology Final," in Robert Fried, *The Passionate Teacher*, 232–33.)

how the parts fit together. They sense alignment and coherence from day to day. They see themselves moving in harmony alongside students.

Something else happens. Backward design thinking invokes the spirit. Teachers when fully immersed not only become engaged but emotionally committed. Unlike developing traditional curriculum units, UbD insists on engagement, not compliance. Teachers seek to collaborate with one another. Classrooms literally come alive. They let students in on the process; they explain where they are headed, how they will be assessed, and what they will do along the way. Some teachers ask students to join in the design process itself, for example, creating projects and scoring rubrics.

Once participants grasp the principles of UbD, Harold clarifies how they can approach their end-of-the-year reflection for their portfolios:

> Visualize the end-in-view you are aiming for? See the big picture you want for your students? Articulate the overall purpose of your teaching in this context—the purpose that all your units and lessons will point toward? What is your ultimate backwards design? Trust that after completing this reflection, you will be better able to design coherent units and lessons. Successful change—as I hope I have made clear by now—after all, begins at the end.
>
> Remember, you are in the business of change. Your students change before our eyes. Your lessons change, too, often minutes after beginning. You know that once a lesson comes in contact with students, who knows where it might go? Plan to design learning towards worthwhile and productive goals. Having a vision of the whole is a gift to your students—and to you. Together you will have better opportunities to stay on track towards worthwhile learning.
>
> Write well. I look forward to reading what you have to say.[4]

Harold concludes his workshop by sharing the now-classic essay found on the Internet, "Big Rocks." The story speaks for itself.

> An expert is speaking to a group of business students, and to drive home a point, he uses an illustration those students will never forget.
>
> As he stands in front of the group of high-powered overachievers, he says, "Okay, time for a quiz." He pulls out a one-gallon, wide-mouthed mason jar and sets it on a table in front of him. Then he produces about a dozen fist-sized rocks and carefully places them, one at a time, into the jar. When the jar is filled to the top and no more rocks fit inside, he asks, "Is this jar full?"
>
> Everyone in the class says, "Yes."
>
> Then he says, "Really?" He reaches under the table and pulls out a bucket of gravel. He dumps some gravel in and shakes the jar causing pieces of gravel to work themselves down into the spaces between the big rocks. Then he asks the group once more, "Is the jar full?"
>
> By this time, the class is onto him. "Probably not," one of them answers.
>
> "Good!" he replies. He reaches under the table and brings out a bucket of sand. He starts dumping the sand in. It falls into all the spaces left between the rocks and the gravel. Once more, he asks the question, "Is this jar full?"
>
> "No!" the class shouts.
>
> Once again, he says, "Good!" Then he grabs a pitcher of water and begins to pour it in until the jar is filled to the brim. Then he looks up at the class and asks, "What is the point of this illustration?"
>
> One eager beaver raises his hand and says, "The point is, no matter how full your schedule is, if you try really hard, you can always fit some more things into it!"
>
> "No," the speaker replies, "that's not the point. The truth this illustration teaches us is: If you don't put the big rocks in first, you'll never get them in at all."

What are the big rocks in your life? A project you want to accomplish? Time with your loved ones? Your faith? Your education? Your finances? A cause? Teaching or mentoring others? Remember to put these big rocks in first or you'll never get them in at all.

So, when reflecting on this story, ask yourself this question: "What are the big rocks in my life or in my teaching?" Then, put those in your jar first.[5]

As the Mad Hatter said, "If you don't know where you are going, any road will take you there." Given the short time teachers have with students, they need to know the road they will take together for every course, unit, and lesson. Whether or not they find a less-traveled road, they can have the confidence that they will make a difference.

REFLECTION

When Dan Hilliard reads about Dan Bisaccio's "Biology Final," he has an epiphany. "What a difference, having a final exam as an indicator of the quality and depth of thinking, rather than as a scorecard of what students remember! I can take this idea and merge my teaching with the intended outcomes for my students.

"I will invite my students into the circle of my intentions. We will explore the ever-growing and changing knowledge, understandings, and skills for the twenty-first century. We will be learning together. I will see them maturing throughout the year. They will leave my classroom better able to teach themselves."

He couldn't wait to tell his colleagues about Bisaccio's "Final." He sends an email to them, with it attached. Obviously, it will raise many questions. He wonders about the applicability of Bisaccio's final-exam concept for teachers who do not give exams. He suspects, however, that sharing it will stir everyone to think—and perhaps clarify their direction and purpose.

POINTS TO PURSUE

What Are the Rhythms of Your School Life?

Dan Hilliard took advantage of his understanding of Bisaccio's "Biology Final." He began to consider other aspects of his teaching, hoping to better integrate his lessons with his intended outcomes. He did not want to become stuck in outmoded patterns.

In your classroom, do you do the same thing every day, every year? Are your rhythms based primarily on your needs? Or, do you consciously create new rhythms to spur curiosity and inquisitiveness? Take a "rhythm inventory" to find out.

Should your school reconsider its rhythm? Would doing so upset the community?

Imagining Standing by Your Door at the End of the Year

Have you ever "dropped anchor" by writing an end-of-the-year reflection? Take some time—even in the middle of the year—to imagine standing at your door on the last day of school. Imagine your students passing by and taking "you" with them. What do they leave with? What differences have you made? This process is well worth your time.

You could offer your students an opportunity to write a reflection of how they see themselves in your classroom at the end of a month or a marking period. It might help them focus. An interesting idea.

Consider Giving Your Final Exam on the First Day of School

Despite the predicted resistance, Harold Dennison values his introduction of Bisaccio's "Final" to participants in his workshops. For one, it opens minds to not only a radically different perception of exams but also to the purpose of teaching.

How do you react to Dan Bisaccio's giving his students their final exam on the first day of school? How might you—at any grade level, in any position—implement Bisaccio's thinking to deepen your teaching? Explore his idea with colleagues to elicit their reactions. Who knows where the conversation might lead.

Consider the Impact of "Big Rocks" for Your Classroom, for Your School

Share "Big Rocks" with colleagues. It is such a simple, yet profound, story. Better yet, share it with your students and allow time for thoughtful consideration. Given that their lives are filled with distractions, finding their "Big Rocks" might help them sort out their primary concerns.

Write your own "Big Rocks" story in which you set your priorities.

NOTES

1. This idea of "being pulled" comes from Rumi, "The Universe Is for Satisfying Needs," in *The Rumi Collection*, ed. Kabir Helminski (Boston, MA: Shambhala, 1998), 66.

2. Robert Fried, *The Passionate Teacher: A Practical Guide* (Boston, MA: Beacon Press, 1995), 232–33.

3. Grant Wiggins and Jay McTighe, *Understanding by Design* (Alexandria, VA: ASCD, 1998).

4. For more information, see Jay McTighe's annotated list of free resources that support curriculum unit planning using the UbD framework at www.jaymctighe.com (click on Resources at the top and then the website's icon).

5. Adapted from a story by an unknown author on the Internet. Thanks to Jennifer Antonucci who found it.

CODA

Make a Difference

The real gift was one I never imagined.

We teach to make a difference, as our teachers did for us. We have stories of students who write or call to thank us. But, we demur from taking credit, because we are modest. Taking credit, perhaps, opens us for taking blame as well.

We act on behalf of our students. We encourage them at every opportunity and discourage them only when necessary. We see their potential, not just their limitations. We offer opportunities rather than close doors. And, we treat them as individuals, never the same as anyone else. We do not, however, orchestrate to make a difference.

We do not often hear from former students, particularly when we teach in grades below high school. When we do we are often surprised—and certainly honored. Warm comments from parents and the occasional letter from a student remind us of the differences we made.

One instance in my later years stands out, not only because it warmed my heart, but also because it taught me that I was not in charge of the outcome. I wrote this story in response to an appeal for Christmas stories from National Public Radio (NPR) several years ago.

The real gift came many years later.

It began with my wish to give a winter coat to a newspaper girl. It was late November 1992 when the cold hit hard in Worcester, Massachusetts. Each Sunday on the way to church, my wife and I would pass through the intersection of Park and Highland Streets, where she helped her father sell the *Telegram &*

Gazette. A small, dark-haired girl, about ten, she was with him every Sunday. Occasionally, I would buy a paper.

As the weather intensified, I noticed she only had a thin fall jacket. When the first blizzard came, she still wore the same jacket. I decided, then, to find her a warmer coat. I did not have the money to buy a new one, so I invited my eighth graders to help me. While I am not clear as to why I asked them, it must have been the right idea. One of my students, Katy, arrived the next day with a lilac down parka—in the perfect size.

I placed the coat in a colorful bag with an unsigned card. As I drove to church, I was nervous about whether I was doing the right thing. At school, we had asked students to bring Christmas gifts to be distributed by Social Services. My students and I bought gifts at a local mall and wrapped them for a little boy. Now, I was having second thoughts about giving the girl the coat myself.

I prayed for the light to turn red at the intersection. It did. I jumped out of the car, ran up to her, handed her the bag, said "Merry Christmas" to her and her father, and jumped back into the car. When I told the story an hour later, I could not hold back tears.

Giving her the coat had been an obsession. That she chose not to wear it for the rest of the winter Sundays, however, became a mystery. I struggled to accept that my gift of the coat, as all gifts, needed to be unconditional.

Eight years later and a couple of weeks before Christmas, I held my final class teaching a group of beginning teachers that I had been working with since September. As part of our closing, I gave them stationery and envelopes on which to write a thank-you letter to someone who made a difference to their becoming a teacher, someone whom they had not yet thanked.

When I returned home that evening, I found a letter from Katy, the student who had given me the coat. Needless to say, I was deeply touched not only because she had taken the time to write but also by her gratitude.

After expressing thanks for helping her survive eighth grade, she wrote, "At one point when you were my advisor, you encouraged me to donate a coat to a young girl you saw out in the cold each Sunday selling newspapers. I cannot even begin to tell you how much this changed my life. Years later when I was deciding what to become in my life, I thought back to that time and realized my calling to become a nurse."

The real gift was one I never imagined.

I had been obsessed with giving a coat to a freezing newspaper girl. Instead, the real gift belonged to Katy, whose action, unbeknownst to her at the time, changed her life. As the Bhagavad Gita says, we should not become attached to the results of our actions. Such understanding frees us to do what we need to do and move on. It reminds us that teaching is not about us, but about our students.

In essence, we simply don't know when and how we make a difference. We can, however, make it our intention to have an exciting classroom. We do not need to talk at our students, insist on having them take notes, and hiss at them to be quiet. When we see them as learners, we concentrate on connecting. If we're lucky, we see their light and let it shine. We are confident that we are creating possibilities for joy—hopefully theirs and certainly ours.

REFLECTION

As we seek to know ourselves, we acknowledge we make a difference. We recognize, more often than not, that we will never know when or how. We can never underestimate the impact we have on others. Ironically, we cannot make this our focus. Rather, we teach well each day—and trust that we do. We may sense the differences we make—or think we may be making—but we do not seek to make them.

Epilogue

Hidden Expectations

Perhaps, in the end, I write to make the invisible visible to my readers—and to myself.

I awoke at four o'clock in the morning and scribbled on a Post-it Note: "The time of inaction merges into action to discover the hidden expectations of the reader." A couple of days later, I found the Post-it Note. "What does this mean?" I asked myself. "What was I thinking?" I didn't have a clue. I could only begin to speculate. I felt, however, it had to do with writing this book.

Perhaps it was about identifying with my future readers. As I write, I often pause to contemplate as I search to anticipate readers' internal needs, wishes, and purposes. Ironically, this is about tapping into their deepest desires, an urge not yet articulated in my mind. Writing without readers, after all, is like playing catch with oneself. The poet writes alone in an attic but her poem becomes alive when read. The artist paints by herself but the painting emerges in the viewer. Is it not the same for the writer?

I sit nearly every day placing my index fingers on my keyboard and write primarily to educators. I explore ideas and peruse the imaginable—and sometimes the unimaginable. I am speaking to my readers as I write, but all along I am waiting for them to open the book. When they do, the book will have arrived.

I discovered this truth when parts of my lost manuscript on teaching and living in the Soviet Union—which I wrote in the late 1980s—appeared on a Kazakh blog in 2008! One September day, by chance I Googled my name and there it was—my insights on the ubiquitous cheating in Soviet classrooms, in eight installments entitled, "Encounters with Soviet People."

A young American university professor—I later discovered—had retyped sections that she had found to share with her Kazakh students. She hoped to end their continuing practice of this old Soviet behavior. A piece of my manuscript had come alive, connecting to readers awaiting its message. (How she discovered the manuscript is another story.)

But then I wondered, perhaps my early morning rumination on the Post-it Note was really about me. The phrase, "time of inaction merges into moments of action," speaks to the writer's process. Fingering the keyboard inside innumerable pauses, I write, so I think, to discover my readers. But perhaps I am really discovering myself.

Returning to the discovered lost manuscript, I did not invent the message the blogger attempted to convey to her Kazakh students. Yes, I observed blatant cheating at all levels in Soviet schools, both for tests and in prompting one another during lessons. But my choice to write and expose this practice did not begin with me but derived from people who taught me the value of honesty—and maybe from my distaste with my own dishonesty.

What does it mean, then, for a writer to have the urge to discover the hidden expectations of his readers? Perhaps my call to write—and it's clearly a calling—comes in part from a deep desire to tap into the awaiting minds and hearts of my future readers. I see them waiting to make discoveries. Do my invitations already exist in their minds but are, at this point, hidden and untapped?

Invitations were hidden from me, too, when I began writing this book. I write often about myself in the third person, which makes readers guess who I am. My writing is a process of self-discovery. It is also anticipating the self-discovery of my readers. Given that the acts of giving and receiving are equivalent, so, then, might a similar equation exist between a writer and his readers?

In the end, I write to make the invisible visible to my readers and to me. My purpose is to awaken, as I've been awakened by books, teachers, students, colleagues, friends, parents, children—and by my own writing. We arrive in this life on a mission to become one with who we already are. We do it through our practice. Whenever we encounter a provocative book, a difficult child, a challenging class, or an unexpected crisis, are we not given the opportunity to discover our own hidden expectations?

We choose our life paths as teacher, doctor, restaurateur, carpenter, writer . . . or better yet they choose us. We enter doors of self-discovery. Maybe the metaphor with which I awoke that morning really does cut both ways. It is about me *and* about you, my future readers.

To extend this metaphor: Could it be true that we take the "time of inaction merging into moments of action to discover the hidden expectations" of our students? Could their hidden expectations be our challenge? Are we not responsible for teaching to these hidden expectations—at least do our best to anticipate them? And should we not at the same time seek to discover our own? After all, we all are heading into a changing future faster now than at any other time in human history. Knowing ourselves anchors us as we face the unforeseen.

The time of "inaction," then, is essential. We cannot carry on mindlessly. We must pause to consider the new and unimagined. We then discover what we know and value and integrate it with how students perceive us. We return to inaction when what we are doing is not working—and when students tell us it's not working. Plowing on, pushing through, covering material, completing the textbook on time, drilling for tests . . . these are the enemies of becoming who we are—and for our students becoming who they are.

Appendix

Teaching Manifesto

To change practice from traditional habitual routines, teachers need guidelines. By signing the Teaching Manifesto, a teacher commits to making her classroom engaging and exciting.

I sign this Manifesto as my commitment to become a better teacher:

For myself:

- I use invitations in my teaching and will be relentless in finding ones that work.
- I make the love and joy of learning the centerpiece of my instruction.
- I listen more and talk less. I will ask more questions and give fewer answers. My questions will elicit thinking and not right responses.
- I refrain from always repeating what students say to indicate my respect for their voices.
- I listen for the wonder in each child and nourish it every day. I do my best to see the world from a child's point of view.
- I respect different learning styles and seek pathways to assure successes for each student.
- I incorporate relevant conclusions of brain research for my classroom.
- I teach by invoking high expectations for all students. Every day, I will reexamine my perceptions of each child's potential.
- I articulate the learning intentions inside the big picture surrounding each lesson—and will make sure each student understands where we are headed and why.
- I teach meaningful and worthwhile content, skills, and values, including important ideas from the past, issues in the present, and anticipations for the future.

- I bring big ideas and enduring understandings into the classroom and value my students' interpretations of them.
- I understand my fundamental responsibility at whatever grade level I am in to teach for lifelong learning: to teach students to teach themselves.
- I seek what is authentic in myself and in my teaching, and commit to discovering my passions and invoke them in my classroom.
- I aim to understand the reality of the world in which we live so I can offer honest and informed perspectives.
- I model risk-taking to teach my students the value of frustration and struggle in learning challenging material.
- I seek to be open to innovative ideas, concepts, and pedagogies.
- I build on methods that work with my students and jettison those that do not.
- I commit to stay current in the growing knowledge base of the profession and in my content areas.
- I seek to collaborate with colleagues to integrate best practices into my teaching.
- I welcome colleagues, parents, and interested citizens into my classroom. I know I cannot teach alone and cannot teach well without feedback and support.
- I commit to encourage students to learn every day, in every class.
- I see my teaching as a calling, not a job.

With my colleagues:[1]

- We pay attention to what works and what does not.
- We take every word, every event, every failure and turn them to the advantage of our students. We sweep nothing under the rug.
- We recognize our part when students struggle. Together we find ways for them to achieve success.
- We do not blame officials, parents, or students for our lack of success. If we cannot enlist their commitment, we will be relentless in doing all we can to overcome challenges and difficulties. No excuses.
- No hurdle, no matter how high, will prevent us from invoking our intelligence, compassion, and love to serve our students' best interests.

And, in addition, I/we . . .

Signed: _____ Date:_____

NOTE

1. The ideas in this section have been inspired by "The Stockdale Paradox," developed by Admiral Jim Stockdale during his years in prison in Vietnam, as described in Jim Collins in *Good to Great: Why Some Companies Make the Leap . . . and Others Don't* (New York: Harper Collins, 2001), 83–87; in particular Stockdale's words: "Retain faith that you will prevail in the end, regardless of the difficulties and at the same time confront the most brutal facts of your current reality whatever they might be," 86.

Acknowledgments

Teachers stand on the shoulders of countless others. From first grade through middle school. From high school to college. From colleagues and mentors. From friends. From books, movies, and travel. The compendium of people and places in my life are almost limitless. I have been blessed with so many who have given me, whether they know it or not, so much to be grateful for.

Let Miss Karasack represent grade school, Thomas Donovan, high school, Orville Murphy, college, and Reginald Archambault, graduate school. Del Goodwin, Barrie Rogers, Vin Rogers, and David Mallery, mentors. Let these few colleagues represent the many wonderful people I've worked with over my forty years in the classroom: Terry Ortwein, Bill Murphy, Ford Daley, Bonnie Miller, Irina Nicholaevna, Raisa Vladimirovna, Winslow Myers, and countless others.

Pat Karl, Bob Milley, Jill Mirman, Rob Traver, Cheryl Bromley-Jones, and Pam Penna from my twelve years as a consultant. And Barbara Barnes, Barnes Boffey, Bonnie Miller, Rebecca Langrall, Mayme and Lafayette Noda, and Misha Bauchev among countless friends.

Finally, I must acknowledge the wise and insightful counsel of the late Christina Ward who set me on the path toward my first publication. She wisely shepherded me through the process. And a special appreciation to my wife, Kathleen Cammarata, whose art inspires me and her words urge me to be honest with myself—and to my readers.

Frank Thoms
San Miguel de Allende, Mexico

Index

Abaid, Mehmed: deep stuff for, 137–38, 139; as if thinking of, 135, 136, 139
ability grouping/tracking, as harmful, 83, 84, 89
acorn theory: Dennison for, 161–62, 164; of Hillman, 161–62, 164
ADD/ADHD, 7
administration: classroom interruptions of, 103, 104, 106; coverage focus of, 112, 137; teachers working with, 101; teaching role of, 106, 119
anchors: against classroom chaos, 190; end-of-year reflection as, 195
Anderson, Ronald, 167, 172
Appleton, Mr., 111, 112, 113, 115
Armstrong, Coleen, 103, 104, 106
The Art and Science of Teaching: A Comprehensive Framework for Effective Instruction (Marzano), design questions/action steps in, 138, 139
as if: as defining moments, 139; teaching practices of, 135, 136; thinking of Abaid in, 135, 136, 139
Attenborough, Richard, 57

backward design: pathway of, 190; teachers in, 192–93

Baker, Mrs., 111, 112, 113, 115
balanced-equation classroom, 27–28
Beat the Odds (BTO), 182–83
begin at end: final exam on first day as, 191, 195; as pathway of backward design, 190
Bernardi, Allegra: history lectures of, 3, 4; liking Eisner/Marzano ideas, 138, 139; for no interruptions, 108; 10-2 implementation of, 8–10; using highlighters, Flags, Post-it Notes, 16, 17
Berry, Thomas, 156, 157
big picture thinking: habitual practices restricting, 45, 46; of innovation, 43, 45; as taking long view, 119
Big Rocks story, 193–94, 195
The Big Shift, 47–48, *48*, 49, 52, 53
Biology Final (Bisaccio), 191, *192*, 194
Bisaccio, Dan, 191, *192*, 194
Black, wisdom of, 167, 169
Blackman, Pat, 171
brain research, 68, 112
A Brief History of Everything (Wilber), 156, 157
Bruner, Jerome, 89
BTO. *See* Beat the Odds
the Buddha, 5, 26, 56, 59

calling: as Dennison teaching, 161; as Hilliard teaching, 164; for teaching, 159
Cassell, Ms., 111, 112, 113, 115, 116
CCSS. *See* Common Core State Standards
Center for Constructive Change, 147
change: Center for Constructive Change in, 147; from culture, 1; Gandhi on, 156; intention for, 30; students resisting, 99; support for, 64; for teachers, 47, 63, 64, 119, 149; tenure as obstacle to, 96, 100; unions resisting, 93–95
Christianson, John, 129
classrooms: administration interruptions of, 103, 104, 106; anchors against chaos of, 190; as balanced-equation, 27–28; control of, 3; culture beyond, 119; digital isolation of students in, 154, 180; excitement from DI, 113–14; as exciting, 1, 4, 35, 43, 112, 113–14 199; as 4-star restaurants, 104, 109; gadfly for excitement in, 122, 124; hybrid flipped model of, 66; interruptions harmful for, 103, 104; invoking play for, 165; isolation harming, 43, *48*, 81, 121, 122; isolation lessened in, 107, 122, 123; learning inside or outside of, 114; Rip Van Winkle in, 78; routine of, 3; as sanctuaries, 107, 108–9; as uninterrupted in Japan, 103–4; visualizing ideal of, 147–49, 150–51
colleagues, consult with, 30
Collins, Marva, 86–87, 91, 152
Common Core State Standards (CCSS), 182, 183
competency, student levels of, 4, 14, 17
Confucius, 26, 56, 59
connected world: of digital age, 4, 46, 180; student isolation in, 154
control, of classroom, 3
Cosmos, 156, 157
Cosmos: A SpaceTime Odyssey, 157

coverage: as administration focus, 112, 137; as teaching practice, 112; time away from, 137
crabs-in-the-cage metaphor: leaping out of, 101; principals start of, 99–100; for teachers, 93, 95, 96, 97, 99; union role in, 100, 101
creativity: culture of, 148; "How schools kill creativity" to, 179; teachers with, 43
Cuba, girl teaching in, 163–64
culture: of creativity/innovation, 148; education needs changed by, 1; as fast-changing, 47, 53, 98, 119; as invasive, 154, 156; as media-driven, 46; beyond schools, 119
curriculum, as interruptions, 108

Dalai Lama, 56, 132, 169, 170, 175, 177
Damon, William, 97
David, among Goliaths, 77, 78, 79
David-Lang, Jenn, 68–69, 71
Dead Poets Society, 25, 26, 28–29
death, and dreams, 173
Death Valley metaphor, 179
deep stuff: for Abaid, 137–38, 139; of Eisner, 137–38, 139
defining: of best teaching assignment, 61; moments of as if, 139; moments of Dennison, 163
Dennison, Harold: for acorn theory, 161–62, 164; as BTO advocate, 182–83; as called to teach, 161; for CCSS, 182, 183; daimon/guardian angel concept and, 162; defining moments of, 163; education philosophy of, 167–71, 172; for Engel viewpoints, 181–82; on Google influence, 181; intentions of, 177; as No Child Left Behind critic, 179, 182; Pausch "Last Lecture" for, 173, 176; Pausch "six months left" for, 173–75; as Race to the Top critic, 182; seeing Cuban girl

teach, 163–64; teaching Marxism/ Communism, 162–63; for TED Talks of Robinson, K., 179–80; for UbD planning, 191, 192; for Updike, 164
Dewey, John, 139, 167, 169, 171
DI. *See* Differentiated Instruction
difference making, 197, 198, 199
Differentiated Instruction (DI), 111; for classroom excitement, 113–14; teaching ideas from, 115, 128
digital age: classroom interruptions in, 105; connected world of, 4, 46, 180; digital native students in, 4, 7, 20, 21, 25, *48*, 74, 76, 180; media literacy in, 4, 21; online learning in, 149; potential limitless in, 66; student isolation from, 154, 180
digital devices: classroom interruptions from, 105; effective use of, 149; student isolation from, 154, 180; of students, 66
digital immigrants, teachers as, *48*
digital natives: one-size-fits-all not serving, 112; student isolated as, 154, 180; students as, 4, 7, 20, 21, 25, *48*, 74, 76, 180
"Digital Natives, Digital Immigrants" (Prensky), *48*
discussion skills, 20
DNA, 83, 84, 176
dreams, and death, 173
Durant, Paul: escaping textbook tyranny, 128; teaching out-of-the-box, 127–28, 131
Dweck, Carol, 87–88, 90, 91

the easier road in teaching: activities of, 75–76, 78; letting go of, 79; as reaching few students, 74, 75, 76, 77; teacher talk in, 73, 112, 175
education: elephant in room in, 175, 177; "How to escape from education's death valley" for, 179;

Marzano reforming, 137, 138, 139; as theocracy, 135–36, 138
educational standards: CCSS for, 182, 183; Hilliard for, 176, 177
educational theocracies, 138; factory-school origins of, 51, 81, 86, 121, 136; of Pullman, 135–36
education methodologies: IEPs as, 75; not designed for students today, *48*; staying current on, 68–69; teacher/student time paramount in, 103, 104
education philosophy: of Dennison, 167–71, 172; of Hilliard, 171
education research, 68–69, 98
Edutopia research, 98
Efficacy Institute, *51*, 52
Eisner, Eliot, 137–38, 139
elementary level, 10-2 at, 6–7
elephant in room, 175, 177
embedded practices: as anachronistic and irrelevant, 119; breaking, 131; gadfly against, 122; as harmful, 81, 113, 175
"Encounters with Soviet People" (Thoms), 201–2
end-of-year reflection, as anchor, 195
energy activators, teachers as, 155
engagement: exit/recap cards for, 32–33, 34, 35, 40–41; give one/get one for, 35–38, 40, 41, 114; listening contrasted with, 5–6, 25, 26, 27; media literacy for, 4, 21; as purposeful, 113; strategies for, 31–41, 40, 41, 52–53; of students, 25, 26, 27; 10-2 for, 113; Thomas, S., novelty of, 25, 26, 27
Engel, Susan, 181–82
entity theory versus incremental thinking, 50–52, *51*, 53–54
Escalante, Jamie, 85, 86–87, 152
Esquith, Rafe, 86–87, 152
excitement: for classroom from DI, 113–14; in classrooms, 1, 35, 43, 199; classrooms with, 4, 112,

113–14; gadfly for classroom with, 122, 124
exit/recap cards, 42n4; for engagement, 32–33, 34, 35, 40–41; sharing success of, 41
expectations, of readers/writers, 201, 202, 203

factory model schools: industrial origins of, 51, 81, 86, 121, 136; teaching principles from, 51; as unionized, 81, 93
faculty room: collegial welcome in, 144–45; Hilliard and Bernardi in, 9; negativity of, 93, 95, 101
families, teachers connect with, 119
Fellows, Margaret: gadfly for, 124; interruption solution of, 107–8; visualizing ideal classroom, 150–51
final exam on first day, 191, 195
Fish! A Remarkable Way to Boost Morale and Improve Results (Lundin, Paul, Christianson), 129
Flags/Post-it Notes, as learning tools, 16, 17
4-star restaurants/4-star classrooms, 104, 109
Frost, Robert, 55, 61, 190

gadfly: activity of, 123; for department/grade, 125; exciting classrooms through, 122, 124; for school, 124; Socrates as, 121; teacher as, 121–24
Gandhi, 57
Gandhi, on change, 156
Gibson, Drew, on stakeholders, 180–81
give one/get one: for engagement, 35–38, 40, 41, 114; pursuing, 41; sample form for, *36*; sample use of, *37*
Gladwell, Malcolm: Golomb story by, 89; *Tipping Point* of, 127, 131
Golomb, Robert, 89

Gonzalez, Javier: student social contract of, 127–28; teaching out-of-the-box, 127–28, 131
Goodman, Delaney, 94, 95–96, 99
Goodwin, Del: Hilliard mentored by, 144; skills teaching of, 13, 17
Google: Dennison on influence of, 181; googling as non-thinking, 46; knowledge formula changed by, 65–66; what is worth knowing and, 148, 181
grading: alternative to, 137; role of, 148–49, 151
Graham, Martha, 130
growth mindset, pursuing, 91

habitual practices, as restricting, 45, 46
Hafiz, 56, 60
Haidt, Jonathan, 63
half-listening, of students, 5
The Happiness Hypothesis (Haidt), 63, 64, 68, 69, 70
harmful practices: ability grouping/tracking as, 83, 84, 89; digital isolation of students as, 154, 180; isolated classrooms as, 43, *48*, 81, 121, 122; whole-class lessons as, 45, 81
Hawken, Paul, on intent, 129
Healey, Tim, 107
Heath, Chip and Dan, 129–30
Herrick, Robert, 26
heterogeneous student grouping, 54
higher road in teaching: as David among Goliaths, 77, 78, 79; as discussions not lecturing, 73; as exploring student thinking, 74; as hard, 77; principles of, 77; students reached by, 74, 75, 76; taking, 79; as taking long view, 119; Teaching Manifesto as, 78, 114–15, 116; as years to become good, 142
highlighters: Mezzo instruction on, 14–16; as tools for learning, 14–16, 17

Hilliard, Dan, 4; activity-centered style of, 150; best practice seminar of, 41; Biology Final intent of, 194; *A Brief History of Everything* and, 156; as called to teach, 164; education philosophy of, 171; engagement strategies of, 40, 41, 52–53; for gadfly concept, 124; Goodwin mentoring of, 144; hearing Sagan lecture, 156, 157; for as if, 138; interruption solution of, 107–8; invitation to learn of, 28–29; liking DI and UbD, 131; liking Pullman/Eisner/Marzano ideas, 138, 139; *The Main Idea* for, 70; *Marshall Memo* for, 70; recommending *Made to Stick*, 131; rider and elephant metaphor for, 69; teaching literacy, 22; for teaching standards, 176, 177; 10-2 implementation of, 8–10, 78; as tracking resistant, 90; union concerns of, 100; *The Universe Story* and, 156; as using alternative ideas, 60, 69–70, 78, 115–16; using highlighters, Flags, Post-it Notes, 16, 17; visualizing ideal classroom, 150

Hillman, James: acorn theory of, 161–62, 164; daimon/guardian angel concept of, 162

history, lectures of Bernardi, 3, 4

Hoff, Benjamin, 56

holon and holons, 156, 157

holons, of Wilber, 156, 157

homework: challenges of, 4, 13, 14, 17, 26, 27; redefining, 6, 9, 45, 46

Hong, Lorraine: on classroom interruptions, 104; 4-star restaurant classroom of, 104, 109

Hopkins, Mark, 121

Howard, Jeff, 50–52, *51*

How People Learn, *49*, 49–50, 52

"How schools kill creativity" (Robinson, K.), 179–80

"How to escape from education's death valley" (Robinson, K.), 179–80

hybrid flipped classroom model, 66

IEPs. *See* independent educational plans

imagine ideal: as visualizing classroom ideal, 147–49, 150–51; as what is worth knowing, 148, 181

imagine the ideal, Sinclair, S., to, 147–49

The Imitation Game, 86

incremental thinking versus entity theory, 50–52, *51*, 53–54

independent educational plans (IEPs), 75

innovation: big picture thinking for, 43, 45; culture of, 148; habitual practices restricting, 45, 46; sharing success of, 123; from unions, 102n2; unions obstacles to, 93–95

Institute of Religion and Science (IRAS), 153

intentions: for change, 30; clarity of, 30; of Hilliard for Biology Final, 194; as important in teaching, 129, 175, 177; as making a difference, 197, 198, 199; as purposeful in teaching, 114; for TAPS, 41; for walkthroughs, 100

interactive strategies: effective teaching through, 20, 183; TAPS for teaching with, 38–40, 42nn9–10; 10-2 as, 6

interruptions: Bernardi against, 108; classroom isolation from, 107; curriculum as, 108; data on, 108; as harmful, 103; from invasive culture, 154, 156; PA as, 104, 106, 107, 108, 109n6; special as less, 109; special programs as, 104, 105, 107, 108; stopping, 103, 107–8

invitation, to learn, 27–29

invoking: of kaleidoscope metaphor, 145; of learning, 53; of play in classroom, 165

216 *Index*

involvement, of students, 2, 29, 30
IQ: fixed/fluid intelligence in, 50–52; intelligence not determined by, 86, 88; self-control contrasted with, 52, 86
IRAS. *See* Institute of Religion and Science
isolation: classrooms relief from, 107, 122, 123; harming classrooms, 43, *48*, 81, 121, 122; teaching in, 43, *48*, 81, 121, 122, 123

Japan, classroom uninterrupted in, 103–4
Jervis, Fred, 147
Johansen, Mark, 65, 68
Jones, Laura Reasoner, 7
Jones, Michael, 97
Jordan, Francis: The Big Shift of, 47–48, *48*, 49, 52, 53; entity theory versus incremental learning from, 50–52, *51*, 53–54; How People Learn from, *49*, 49–50, 52

kaleidoscope metaphor: invoking of, 145; patterns emerge in, 143; of Peters, 141, 142–43, 145
Keating, John, 25, 26, 27, 152
Kemp, Janice, 88
Kingsley, Ben, 57
Klunder, Ben, 93–94, 95–96, 97, 99, 100
knowledge: Google changing formula of, 65–66, 148, 181; as what is worth knowing, 148, 181

Lambourne, Marie: new teacher challenges of, 144; Peters letter to, 141–43
Langer, Judith, 182–83
language arts, 10-2 for, 6
language tyranny, 90
The Last Lecture (Pausch), 173, 176
Lavine, Portia, 106
Lavoie, Richard, 48–49

Lawrence, Bariyyah, 26
leaping out of bucket as, 101
learning: assessment of, 4; inside class or outside for, 114; interruptions harming, 103; invoking, 53; IQ role in, 50–52, 86, 88; online sources enhancing, 149; partnership of, 27; self-control role in, 52, 86; students invited to, 27–29; styles of, 111, 112, 113, 150; 10-2 for, 6; as untaught skill, 13; walkthroughs opportunities for, 106
learning disabilities, 7
learning tools: highlighters as, 14–16, 17; metacognitive discussion as, 20–22, 23; Post-it Notes/Flags as, 16, 17
lectures: of Bernardi, 3, 4; as norm, 4; 10-2 for, 6
Lehman, Mike, balanced teaching of, 59–60
lessons, processing of, 4
listening: engagement contrasted with, 5–6, 25, 26, 27; half-listening in, 5; universe as if, 135, 136, 137, 138
literacy skills: developing student thinking, 20; teaching, 19–22; types of, 4–5
the long view: patterns emerge through, 143; of teaching as artistry and science, 142; of teaching practices, 119
luminaries, wisdom of, 139, 148, 167, 169, 171
Lundin, Stephen C., 129

Macon, Peter: exit card use by, 32–33, 34–35, 40; recap card use by, 33–35, 40
Made to Stick: Why Some Ideas Survive and Others Die (Heath): principles of, 129–30, 131, 132, 133n8; rethinking teaching practices from, 130
The Main Idea, 68–69, 70, 71

"A Manual for the Writing of Research Papers" (Goodwin), 13
"Mapping a Route Towards Instruction" (Tomlinson), 111, 115
Marshall, Kim, 68
Marshall Memo, designated reader for teachers, 68, 70, 71
Marxism/Communism, 162–63
Marzano, Robert: design questions/action steps of, 138, 139; education reform call of, 137
Massachusetts Comprehensive Assessment System (MCAS), 26, 89
McGillis, Mary, 27
Meat, 63, 69
media-driven culture: as fast-changing, 47, 53, 98, 119; social-media in, 60; teacher openness to, 46
media literacy, engaging students through, 4, 21
Messiah, student as, 60
metacognitive discussion, 20–22, 23
metaphors: crabs-in-the cage as, 93, 95, 96, 97, 99, 100, 101; of Death Valley, 179; kaleidoscope as, 141, 142–43, 145; rider and elephant as, 63, 64, 68, 69, 70; as spiral/elliptical galaxy of Swimme, 153–54, 155, 156, 157; time of inaction, 201, 202, 203
methodologies, *48*, 68–69, 75, 103, 104
Mezzo, Abraham, 14–16
mindset, fixed versus growth, 87–88, 90, 91
Mindset: The New Psychology of Success (Dweck), 87–88, 90
motivation: of students, 2; teacher responsible for, 28
Mullen, Bob, 37–38
Mullens, Sean, 105, 106

National Board Certification teaching standards, 176, 177
National Research Council, brain research from, 112

Nhat Hanh, Thich, 56, 58
No Child Left Behind, 179, 182
note taking, 7

one-size-fits-all teaching: alternatives to, 60, 69–70, 78, 115–16; ending, 111, 113–14, 115; as ineffective, 38–39, 45, 111, 113, 115; as not serving digital students, 112
out-of-the-box teaching, 127–28, 131

PA. *See* public address system
Palmer, Parker, 175, 177n2
PARCC, 182
partnership, learning as, 27
Partnership for Twenty-first Century Skills, 4–5, 22, 23
pathways: for backward design, 190; Big Rocks story for, 193–94, 195; to Cassell, 116
Paul, Harry, 129
Pausch, Randy: discovering wisdom, 173; "Last Lecture" of, 173, 176; "only six months left" of, 173–75
Peck, Scott, 59–60
pedagogy. *See* teaching practices
performance reviews, contrast with tenure, 98
Perkins, Ignatius, 106–7
Peters, Pam: for ending one-size-fits-all teaching, 111, 113–14, 115; fixed versus growth mindset for, 87–88, 90, 91; for high expectations of students, 85, 86; kaleidoscope metaphor of, 141, 142–43, 145; Lambourne letter of, 141–43; in take-back-the-classroom, 103, 106, 107; teacher training of, 83
Peterson, Isaiah, 20–21
philosophy of education: of Dennison, 167–71, 172; of Hilliard, 171; for you, 172
Pike's Place Fish Market, 128–29, 131–32

Plato, 148, 167, 169
play, contrast with test taking/ assessments, 165
Post-it Notes/Flags, as tools, 16, 17
potential: digital limitless in, 66; as everyone has, 89
Prensky, Marc, *48*, 186
Pressfield, Steven, 100, 101
primacy-recency, 66–67, *67*, 70
principals: as classroom interrupters, 103; crabs-in-the-cage starts with, 99–100
processing: of lessons, 4; students time for, 8
public address system (PA), as interruptive, 104, 106, 107, 108, 109n6
Pullman, Philip: educational theocracies of, 135–36, 138; as if ideas of, 137, 138; listening to universe, 135, 136, 137, 138
purpose: as important in teaching, 129; teaching with, 113, 114

questions: Google answering, 46, 65–66; Marzano design questions as, 138, 139; teaching through, 43, 45, 46, 56, 57, 58, 59, 61, 65

"The Rabbi's Gift" (Peck), 59–60
Race to the Top, 182
readers/writers, expectations of, 201, 202, 203
reading: fluency in, 20; for meaning and understanding, 19; teaching, of textbooks, 19–20
recap/exit cards, 33–35, 40–41, 42n4
research: for interruption data, 108; staying current on, 68–69
respect, of teachers, 1
rhythms of school, 194
rider and elephant metaphor, 63, 64, 68, 69, 70
Rip Van Winkle, 78
"The Road Not Taken," 55, 190

Robinson, Ken: "How schools kill creativity" by, 179–80; "How to escape from education's death valley" by, 179–80
Robinson, Sarah, 55–60, 61
Rogers, Vincent: pursuing 10-2, 5–8, 9–10; for wait time, 7
routines, of classrooms, 3
Rowe, Mary Budd: 10-2 of, 5, 6, 7, 8, 9, 10; wait time of, 7
Rumi, 55, 56

Sagan, Carl, 156, 157
sanctuaries, classrooms as, 107, 108–9
Sanderos, Carlos, 76–77, 79
Sanders, William, 97–98
Saphier, John, 50–52, *51*
satisfaction: of students, 2; of teachers, 2
schools: book/film club for, 71; culture beyond, 119; gadfly in, 123, 124, 125; "How schools kill creativity" for, 179; industrial factory origins of, 51, 81, 86, 121, 136; rhythms of, 194; teacher/student time paramount in, 103, 104; teaching principles origins of, 51; as unionized, 81, 93; welcoming new teachers, 144–45
Schultz, Ron: metacognitive methods of, 20–22, 23; Peterson coaching of, 20–21; teaching literacy skills, 22
Scortino, Angela, 76–77, 79
seek out great teachers, 152
self-control, IQ contrast with, 52, 86
self-direction skill, 4
sharing success: of exit/recap cards, 41; of innovative methods, 123; of teaching study habits, 14–16, 17, 19–20; of 10-2, 10
Sharma, Amir, 105
Simmons, Marie, 65, 66
Sinclair, Jennifer, 85
Sinclair, Steve: new thinking from IRAS for, 153; spiral/elliptical galaxy metaphor for, 153–54,

155, 156, 157; visualizing ideal classroom, 147–49
"six months left," of Pausch, 173–75
skills for student success: assessment of, 14, 17, 22; classroom rearranging as, 25, 30; gauge competency levels of, 4, 14, 17; highlighter use as, 14–16; interactive strategies as, 20, 183; learning as, 13; learning in or out of class as, 114; literacy skills for, 4–5, 20; from Partnership for Twenty-first Century Skills, 4–5, 22, 23; problem-solving skill, 4; in study habits, 14–16, 19–20; test taking/assessments as, 13; writing as, 20
Smarter Balance Assessment Consortium, 182
social media, 60
Socrates, 121, 159
Sousa, David, 66–67, *67*, 70
special programs: as interruptive, 104, 105, 107, 108; as less interruptive, 109
spiral/elliptical galaxy metaphor, 153–54, 155, 156, 157
stakeholders, teachers as, 180–81
Stand and Deliver, 85
stickiness, 129–30
students: brain growth of, 91; digital devices of, 66; digital isolation for, 154, 180; as digital natives, 4, 7, 20, 21, 25, *48*, 74, 76, 180; education needs changing for, 1; education not designed for, *48*; engagement of, 25, 26, 27; as focus of Cassell, 111, 112, 113, 115, 116; fulfill teacher labeling, 89–90; gauge competency of, 4, 14, 17; googling as non-thinking, 46; half-listening of, 5; high expectations of, 85, 86; homework challenges of, 4, 13, 14, 17, 26, 27; as invited to learn, 27–29; involvement of, 2, 29, 30; as learning partners, 27; Messiah

as, 60; motivation of, 2; potential contrasted with tracking, 89; processing by, 4, 8; pursuing ideas of, 30; as put first by schools, 103; resisting change, 99; satisfaction of, 2; self-direction skill of, 4; skills assessment of, 14, 17, 22; social contract with, 127–28; teachers challenging, 90; teachers connect with, 119; teacher talk alienating, 112, 175; teaching for, 198; whole-class lessons not serving, 4, 45, 76, 81, 83, 115
student/teacher time interruptions, 103, 104
study habits, 14–16, 19–20
success sharing, 10, 14–16, 17, 19–20, 41, 123
support: for change, 64; of new faculty, 144–45
Suzuki, Shunryu, 58
Swimme, Brian: spiral/elliptical galaxy metaphor of, 153–54, 155, 156, 157; *The Universe Story* of, 156, 157

take-back-the-classroom, 103, 104, 106
taking higher road, 79
The Tao of Pooh (Hoff), 56, 59
Tao Te Ching, 56, 59
TAPS Template for Teacher Planning: departing from whole-class lessons, 38–39; as guiding teacher improvement, 115, 116; intentions for, 41; for interactive teaching, 38–40, 42nn9–10; template of, *39*
teachers: assessing student skills, 14, 17, 22; in backward design, 192–93; book/film club for, 71; as challenged when new, 144–45; as challenging students, 90; change for, 47, 63, 64, 119, 149; collegial relations for, 144–45; connecting with students, 119; as crabs-in-the-cage, 93, 95, 96, 97, 99, 100, 101; with creativity, 43; as Davids among

Goliaths, 77, 78, 79; defining as if moments of, 139; defining best teaching assignment, 61; as digital immigrants, *48*; discussing our place in universe, 157; as energy activators, 155; faculty room of, 9, 93, 95, 101, 144–45; families connect with, 119; as gadfly, 121–24; gadfly activity of, 123; give one/get one for, *36*, *37*, 41; helping new teachers, 144–45; as lax on standards, 176; as learning partners, 27; *Marshall Memo* for, 68, 70, 71; personal inventory by, 70, 138, 172; Peters for training of, 83; as pursuing ideas of students, 30; as putting students first, 103; respect of, 1; satisfaction of, 2; seeking great ones, 152; self-assessment for, 116; skills of, 1; as special/unique, 161, 164; as stakeholders, 180–81; student motivated by, 28; students fulfill labeling by, 89–90; TAPS for improvement of, 115, 116; TAPS template for, *39*; UbD benefiting, 128, 191–92, 196n4; as untrained for students today, *48*; working with administration, 101

teacher/student time interruptions, 103, 104

teacher success: engagement strategies for, 31–41; gadfly for, 124; from going beyond habitual practice, 46; homework redefining for, 6, 9, 45, 46; out-of-the-box teaching for, 127–28, 131; Partnership for Twenty-first Century Skills on, 4–5, 22, 23; from sharing innovative methods, 123; sharing of, 10, 17; student engagement as, 25, 26, 27; TVASS on, 97

teacher talk: reducing, 4, 5, 10; student alienation from, 112, 175; in teacher DNA, 83, 84, 176

teaching: administrators as, 106, 119; as calling, 159, 161, 164; in isolation, 43, *48*, 81, 121, 122, 123; reading as, 19–20; as about students not teachers, 198; of study habits, 14–16, 19–20

Teaching Manifesto, 78, 114–15, 116

teaching practices: 10-2 principles for, 5–6; activity-centered style of, 111, 112, 113, 150; as artistry and science, 142; balanced teaching as, 59–60; best practice seminars as, 41; breaking embedded, 131; changing, 1; colleague consultation as, 30; coverage as, 112, 137; DI and UbD improving, 115, 128; easier road of, 73, 74, 75–76, 77, 78, 79, 112, 175; embedded harmful forms of, 81, 113, 119, 122, 175; entity theory versus incremental learning as, 50–52, *51*, 53–54; from factory model schools, 51; gadfly for improving, 124; grading, 137, 148–49, 151; as habitual, 45, 46; higher road of, 73, 74, 75, 76, 77, 78, 114–15, 116, 119, 142; How People Learn as, *49*, 49–50, 52; as if as, 135, 136; for immediate action, 1; intentions important as, 129, 175, 177; in literacy skills, 19–22; long view of, 119; one-size-fits-all ineffective as, 38–39, 45, 111, 113, 115; out-of-the-box as, 127–28, 131; personal inventory of, 70, 138, 172; as purposeful, 113, 114, 129; rethinking, 130; standards of, 176; for student brain growth, 91; as taking writing seriously, 172; Teaching Manifesto for, 78, 114–15, 116; as teaching through questions, 43, 45, 46, 56, 57, 58, 59, 61, 65; teach-to-the-test as, 123; tenure as obstacle to change, 96, 100; test taking/assessments as, 3, 4, 5, 9, 13, 16, 22, 23, 26, 75, 84, 88 technology: effective use of, 149; social-media as, 60; teacher openness to, 46; Unlearn, Learn, Relearn need in, 48–49

TED Talk: Dennison recommending, 179–80; "How schools kill creativity" as, 179; "How to escape from education's death valley" as, 179

10-2 Thinking: ADD/ADHD helped by, 7; at elementary level, 6–7; for engagement, 113; facilitating note taking, 7; Hilliard implementing, 8–10, 78; implementation tips for, 8–10; interactivity promoted by, 6; in language arts, 6; for learning, 6; principles of, 5–6; Roberts with, 5–8, 9–10; Rogers pursuing, 6–8, 9–10; by Rowe, 5, 6, 7, 8, 9, 10; sharing success of, 10; Webb, Sheila with, 7

Tennessee Value Added Assessment System (TVASS), 97

tenure: as obstacle to change, 96, 100; as obstacle to performance reviews, 98

test taking/assessments: BTO versus TP in, 182–83; coverage for, 112, 137; emphasis on, 3, 5, 9, 13, 16, 22, 23, 26, 75, 84, 88; Google and what is worth knowing, 148, 181; MCAS as, 26, 89; measuring clerical-level thinking, 179; play contrasted with, 165; teacher peer-assessment as, 116; teacher self-assessment as, 116; teach-to-the-test for, 123

textbooks, 19–20, 128

theocracy of education, 135–36, 138

thinking skills, 4; googling as non-thinking, 46; literacy developing, 20; Sinclair exploring new, 153; tests measure clerical-levels of, 179

Thomas, Annie: DI and UbD of, 128; *Made to Stick* principles of, 129–30, 132, 133n8; for Pike's Place Market, 128–29, 131–32; stickiness for, 129–30; student social contract of, 127–28; tipping points for, 129

Thomas, Steve, 25, 26, 27

Thompson, Mary, 106

Thoms, Frank, 201–2

time of inaction metaphor, 201, 202 203

Tipping Point (Gladwell), 127, 131

tipping points, 127, 129

Tomlinson, Carol Ann, 111, 115, 128

tools for learning: highlighters as, 14–16, 17; Post-it Notes/Flags as, 16, 17

"To the Virgins, to Make Much of Time," by Herrick, 26

TP. *See* Typically Performing

tracking/ability grouping: as harmful practices, 83, 84; Hilliard resisting, 90; as language tyranny, 90; student potential contrasted with, 89

Turing, Alan, 86

TV, movies, video: *Cosmos* as, 156, 157; *Cosmos: A SpaceTime Odyssey* as, 157; *Dead Poets Society* as, 25, 26, 28–29; *Gandhi* as, 57; "How schools kill creativity" as, 179; "How to escape from education's death valley" as, 179; *The Imitation Game* as, 86; *Meat* as, 63, 69; Pausch "Last Lecture" as, 173, 176; *Stand and Deliver* as, 85

TVASS. *See* Tennessee Value Added Assessment System

twenty-first century student skills, 4–5, 22, 23

Typically Performing (TP), as test prep method, 182–83

tyranny: of language, 90; of textbooks, 128

Tyson, Neal deGrasse, 157

Understanding by Design (UbD), 128, 191, 192, 196n4

unions: Hilliard concern for, 100; as obstacles to change, 93–95; positive example of, 102n2; role in crabs-in-the-cage activity, 101; in schools, 81, 93
universe: as if listening, 135, 136, 137, 138; our place in, 157; Pullman listening to, 135, 136, 137, 138; seeking and teaching wisdom of, 55, 56–60; Wilber on intelligence of, 155
The Universe Story (Swimme and Berry), 156, 157
Unlearn, Learn, Relearn, 48–49
Updike, John, 164

visualization, of ideal classroom, 147–49, 150–51
Vreeland, Tom, 89

wait time, 7
walkthroughs: intentions for, 100; as learning opportunities, 106; Wesson on, 121
Webb, Sheila, 7
Wesson, George: teacher gadfly of, 121–24; walkthroughs of, 121
Whitehead, 167, 169
whole-class lessons: as harmful practice, 45, 81; not meeting student needs, 4, 45, 76, 81, 83, 115; TAPS departure from, 38–39
Wilber, Ken: *A Brief History of Everything* by, 156, 157; holons of, 156, 157; on intelligent universe, 155
Wilcox, Jesse, 73
Wiliam, Dylan, 6
Williams, Robin, 25
Williamson, Marianne, 87
Wilmot, Jared, 78
Wilson, Josh, 65; brain research followed by, 68; primacy-recency through, 66–67, *67*, 70; rider and elephant metaphor for, 63, 64, 68, 70
Wineburg, Stephen, 183
wisdom: of luminaries, 139, 148, 167, 169, 171; Pausch discovering, 173; seeking and teaching, 55, 56–60
Wiseman, Frederick, 63, 64, 69
writers/readers, expectations of, 201, 202, 203
writing skills: for student success, 20; as taken seriously, 172

Zen Mind, Beginner's Mind (Suzuki), 58

About the Author

Frank Thoms is a lifelong classroom teacher, consultant, and writer. He devotes himself to improving the teaching profession, one teacher at a time. He's relentless in finding ways to meet the challenges of today's digitally wired, techno-literate students. He advocates that teachers become their own change-makers. He believes invitations offer the most powerful impetus to effect change, in stark contrast to federal, state, and local mandates that often cause resentment and resistance.

Frank has taught in public and private schools in the United States, as well as in schools in England, Russia, Kazakhstan, and Mexico. He was a founding member of the exemplary Upper Valley Educators Institute, one of the nation's first alternative teacher-certification programs, now in its fifth decade. He developed a model open-education classroom that served as a resource to New England schools. He has consulted for PBS, AFS Intercultural Programs, I/D/E/A Kettering, Association of Independent Schools of New England (AISNE), and the Vermont State Department of Education.

In his last twelve years as a consultant, he served in more than 125 schools, providing keynotes, workshops, pedagogical courses, mentoring, and teacher coaching. His unique style blends serious content and processes in an interactive format that serves as a model for the teaching he advocates throughout his writings.

Contact Frank at frankthoms3@gmail.com and visit his website www.frankthoms.com.

Made in the USA
Middletown, DE
05 August 2019